Geographical Indications and International Agricultural Trade

Also by Louis Augustin-Jean

ASIAN ECONOMIC DYNAMISM IN THE AGE OF GLOBALIZATION (*co-edited with Edward K. Y. Chen and Anne Androuais*)

HONG KONG. ECONOMIE, CULTURE, SOCIETE (*co-edited with Florence Padovani*)

Geographical Indications and International Agricultural Trade

The Challenge for Asia

Edited by

Louis Augustin-Jean
Associate Professor, University of Tsukuba, Japan

Hélène Ilbert
Professor and Researcher in International Economics, University of Montpellier, France

and

Neantro Saavedra-Rivano
Professor Emeritus, University of Tsukuba, Japan

palgrave
macmillan

First published 2012 by
PALGRAVE MACMILLAN

Palgrave Macmillan in the UK is an imprint of Macmillan Publishers Limited, registered in England, company number 785998, of Houndmills, Basingstoke, Hampshire RG21 6XS.

Palgrave Macmillan in the US is a division of St Martin's Press LLC, 175 Fifth Avenue, New York, NY 10010.

Palgrave Macmillan is the global academic imprint of the above companies and has companies and representatives throughout the world.

Palgrave® and Macmillan® are registered trademarks in the United States, the United Kingdom, Europe and other countries.

ISBN 978–0–230–35575–0

This book is printed on paper suitable for recycling and made from fully managed and sustained forest sources. Logging, pulping and manufacturing processes are expected to conform to the environmental regulations of the country of origin.

A catalogue record for this book is available from the British Library.

Library of Congress Cataloging-in-Publication Data
Geographical indications and international agricultural trade : the challenge for Asia / edited by Louis Augustin-Jean, Hélène Ilbert, and Neantro Saavedra-Rivano.
pages cm
Includes bibliographical references.
ISBN 978–0–230–35575–0
1. Agricultural produce—Developing countries. 2. Agriculture and state—Developing countries. I. Augustin-Jean, Louis. II. Ilbert, Hélène. III. Saavedra-Rivano, Neantro, 1946–

HD9018.D44G46 2012
382'.41091724—dc23 2012016690

10 9 8 7 6 5 4 3 2 1
21 20 19 18 17 16 15 14 13 12

Printed and bound in Great Britain by
CPI Antony Rowe, Chippenham and Eastbourne

Contents

List of Tables and Figures

Tables

Figures

Notes on Contributors

Gilles Allaire studied agronomics and rural economics in Toulouse. He is currently senior researcher at the Institut National de la Recherche Agronomique (INRA). He has recently been scientific coordinator of the European research program SINER-GI (Strengthening International Research on Geographical Indications: from research foundation to consistent policy; www.origin-food.org). His current research topics are market functioning, and policy analysis (the globalization of agrofood systems, quality, and rural development).

Louis Augustin-Jean is Associate Professor at the University of Tsukuba where he is teaching international development, Asian economic development and economic sociology. He has been living in Asia for 15 years and his research is on China's rural development and food systems. He was the co-editor of the recent volume *Hong Kong. Economie, société, culture* (2007).

Nicolas Baumert is Associate Professor at Nagoya University. He is a geographer, and a specialist in the cultural and historical geography of Japan. He obtained his PhD from Paris-Sorbonne University in 2009. He is a member of the Espaces, Nature et Culture laboratory and an Associate Researcher with the Maison Franco-Japonaise, Tokyo.

Selina Ching Chan has a DPhil. in Social Anthropology from Oxford University. She worked at the National University of Singapore before joining the Sociology Department as Associate Professor and Associate Director of the Contemporary China Research Center at the Hong Kong Shue Yan University. She is a social anthropologist who has conducted fieldwork in different Chinese communities in Hong Kong, Taiwan, China and Singapore. Her articles have appeared in the *China Quarterly, Modern China, Identities, China Information, Ethnology, European Planning Studies* and the *Asian Journal of Social Science*.

Hélène Ilbert is a Research Director at the CIHEAM-IAM-M, member of the research team "Markets, Organizations, Institutions and Stakeholders Strategies" (MOISA) at the University of Montpellier. She works in the field of global international economics and her research interest focuses on geographical indications and Mediterranean economic integration. She has been awarded the Mobius prize by the

National Scientific Research Institute and the Commission of the European Communities.

Jean-Louis Rastoin is Emeritus Professor at Montpellier SupAgro, France, with Unesco Chair in World Food Systems' tenure. He is an international expert in agricultural and food economics and management. He was Full Professor in this academic institution and founder and Director of the economics and management research unit 'MOISA', in Montpellier. He has more than 35 years of professional work experience, including extensive experience in developing countries. His research has concentrated on economic policy analysis and firms' strategies related to agriculture, agro-industries and agrofood value chains. He has published extensively in these areas, including four books and more than 200 professional publications.

Neantro Saavedra-Rivano is Professor Emeritus of the University of Tsukuba and Deputy Director of its Program in Economic and Public Policy Management. He holds PhDs in Economics from Columbia University and in Mathematics from the University of Paris. His research interests include human capital financing and economic development, regional economic integration in East Asia and the Americas, and international trade.

Suyako Sekimoto completed her Master's degree in South Asian Studies at the University of Tsukuba with the subject of her thesis being about the Philippines. She currently works for a manufacturer of agricultural machinery.

Kae Sekine is an Assistant Professor at the College of Economics at Rikkyo University, Japan. She studies transnational agribusinesses' behaviour and its consequences (especially in the fresh fruit and vegetable sector) as well as the processes and role of the actors associated with Geographical Indications in Japan and France. She holds a Master's degree and a PhD in Economics from Kyoto University and also studied at the French National Institute for Agricultural Research (INRA), Montpellier, from 2007 to 2010.

Philippe Steiner is Professor of Sociology at the University of Paris-Sorbonne. He works mainly in the domain of economic sociology and the history of social sciences. He has recently published *La transplantation d'organes: un commerce nouveau entre les êtres humains* (2010), *Durkheim and the Birth of Economic Sociology* (2011) and *Les rémunérations obscènes* (2011).

Guihong Wang holds a PhD in Economics from Toulouse University where she studied the implementation of the protection system for Geographical Indication Products in the context of the economic transition of China. She has participated in the European Research Program SINER-GI and was consultant for the FAO Asia on agro-food quality products linked with Geographical Indications. Her research deals with institutional adjustment, food certification and agricultural development, with a focus on economic, social and environmental aspects of food quality.

Introduction: The Globalization of Geographical Indications: The Challenge for Asia

Louis Augustin-Jean

I.1 The Fordist model of food production and its limits

Since the end of the Second World War, the dominant model of food production has been characterized, at least in developed countries, by economies of scale, the production of standardized goods, and mass consumption. By no means limited to agricultural products, this standardization implies a high degree of coordination between the agricultural and industrial sectors, leading to the emergence of an agro-food complex – with the aim of producing more at cheaper prices.

Nevertheless, after the period of reconstruction that followed the end of the war, this model of production was affected by several factors. The emergence of productive agricultures in Europe and in the New World created a situation of overproduction, in the United States and in Western Europe alike. The consequences were not only the search for new markets, but also, in Europe, an evolution of the CAP (Common Agricultural Policy): policies sometimes shifted as incentives were given to farmers to limit their production (such as milk). At the same time, the promotion and the production of 'quality' products was encouraged with the increase of specific labels (on quality, see below). This new trend was welcomed by consumers who, after a series of food safety incidents that have been on a rising trend in recent years, started to question the validity of this mass production model. It is especially prominent in North America, Europe or Japan, but it is also gaining ground in developing Asia, where revenues are rapidly increasing.

Thus, the model of mass production and mass consumption (which can be roughly defined as the Fordist mode of production), while remaining dominant, came to a crisis that has become more acute in recent years – what Philip McMichael and Harriet Friedmann call the crisis of the post-war (or second) food regime (Friedmann and McMichael, 1989; McMichael, 2009a and 2009b). In response to this situation, under the impetus of a minority of consumers and producers, alternative modes of production to Fordism gained momentum. Of these, organic food, fair trade, products of origins, and products of *terroir* are perhaps the most significant. They all share a certain perception of 'quality' (a notion that will be discussed below), in accordance with the shift of the CAP mentioned earlier. In addition, these alternative productions now have to adapt to the global agro-food trade requirements, in which organizations which control private standards adapt the compliance of their own system with the food safety regulations of international trade. Supermarkets include quality and small-scale producers in their business practices. Public policy evolves and includes quality controls, while private lobbies and public regulations are under pressure from consumers. In such a context, products of origins and *terroirs* add a geographical dimension which is the source of debates in the academic and political fields, and also in international negotiations.

I.2 A specific regime: geographical indication products and products of *terroir*

While products of *terroir* (PT) and geographical indication products (GIP) have a slightly different meaning, they both express the same reality: the emphasis on geographical locations, which gives a premium to local producers. The legitimacy of the premium generated by the producer is subject to debates. But before developing that point, it is necessary to detail the notions of *terroir* and GIP further.

Terroir is a relatively old notion that was created in Southern Europe at the beginning of the twentieth century for wines (it is related to the French 'Appellation d'origine contrôlée', and was later extended to other agricultural goods such as cheese, meats, and other foodstuffs). PT is a concept with no legal existence, GI being the form of intellectual protection that is attached to PT (Josling, 2006, p. 338). In recent years, GIPs and PTs (and other speciality products) have multiplied, not only in Europe, but also in other parts of the world. The reasons should be searched in changes in both supply and demand for agro-food products.

First, from the supply side, the development of GIPs can be seen as a reaction from producers who want to obtain an extra value from their production. PTs and GIPs can therefore be considered as tools for producers who seek to differentiate their goods from 'generic' commodities and mass production. For this reason, the emphasis on GI has sometimes been perceived as unfair competition since by definition, producers located in other areas are unable to enjoy this specific (locational) advantage. The arguments put forward by the proponents of PT and GIPs, who emphasize the importance of tradition and previous investments in quality do not seem convincing enough to brush away the previous statement – especially since the cumulative investments related to the promotion of the GI are difficult to estimate. The debate is obviously related to the definition of 'quality' and its operational mode, which will be presented in the next section.

A possibly more powerful argument in favour of the GIPs is from the demand side. GIPs are gaining a growing market share, especially in the developed world – not only in Europe, but also in Japan and in North America. As will be seen below, the search for 'authenticity' or 'tradition' by customers demonstrates that the existence of PTs and GIPs corresponds to a real need, and GIs are much more than an artificial tool in the hands of producers. This trend is to be related to broader social and economic factors. Since the end of the 1970s, the rising living standards in the developed world have boosted the demand for such personalized services and products, in agro-food as in other industries. In more recent years, the multiplication of food safety crises, such as the BSE or avian flu, has eroded the confidence of consumers, who become more inclined to demand these 'genuine' products – that is, 'natural products', 'traditional products', 'products that can be trusted', and so on.

In other words, in the quest for this (reconstructed) 'authenticity', many consumers are looking for a gamut of products that are not provided by the Fordist mode of production. This problem of differentiation between these two kinds of products leads to a redefinition of the notion of quality.

I.3 PGIs/PT vs Fordist production: a differentiated definition of quality

In short, the agro-food complex, as it has emerged since the 1970s, exhibits two main tendencies. The first is the 'commodification' of agro-food industries which can be traced back to at least the mid-nineteenth century, but found its most advanced form with the development of Fordism from the end of the Second World War onwards. The development of commodity markets implies an *ex ante* definition of quality (like for any market – for the classical example of second-hand cars, cf. Akerlof, 1970). Quality, as it is understood here, is based on the early efforts for standardization and the establishment of industrial norms (that is, it is based on a precise measurement). Quality has to be homogeneous, and products from region (or producer) A must be perfectly substitutable for products of region (or producer) B. The technical specificities for these products are described precisely – for example, in sample contracts issued by the Chicago Board of Trade. That understanding of quality finds its most perfect achievement with the implementation of futures markets for commodities, in which products from different origins are perfectly substitutable, provided they match the technical description written in the contracts (as well as conditions for delivery, a topic which is beyond the scope of this presentation). Therefore, the quality is generally defined outside the production areas, sometimes in very distant places.

The second tendency, opposite to mass production, is differentiation – *terroir* being only one possible way to achieve differentiation. The new fashion to promote old traditional products can also be perceived as an element of differentiation that cannot be totally assimilated to GIs and PTs. The promotion of the 'One Town, One Product' movement, first in Japan and later developed in other parts of Asia, exemplifies perfectly this tendency. Similarly, the recent development of agro-tourism is also related to this search for (reconstructed) 'authenticity' (for an Asian example, see Selina Chan on Taiwan, 2010).

In this second pattern, quality is not (only) defined by precise technical criteria: tradition, know-how, culture, and so on are elements that cannot be precisely measured, but are important factors that influence the perception of consumers. Quality is therefore a process that is (at least partly) negotiated *inside* the region and by consumers. The elaboration of the definition involves most actors that are parts of the system of production (for example, the definition has to incorporate the tension that exists between 'authenticity' and industrial constraints). The result is a compromise that has also to take into account the tastes, preferences and regulations that exist in the consumption areas. Even though a dominant agent (for example, a multinational corporation) might play a key role in the negotiation process, the quality has still to be negotiated and legitimated by the actors at the local level – to make it short, inside the *terroir* (Eymard-Duvernay, 1989; Allaire, 2004). Thus, quality is here defined by the interaction of three related parameters: geographical – a geographical location that customers can trust; historical – a product of 'tradition'; and industrial – traceability, norms of quality, labels, ISO standards, and so on, for which consumers generally do not understand the technical elaboration, but for which they trust the organism of certification.

Therefore, a key question concerns the degree of compatibility of these two definitions of quality (the one that applies to mass consumption products, and the one that applies to GIPs) – a question that has generally been confined to a discussion about the legitimacy of the second definition. However, before developing this point further, it is worth noting that both cases (differentiation and mass production/consumption) imply a high degree of geographical concentration of the production. Therefore, it remains to be seen how these local production zones (whether they are *terroirs* or not) are integrated or linked with other, larger, geographical entities (the state, the region, the world, and so on). This is of particular importance, as the two dimensions or quality and territorial organization are embedded in a complex way that affects not only the production of goods, but also their consumption and their (international) trade. The debates surrounding these definitions of quality in the international trade will be developed in the next section.

I.4 Geographical Identification and international trade

The divergences between the two concepts of quality – and their potential points of convergence – can best be perceived when they are subject to debates and when arguments that justify or criticize each of them are put forward (Boltanski and Thévenot, 2006). In this respect, because of the importance of agriculture in multilateral discussions, the international arena offers the best prospect for explaining the tension between the 'Fordist' and 'GI' definitions of quality, and highlights the ambivalent position of some countries.

First of all, the establishment of norms and standards at the global level is not a straightforward process, and leads to endless bargaining among countries. Norms for GIPs, as well as for agro-food in general, are subject to tough negotiations at the World Trade Organization (WTO), as is demonstrated by the recent failure of the Doha Round (mainly due to the agricultural sector). If the debate is limited to the GIPs only, different countries have different rules, related to their specific history, culture, economic organization, and other factors. For example, while PGIs are well specified in Southern Europe, their definition is sometimes lacking in other countries, including those, like Japan, where consumers are extremely concerned about the geographical origins of their products and where traditional agricultural products can be found (Kobe beef, Aomori apples, and so on).

Second, and in relation to the previous point, differences between regulations create territorial gaps and accelerate competition between countries. The countries which are 'friends' of the *sui generis* geographical indications system (mainly in Europe) are struggling to create an international notification system, while others (North America, Australia and so on) do promote brands or collective marks. This ongoing conflict between the 'New' and the 'Old' world generates permanent tensions between governments at a global level (as is well illustrated by the WTO panel on GI; see Ilbert's chapter in this volume). As rules are being slowly built by governments, international food standards as well as private companies procedures challenge public regulation.

Private standard settings, such as GlobalGap or the International Food Standard, facilitate compliance with food safety in a very flexible and effective manner: companies build their own standard-setting coalition and formulate their own corrective actions. The guidelines, the monitoring, and the control processes are based on a technical approach of quality in order to simplify accreditation and certification processes. The implementation, conformity and enforcement system gives an immediate response to markets and is embedded with international food safety rules such as the Codex guidelines (S. Henson and J. Humphrey).

This private international diplomacy for quality standards is also at work for intellectual property rights. Companies with strong market power do combine brand and GI in order to reinforce their monopoly.

Therefore, even though GIPs occupy only a small niche in international trade, it has important theoretical implications that cannot be ignored. It relates to the validity of the rule of comparative advantages. The use of international property rights and the increasing interference of quality policies as tools in international competition contribute to the build-up of competitive advantages (see Porter, 1986, 1991) while they create new market failures and affect existing comparative advantages. More importantly, perhaps, the nature of the international trade also changes, since the rise of *terroirs* brings a new form of competition between territories, a 'meso-level' between multinational corporations (MNCs) and the states.

I.5 Geographical Indication and development

As can be seen, this debate is not only between opposing production processes and methods, but also between different conceptions of agro-food production systems. A change in the relative balance between private and public order, as well as between the collective trademark/certification mark and the *sui generis* European models, may also influence the future modes of consumption. If, in recent years, the mistrust of consumers from developed countries has boosted the consumption of products of origins and has questioned the future of the Fordist model, this very same Fordist model can also be seen as a suitable solution to the food shortage in developing countries (Rastoin, 2008).

At the same time, GIPs can be developed as niches in a limited number of places in the developing world, in order to obtain a premium for agricultural products and move along the path of development. The problem here is that the existence of a *terroir* does not guarantee the development of the locality – for example, when the profits are confiscated by middlemen. A related and perhaps more fundamental point concerns the validity of the GIP/PT model. There are currently many traditional products and products of *terroir* in developing countries that are unable to reach the market because of insufficient recognition and/or marketing. If the GI and PT models are proved valid, they offer a suitable solution for these niche products to reach markets, at home and abroad, without competing with mass production goods. Nevertheless, this development, which will be limited to very specific areas, would be possible only if sufficient investments are made in areas such as marketing, packaging and standardization. That brings new challenges.

The first is related to the transferability of a model that was elaborated in developed countries in specific historical circumstances (for Bourgogne wines and the AOC, cf. Laferté, 2006). In order to understand the conditions of transferability, it is therefore necessary to examine (or even to compare) the mode of implementation of GI systems in various Asian economies.

Second, it is necessary to understand the historical process by which traditional products develop and find a place in the market. In this respect, the conditions by which it becomes legitimate to term a given product a PT have to be checked. It is obviously not sufficient for a good to be produced in a specific area; that good also needs to respect certain norms and standards, which have to be negotiated among all of the participants (including consumers, who decide if a PT is worth its price or not). It also calls for a specific certification, which can be given by the private sector or by the state. This is a major difference from branding, which depends mainly on individual firms. More fundamentally, the creation of geographical indications is dependent on social and historical context (see in Chapter 8 the example of Japanese *sake* since the beginning of the 1980s). A related element here is that most PTs are only distributed locally, and do not reach international or even national markets or recognition.

Third, there are still some difficulties in regulating GIs at the global level (the problem of global governance). Some countries have a well-defined system of regulation, while others are only just beginning to understand the interest of GIs. The example of Japan is of special interest, since the government has long emphasized the importance of traditional products (through, for example, the 'One Village, One Product' campaign), while avoiding taking regulatory action in this domain. For example, the famous Kobe beef, which can fetch $50 per 50 grammes in top-class restaurants, is not protected by a specific label of quality, at least internationally (China has recently started to produce its own 'Kobe beef', which has nothing in common with the genuine article). The different regulations and understanding concerning GIs lead to a 'spaghetti bowl' that is confusing for consumers and producers alike. China, which has concurrently several systems of protection for GIs, is a good example of this confusion, as developed by Wang Guihong in Chapter 10.

The fourth and final question is related to the fallacy of composition. As indicated earlier, PTs are sold at a premium, which means they are marketed principally for a small fraction of the world's population. Furthermore, even though the market for such products is growing regularly, it remains relatively small in comparison to the market for mass products. A large increase in the number of GIs and PTs might therefore prove counterproductive.

The questions which are raised from the concentration of agro-food production are diverse, both theoretically and practically. They lead to several forms of (local) development and models of society. The increase in products of origins over the past few years, in developed and developing areas alike, has led to questioning of the pertinence as well as the viability of this form of development. GIs open a small window for developing countries, as a minority of their farmers can receive a premium from their production (cf. the rice produced by farmers in Ifugao province in the Philippines is sold at $12 per kg in the United States).

On the other hand, the inclusion of this local model of development in the framework of international trade and of the WTO also poses problems. For developed countries, the multiplication of these forms of local development induces a new form of competition between geographical entities (Bayonne ham versus Parma ham, for example). In the case of Japan, the problem is even more complex, because, while it has developed many products of origin, it does not have easily recognizable standards that guarantee the intrinsic quality of these products: consumers base their choice on the *kata* – a term that defines a defect-free product and its production process – which in concrete terms means the physical appearance of the products (Bestor, 2004) or on fame (people may know the product but may not always be able to recognize it or its label). Furthermore, products of origins are not uniformly managed, and local governments have considerable leverage to decide how to promote their products of origins, how to protect them and so on (see Chapters 7 and 8 of this book).

In any case, the future recognition of as well as the international trade in these products is increasingly going to be influenced by the situation in East and Southeast Asia. For example, in accordance to what has been indicated above, Japan is currently hesitating between an 'American model' (that, in turn, becomes more flexible) and a 'South European model', while at the same time trying to promote some products of origin in international markets. The direction it finally takes will have some consequences not only on its agricultural exports, but also on the course of international negotiations. Similarly, the position of China, which is perceived by the international community as having difficulties in controlling the quality of its agricultural products, remains unclear, especially since it has implemented several systems of protection for GIs. What makes the situation more complex is that there is no unified direction in each country, the management of the products of origins depending heavily on the product itself and the attitude of local authorities and the state of power among local actors. Nevertheless, there is now a clear awareness in these two countries – as well as in other parts of Asia – of the necessity to make a decision on these issues.

I.6 The organization of this volume

The rapid development of Asia is changing the way policy makers (and researchers) can comprehend these challenges and the future of agro-food systems. Since most Asian countries, including Japan, China and Thailand, have recently been affected by food safety issues, many local consumers are now demanding higher-quality products. That prompted their governments to implement new laws to regulate geographical indications, which was in any case also advocated by the WTO.

But, in turn, that is prone to affect the current international negotiations with regards to GIs. On one hand, the conditions of the transferability of the 'geographical indications model' that has been developed in Southern Europe 100 years ago can be questioned. Can this model, which is already being challenged by the United States, have a better chance of being adopted by Asian countries? And, if the answer is positive, under what conditions? On the other hand, the trademark and certification mark system used in North America cannot be adopted straightforwardly by countries which still have difficulties in fully grasping the concept of intellectual property. In addition, the implementation of a trademark system may lead to conflicting situations with farmers who are producing these traditional goods for generations and do not intend either to discontinue their practice or to pay a membership fee.

In relation to this ambiguous situation, the actions taken by governments vary depending on the local context. It means, in fact, that these actions are also influenced by other agencies such as farmers, enterprises, and so on. As indicated earlier, the growing importance of GIs have induced a new form of territorial competition, which means that local governments, as well as enterprises, have an interest in promoting certain forms of legislation rather than others. As Guihong Wang shows in Chapter 10, conflicts may arise between local governments on one hand and local companies and farmers on the other. Since, in addition, GIs give competitive advantages to local producers, it becomes clear that the implementation of geographical indications in Asia becomes the focus of many divergent interests, locally and internationally.

The following chapters aim to analyse these different points. The way Asian countries can affect international negotiations also depends on the possibilities of GIs in terms of local development. These two factors are related to the way local cultures are 'operationalized' and reinterpreted by the local population in the context of globalization. For example, people, including international negotiators, have a different understanding of the concept of geographical indications based on the history of their country, while existing divergent economic interests (also affected by culture) remain paramount in such negotiations.

These points have both theoretical and empirical aspects. The first six chapters of the volume provide a theoretical framework to allow us to understand why and how the concept of geographical indications can be affected by culture, and what consequences it may have for their development. In particular, the social construction of markets, as well as the different evaluation of quality, affects the understanding of geographical indications. The five chapters that follow consist of case studies of different Asian countries (Japan, the Philippines and China) that illustrate how traditional agricultural products can be transformed into geographical indications, and what consequences they may have in terms of local development and for the future of GIs.

More specifically, in Chapter 1, Neantro Saavedra-Rivano links geographical indications and international trade. He shows that the development of the exports of GIs products challenges the rule of comparative advantage, while PGIs will gain more prominence in global trade. If the status of geographical indications is to be clarified internationally, it may offer some prospects for developing countries to gain global market access. In this respect, an important aspect is the relation between the redefinition of quality and the reorganization of international trade: the establishment of PGIs allows some regions to build up new comparative advantages, and to gain market shares overseas. There is therefore a reorganization of international trade at the local level, with the appearance of new actors (the role of geography in international trade being a well-debated topic since the pioneering work of Paul Krugman, 1991), and a new form of competition between infra-national geographical entities.

Chapters 2 to 4 address the construction of agricultural markets, commodities and quality. In Chapter 2, Philippe Steiner contends that agro-food markets are different in nature from other markets. Developing his argument from the notion of 'fictitious commodities' of Polanyi, he shows that the specificity of agro-food markets lies in the fact that they impact directly on human life. At the same time, since the eighteenth century, there have been considerable increases in the distance between food producers and consumers. These two phenomena have huge consequences, because their collusion also increases the anxiety of consumers about the food they buy, for which they have no guarantee for quality. This may explain the reasons why geographical indications, which are one of the tools to bridge consumption and production, are currently gaining ground, following a series of food safety crises. Louis Augustin-Jean, in Chapter 3, continues this discussion and shows that markets are dependent on the very definition of commodities. While markets and commodities are two sides of the same coin, the existence of market implies the aggregation of goods that are not perfectly similar. This process of aggregation causes the elimination of some characteristics of the product, such as history, geography and so on. On the other hand, the construction of geographical indications leads to the reincorporation of these characteristics inside the product, in order to 'value the unique'. This double process of aggregation and disaggregation is cultural in nature. That may explain why the European model of *terroir* has difficulties in imposing itself globally. In Chapter 4, Gilles Allaire completes this theoretical discussion with an analytical framework of the multidimensional construction of quality. He considers the three dimensions of quality, as judgments, as institutions and in markets, and shows that the construction of food standards, including geographical indications, are the products of a compromise that is tested in several market places and social arenas. Consequently, how intangible qualities combine in effective markets varies according to polities.

Overall, these three chapters concentrate on the cultural dimension of markets, especially with regard to the construction of geographical indications. They indirectly offer a perspective on the conditions for the emergence of a *terroir*, and the way it is invented from the inside, in relation to other geographical entities (from the infra-national to the global level). The emergence of the *terroir* as an analytical category also implies considering the role of other kinds of actors. Phenomena such as civil society movements, consumer groups, mass media and the search for ecotourism, are now playing a significant part in the promotion of GIPs, and increase the pressure on MNCs to take into account these new players. That does not mean, of course, that MNCs are only in a defensive position – it is exactly the contrary, as shown by Jean-Louis Rastoin in Chapter 6.

The last two chapters of the first part build on this construction of agricultural markets and quality. In Chapter 5, Hélène Ilbert first draws a historical trajectory of geographical indications from the twentieth century onwards. She meticulously describes the process of judicial construction of GIs, and the ongoing debates at the WTO. Products and know-how attributes are formally organized in the global network of intellectual property rights: territorial quality trademark, certification marks, and geographical indications are legitimate instruments for protecting a specific dimension of a good or a service. But the international recognition of GIs or *sui generis* rights is at stake. Conflicts between trademarks and collective rights, between mandatory or voluntary legal procedures, between biodiversity protection and exploitation emphasize the bargaining mechanism of the institutional intellectual property rights marketing process. Arguments related to costs, to local know-how protection, to trade barriers, to local innovative traditions or discriminatory measures institute various strategies for marketing property rights. In global competition, the reputation of the goods and the promotion of their attributes, guaranteed by legal means, accelerate the process of creating differentiated markets ruled by monopolistic competition. Within this complex legal and institutional framework, Jean-Louis Rastoin, in Chapter 6, proposes an analysis based on the firms' strategy and the building up of competitive advantage. He shows that, while the 'tertiary agro-industrial model' is becoming dominant through the increasing weight of MNCs, the *terroir* model proposes an alternative that might help to correct some of the deficiencies of the first one, in terms of public health, food safety, and so on – all issues that have been studied in previous chapters. This model, as well as the strategies of firms located in the terroir, can be built on the European institutional and legal framework of geographical indications, which is well defined and complies with the corporate social responsibility.

Part II of the book seeks to present case studies in Asian countries – namely, Japan, the Philippines and China – and show how local products with a geographical label take part in this process. As indicated, the position of Asian countries is likely to affect the future trade of PT and GIPs. In reality, Asia has the potential to develop or promote many of its traditional productions as GIPs or PTs. Nevertheless, at the moment, only a few of them have gained international recognition, even though that does not always equate with a vivid international trade (Kobe beef is renowned across the world, but is only consumed in Japan, as indicated in Chapter 7). The aim is also to confront current practices with the theoretical considerations elaborated in Part I, especially in regard to the history of the creation of the GIPs, their marketing, and the construction and internationalization of *terroirs*. In such a way, it becomes possible to understand the local and global dynamics at work concerning the GIPs in the context of tense international negotiations. In Chapter 7, Louis Augustin-Jean and Kae Sekine consider the examples of the famous Kobe beef and Matsusaka beef, and show that, despite an identical national institutional framework based on a collective trademark, the pattern at the local level is different in the two instances – closer to the collective trademark in Matsusaka and to the European *sui generis* system for Kobe. These differences are linked to the social structure at the local level and give rise to differentiated marketing strategies. Their analysis indicates that Japan is still balancing between the European or the American systems, neither of which is entirely suited to the local culture. Similarly, in Chapter 8, Nicolas Baumert illustrates how the taste of consumers for Japanese *sake* has changed in recent years. While in the past quality had depended on traditional commercial brands, the importance of identifying precise geographical origins has gained ground in recent years. In particular, the region of Niigata, which used to be a minor producer of *sake* in the past, emerged as new region producing quality *sake*. Nevertheless, this evolution does not equate with the development of *terroirs*, for cultural, legal and institutional reasons. In Chapter 9, Suyako Sekimoto and Louis Augustin-Jean analyse the process by which the Tinawon rice, a speciality rice of the Cordillera that was originally not produced for the market, became a commodity following the involvement of an American company. The company incorporated traditions and culture into the quality of the product, which fetches a very high price in specialized North American markets. But then, who should benefit from the added value from these cultural elements? Is it the company, which valorized the product and the local culture? Or should it be the farmers, who maintain the local traditions? Of course, the answer to this type of question will vary, depending upon who is supplying the answer. In conclusion, this chapter shows the advantages of building an analysis based on the commodification process. The last two chapters of the volume are devoted to China. In Chapter 10, Guihong Wang carefully describes the construction of the legal framework of geographical indications through the case of Jinhua ham in Zhejiang Province. She indicates that, having initially avoided making a choice between the American and the European system, China finally implemented both of them. The result has been legal confusion and disputes, which are still in the process of being resolved. Nevertheless, it has been replaced by a different type of confusion, since consumers have difficulties in differentiating among multiple labels. In other words, while the demand for GI products is growing because consumers are seeking higher-quality products, the existing system does not provide suitable information on quality to these very same customers and the system is still under construction, as illustrated in the last chapter. Thus, in Chapter 11, Selina Ching Chan, through a meticulous anthropological investigation, shows how the definition of *longjing* tea, also in Zhejiang, is the product of the confrontation between several types of discourses (historical, legal, and so on). As such, it is a construction, which depends not only on the long history of the tea and its culture, but also on how it is portrayed by local actors – and by national politicians. As in the case of Jinhua, the evolution of the production, during the Maoist era and the reform period, has created confusions regarding the zone of production and in the (re)definition of the product.

The five case studies demonstrate the difficulties in adapting to a given system, whether it is American or European. While China has adopted both systems, in Japan, there are negotiations and testing to see which one is best suited to the country. It is a matter not only of institutional prerogatives (in other words, the result of a debate between the Ministry of Agriculture and the Ministry of Finance), but also of cultural conditions. In the Philippines, the implementation of a GI system is also under discussion, but the example of Tinawon rice indicates that the final system will have to consider existing cultural values and the relationships between local actors, the product and their traditions. With these considerations in mind, the results of international negotiations at the WTO may not be the choice of the American or the European system of protection, but rather the invention of a new one, based on the historical experiences of Asian countries – and their economic interests.

Note

The editors wish to thank three people who have generously taken some of their time to help us in the preparation of this volume. Ms Sherlon Chi-Yin Ip (The Chinese University of Hong Kong) has taken on the valuable and irksome task of formatting all of the chapters, while she also proofread Chapter 10. Mr Cho-hong Choi (University of Hong Kong) has proofread Chapters 3, 7 and 9, and Dr James A. Elwood (The University of Tsukuba), Chapter 6.

References

Akerlof, G. (1970) 'The Markets for "Lemons": Qualitative Uncertainty and the Market Mechanism', *Quarterly Journal of Economics*, 84, 488–500.

Allaire, G. (2004) 'Quality in Economics: a Cognitive Perspective', in M. Harvey, A. McMeekin and A. Warde (eds), *Qualities of Food* (Manchester: Manchester University Press), pp. 61–93.

Bestor, T.C. (2004) *Tsukiji: The Fish Market at the Center of the World* (Berkeley: University of California Press).

Boltanski, L. and L. Thévenot (2006) *On Justification: Economies of Worth* (Princeton, NJ: Princeton University Press).

Chan, S.C. (2010) 'Imagining and Consuming Cultures. Nostalgia and Domestic Tourism', in L. Augustin-Jean (ed.), *Entrepreneurship and Development in Asia*, special section, *The Canadian Journal of Development Studies*, 31(3–4), 367–81.

Eymard-Duvernay, F. (1989) 'Conventions de Qualité et pluralité des formes de coordination', *Revue Economique*, 40(2), 329–59.

Friedmann, H. and P. McMichael (1989) 'Agriculture and the State System. The Rise and Decline of National Agricultures, 1870 to Present', *Sociologia Ruralis*, 29(2), 93–117.

Henson, S. and J. Humphrey (2011) 'Codex Alimentarius and Private Standards', in B.M.J. van der Meulen (eds), *Private Food Law: Governing Food Chains Through Contract Law, Self-regulation, Private Standards, Audits and Certification Schemes* (Wageningen: Wageningen Academic Publishers).

Josling, T. (2006) 'The War on *Terroir*: Geographical Indications as a Transatlantic Trade Conflict', *Journal of Agricultural Economics*, 57(3), 337–63.

Krugman, P. (1991) *Geography and Trade* (Cambridge, MA: MIT Press).

Laferté, G. (2006) *La Bourgogne et ses vins: image d'origine contrôlée* (Paris: Belin).

McMichael, P. (2009a) 'A Food Regime Analysis of the "World Food Crisis"', *Agriculture and Human Values*, 26, 281–95.

McMichael, P. (2009b) 'A Food Regime Genealogy', *The Journal of Peasant Studies*, 36(1), 139–69.

Porter, M. (1986) 'Competition in Global Industries: A Conceptual Framework', in M. Porter (ed.), *Competition in Global Industries* (Boston, MA: Harvard Business School Press), pp. 15–60.

Porter, M. (1991) 'Towards a Dynamic Theory of Strategy', *Strategic Management Journal*, 12, 95–116.

Rastoin, J.L. (2008) 'Les multinationales dans le système alimentaire', *Projet*, no. 306 (La Plaine, St Denis), 61–9.

Part I
The Theoretical Implications of Products of Origins

1

Geographical Indications and International Trade

Neantro Saavedra-Rivano

1.1 Introduction

Although geographical indications (GI) occupy a small niche in world trade they raise important issues in the theory of international trade such as the overall validity of the principle of comparative advantage. In a dynamic context, where basic food products are increasingly being produced through international production chains thereby raising food safety concerns and where luxury food products are appealling to wider segments of the populations everywhere, the place of GIs in world trade is set to become more prominent. On the other hand, international trade considerations are paramount from a GI perspective. For one thing, most of the disagreements on GIs take place in the international domain. Not that there are no disagreements within respective national environments but nations usually possess institutional mechanisms that can, in principle, be activated to deal with them. The situation is not so clear internationally and this chapter will look at how the World Trade Organization (WTO) has handled them so far. In addition to the controversies and disputes surrounding GIs we will also look at the connection between them and development policies in developing countries, especially the use of GIs in development strategies that seek to generate export revenues through the exploitation of their 'hidden' treasures.

1.2 The historical background

Although the term geographical indications is a relatively new one the roots of them are ancient, as old in fact as the traditions that led to products now covered by them. In an age when communication between different communities was difficult and infrequent it was natural that techniques of production would evolve in ways that were differentiated. Those differences corresponded not only to differences in local customs and traditions but also to the specific characteristics of the territory, such as topography, climate, biodiversity, soil quality and landscape among others. The French word *terroir* captures the idea of a locale endowed with such a set of attributes and, consequently, the term *products of terroir* refers to those products embodying them. This kind of very localized and culture-specific development of production techniques affecting goods of common use, mainly foods and beverages, happened everywhere in the world and was parallel to the development of other cultural manifestations such as handcraft, cuisine, and popular arts. Limited mobility and interaction between communities implied that knowledge and appreciation of these products was circumscribed to the immediate vicinity of those communities that produced them. It is also important to notice, as in Bérard (2005), that a similar development took place in the modalities of consumption of these products, to such an extent that in some cases it was hard for outsiders to understand how any satisfaction could be derived from their consumption.

Over time, as there were improvements in mobility and communications, it became increasingly common for individuals to become aware of the existence of products that did not correspond to their own local traditions and environment. Natural selection and cultural affinities led to some of these products becoming popular outside of their *terroir* and in this way a regional and national demand for them appeared. The emergence and growth of urban centres with heterogeneous populations of migrants originating from a variety of regional backgrounds was also conducive to the projection of *products of terroir* to a broader public and to the development of a wider demand for them. This demand brought with it a bonus in their price as a reward for their specific characteristics and origin. In turn this bonus would entice imitators eager to appropriate it. It was only natural for original producers to seek protection from this assault on their perceived rights. In the process they developed cooperative structures that would make their lobbying more effective. Gradually, regulations governing the production of these goods began to appear in national jurisdictions. The rationale behind them consisted, as is usually the case when dealing with intellectual property rights, of two main components. One was to reward producers for their industry and innovation and, in this way, to signal to other potential innovators that their effort would not be wasted. The other, also present from the beginning, was to protect consumers from misleading information.

This process of dissemination to wider economic spaces of products originally pertaining to very localized territories eventually moved from its national stage to its next stage of internationalization. Once again, the continued development of communications and technology supplied the background that made this possible. Products that had a more universal appeal or whose consumption became associated with cultures or ways of life that inspired imitation elsewhere were sought globally. International migrants, anxious to reproduce, even if partially, their original habitat in the distant lands they had adopted, were instrumental in reinforcing this movement. They also contributed actively to the generation of imitation products to the original products. Protection at the international level became an issue but one of a much higher level of complexity than protection at the national level. The most obvious reason for the difficulties in building a meaningful system of protection for these kinds of products are the imperfections – or even the plain absence – of international institutions that could be used for this task. An additional hindrance has been that the knowledge behind a *product of terroir* is undeniably of a quite different nature than that underlying other forms of intellectual property such as a work of art of a modern invention. Let us say that we compare a product of *terroir* such as Cognac, a work of art such as *La Gioconda*, and a modern invention such as the blue light-emitting diode (LED). *La Gioconda* is perhaps the best-known work of Leonardo da Vinci and its fame is such that attempts to counterfeit it would be most likely laughed off and, if at all successful in misleading a buyer, swiftly pursued as a crime. Although not as famous, many people are familiar with Shuji Nakamura, the Japanese scientist who invented the blue LED in 1995 while working at Nichia Corporation and with the legal dispute with his employer that ended ten years later with the award of a substantial monetary compensation for that ground-breaking and profitable innovation (see, for instance, Taplin, 2008). Attempts to manufacture products using this knowledge have been fought vigorously by Nichia Corporation in the courts using the technical specifications codified in registered patents and by the international system for their protection. On the other hand, no one name could be easily associated with the invention of Cognac. Even the notion of 'invention' seems hardly appropriate for this kind of product, characterized not only by a process of elaboration which has evolved through the ages but also by a variety of inputs which are specific to the region of Cognac. Cognac is, despite these differences, a relatively successful case of a *product of terroir* that has achieved widespread international protection. The protection afforded to Cognac is part of the agreements reached at the end of the Uruguay Round of trade negotiations of the General Agreement on Tariffs and Trade (GATT), which led to the creation of the World Trade Organization. Article 22 of the Agreement on Trade-Related Aspects of Property Rights (TRIPS), a component of that package which came into effect on January 1995, deals specifically with the protection of GI, while Article 23 strengthens it in the case of wines and liquors. Those articles, in addition to firmly establishing the use of the term 'Geographical Indications', have defined the background for international negotiations on their protection. Although these issues are discussed in more detail in Chapter 5 of this book, it should be mentioned here that international negotiations on GI started at a much earlier time, with the historical precedents of the Paris Convention (1883), the Madrid (1891) and Lisbon (1958) agreements and other negotiations in the context of the World Intellectual Property Organization (WIPO) prior to the TRIPS.

It may be instructive to follow these historical developments by considering the case of a particular *product of terroir* and, for this purpose, we will choose the Roquefort, one of the oldest and best-known French cheeses. According to Frayssignes (2011), the origins of Roquefort cheese can be traced back to 3500 BC. The cheese is produced in the village of Roquefort-sur-Soulzon in the Aveyron department in the south of France. History has it that it was a favourite of Charlemagne and that he granted to the village the monopoly of ripening of the cheese in 1411. Roquefort was the first cheese to be granted the status of Controlled Appellation of Origin (AOC) by a law of 1925, obtaining in this way full protection within France. Since 2008 it has been registered as a Protected Designation of Origin (PDO) of the European Union, thus extending the area of protection to Europe. Being included in both schemes of protection opens the way for even wider protection to be negotiated under the umbrella of Article 22 of the TRIPS.

1.3 The international fault lines

GIs may not be the most important among the many contentious issues in international trade relations but it is undeniably one of the most fascinating. It is related to discussions on the agricultural sector, certainly one of the most intractable areas in negotiations to date. It also invokes intellectual property issues, recently incorporated into multilateral trade agreements through the TRIPS, but still subject to a host of confrontations involving national and multinational interests. And it is perhaps through the skirmishes on GIs that some of the most significant fault lines in international trade relations are revealed. We are thinking about the following three fault lines: the '*Transatlantic fault line*', separating the United States from the European Union; the '*Historical fault line*', separating the New World countries from the Old World countries; and the '*Developmental fault line*', separating developing countries from developed countries. These characterizations are, of course, simplistic, but they are useful to portray the main issues involved. Each one of these fault lines could be associated with a central theme of disagreement, around which other related themes are played.

Liberalization is the core issue associated with the *Transatlantic fault line*. The United States is usually perceived as the main champion of the cause of liberalization, not only on matters related to international exchanges but also on those pertaining to the national economy, such as the scope of regulation and, more generally, the role and size of government as an economic agent. Although in practice the United States is far from being a model of liberalization and, in particular, its authorities resort unabashedly to protectionist practices whenever that suits the perceived national interest, liberalization remains an ideal to long for and regulation, as well as other government constraints on economic activity, are seen as a necessary evil. On the other hand, European countries, especially Continental Western European countries, tend to view government as a natural and leading agent in all domains of economic activity. That view needs to be tempered by the fact that economic liberalism has been making inroads in Europe for at least the past 40 years. We can thus say that there has been a narrowing of views, if not necessarily a process of convergence. In the case of GIs the debates concern both consumers and producers of these goods. Everybody accepts as an important issue the need to protect consumers from misleading information. Not even the most extreme advocate of liberalization would defend the 'right' to sell products on the basis of deceptive labelling or advertising and national commercial regulation generally protects the consumer. That principle has also been present in international agreements since the Paris Convention (1883), whose Article 10 refers explicitly to the seizure of 'goods bearing false indications as to their source or the identity of the producer'. There is, however, another aspect of consumer rights, namely the faculty to *knowingly* acquire goods labelled in a way that evokes a different origin than their actual geographical origin. An example would be the consumption of local brands of *parmesan* cheese in the US or *parmesano* in South America (*parmesão* in Brazil), products that clearly evoke the name of the original *Parmigiano Reggiano*. The capacity to exercise this freedom of choice by consumers is, naturally, closely linked to the corresponding ability of producers to enter the market for products that, although being well established in terms of their geographical origin, could be replicated in other places in terms of their quality and other physical characteristics and, in addition, to use marks that relate their own products with those they are imitating. It is at this point that the rift between the United States and the European Union becomes apparent. Going back to Parmiggiano Reggiano cheese, that product carries a PDO from the European Union. In 2008 the European Court of Justice ruled, in a case brought by Italy against German producers, that that protection extends to the use of the term 'parmesan' (European Court of Justice, 2008). On the other hand, although the Parmigiano Reggiano Cheese Consortium has been able to successfully defend the name 'parmigiano reggiano cheese' in United States courts, it has been unable to do so for the name 'parmesan cheese'. Even now there is a host of producers in the United States marketing 'parmesan cheese' under their own trademarks. The freedom that the principles of liberalization grant to non-original producers has as its counterpart a cost to the original producers. To the extent that the reputation or image of the original products allow their producers to reap a bonus they are clearly affected by the entrance of other, non-original producers. As has often been noted (see, for instance, Fink and Maskus, 2006) this effect has at least two components. The most obvious one is the reduction in market share that the entry of non-original producers has on original producers. That component may not be as important as it would appear at first sight; the reason is that the incorporation of new producers and the advertising it usually entails have the potential of expanding the market for that product. In theory, it might even be conceivable that sales by original producers would be even higher in the expanded market than they were in the protected market, although whether this is observed in practice is highly debatable and remains to be proved. The second component is more insidious and the damage it causes is lasting. It affects mostly those goods whose consumption carries a special image or connotation, the so-called *status goods*. Entry of non-original producers has the potential of reducing or even erasing the special aura associated with the good and substantially reducing the premium consumers had been willing to pay until then.

The *Historical fault line* is perhaps the most interesting and less conventional of the three, and it is also the most relevant to GIs. The New World refers, of course, to countries of recent settlement, as is the case of Australia, Canada, New Zealand and the United States. Several Latin American countries also fit into this category, and this is clearly the case for Argentina, Brazil and Chile, whose populations to a large extent have been transplanted from other lands over the past five centuries. Other Latin American countries, such as Bolivia, Mexico and Peru, are arguably part of the Old World as they are cultural heirs to ancient civilizations. The same is, of course, true in the case of European and Asian countries. One of the surprises of the current era of globalization is that, despite all the discourse of post-modernity, the presence of ancient civilizations can be felt everywhere and defines much of our current world. A similar assertion holds for international relations where history, sometimes going back for several centuries, weighs powerfully in drawing current confrontations and rivalries. When looking at the spread of globalization, we see that the main agents of the process are New World countries, chiefly the United States, and that the tools that allow for it, communication and transportation technologies, are thoroughly modern. On the other hand, much of the content of globalization, as for instance in the popular arts and fast food, is derived from ancient traditions of the Old World. In schematic terms it could be said that the New World countries wish to move forward with the assimilation and processing of traditions from the Old World countries and to continue reaping the economic and strategic benefits from distributing them globally. Old World countries are thus pressed to choose between taking themselves the initiative of packaging and adapting their traditions so as to sell them globally or rather continue trying to protect their integrity and to closely control the international markets for related products. Thus far those Old World countries better placed in the struggle for control of the globalization processes seem to have selected the second option. GIs are on the frontline of this clash of perspectives on the shape and control of globalization and the World Trade Organization is the main theatre for national actors to further their positions. Given the general stalemate of the Doha Round of trade negotiations there has been little progress in advancing towards a global and comprehensive treatment of GIs that would go beyond the modest measures embodied in Section 3 (Articles 22 to 24) of the TRIPS. Instead countries have moved towards the consolidations of their own treatments of the issue in line with their overall commercial and economic strategies. The United States considers geographical indications as being 'a subset of trademarks' (USPTO, 2011) and, accordingly, it deals with them using the administrative system it has already set for handling trademarks. This means there is no specific recognition of GIs as such or, in particular, a registry for such products. As a matter of fact the United States Patent and Trademark Office (USPTO), the government unit supervising that system, states explicitly that it 'does not protect geographic terms or signs that are generic for goods/services' (USPTO, 2011). This opens the way for arbitrary treatment of many products, a good example being the case of cheeses. As previously mentioned, local (or international) producers can freely use the term 'parmesan cheese' under their own trademarks while the exclusive rights of 'Parmigiano Reggiano' have been judicially recognized. On the other hand there are no US producers of 'Roquefort' cheese, and the name is protected by a USPTO certification mark, the device available under the United States system to register the regional origin of specific products. Certification marks can also be used to register, in addition to place of origin, other characteristics of goods or services, such as, for instance, specific features of the process of production, or the fact that labour for the production was performed by members of a specific union or guild. Certification marks differ from trademarks in that their owners cannot themselves engage in production of the good or service carrying the mark and that they do not identify its particular producer but instead the nature and qualities that defined the mark in the first place. The Canadian treatment of GIs is similar to that of the United States and, in particular, it uses the system of certification marks to identify the geographical origin of those products that come to be protected by them. Wines and spirits receive a differentiated treatment, both in deference to Article 23 of the TRIPS and because of the *Canada–European Community Wines and Spirits Agreement* signed in September 2003 (Daley, 2008). That treaty establishes that Canada will remove over the following 12 years a number of GIs for wines and spirits from their 'black list' of so-called generic names. It represented a significant victory for the European position of repatriating or 'clawing back' names that are in use elsewhere and that evoke traditional European GIs. On the other side of the historical fault line, the European Union has been the most vocal advocate of considering geographical indications an entirely new category of intellectual property rights, one not to be confused with trademarks and not particularly well served by the system of certification marks. Since 1992 it created two categories of intellectual property, Protected Designation of Origin (PDO) and Protected Geographical Indication (PGI), as well as mechanisms for registration and for protection within the European Union. In addition it pursues vigorously protection of these products through several avenues. Efforts at a global level, at the World Trade Organization, in particular at the

TRIPS Council, have had rather modest results. Most effective have been those conducted on a bilateral basis, leading to specific agreements with Australia, Canada, Chile, Mexico, South Africa and the United States. In the case of Chile and South Africa these agreements were negotiated as part of wider bilateral cooperation treaties.

The *Developmental fault line* separating developing and developed countries on issues of international trade has gained increased relevance after the launch of the Doha Round of trade negotiations and with the adoption of its associated Doha Development Agenda (DDA). As pointed out by Moore (2002), who was at the time Director-General of the World Trade Organization, the DDA placed development issues and the interests of developing nations at the very heart of trade negotiations. However positive the new emphasis on development and global inequalities it is also one of the main reasons for the prolonged impasse of that round. The stalemate, most recently highlighted by the disappointing results of the Eighth WTO Ministerial Conference (Geneva, 2011), has led many to propose the recognition of failure of the trade round (see, for instance, Schwab, 2011). The current deadlock in negotiations is largely explained by the shift in the strategic distribution of power among regions of the world. Power is being transferred progressively from the traditional centre (the United States, Western Europe and Japan) to the emerging countries (China, India, Brazil) while at the same time the global governance system established at the end of the Second World War is showing its age. The lack of agreement on international trade issues is just one aspect of broader and disturbing differences about the world system among its main players. Confining ourselves to the area of trade the most important issue from the perspective of developing countries is certainly market access, especially for agricultural products. GIs are, of course, a subset of these, minor although potentially important. Albeit most discussions about *products of terroir* bring to mind products predominantly from France and other Southern European countries the truth is that they are present in many other countries, developed as well as developing. Part II of this book offers a detailed discussion of some of these products for Asian countries, namely China, Japan and the Philippines, and provides a glimpse into the wealth of products of *terroir* in that part of the world. Latin American countries also possess a large variety of products of *terroir*, albeit systematic efforts to develop that potential, pursued within the last couple of decades, are still lagging. For example, Peru, heir to one of the most advanced pre-Columbian civilizations and endowed with an exuberant fauna and flora, has so far registered only eight Denominations of Origin, and only two of them are controlled by a Council representing the producers of the corresponding good. One of these two Denominations of Origin was given to Pisco, a grape brandy produced in selected areas along the Southern coast of Peru. A very similar spirit, carrying the same name, is also produced in winemaking areas of Chile, and both countries have been claiming the origin of the product for many years, a dispute that so far has prevented either of them from seeking international recognition and protection for that GI. Despite these difficulties, the fact remains that Latin American countries, as well as developing countries elsewhere, possess a large potential stock of geographical indications based either on their biodiversity or on their traditional products. As this potential is progressively realized the issue of market access for GIs from developing countries becomes more pressing. In this specific case that access includes equal treatment to the mechanisms of protection and registry of GIs in developed countries. There are encouraging signs that the European Union is moving towards a friendlier position towards access to their markets for GIs from developing countries, possibly sensing that both groups of countries can work together in the World Trade Organization to design a more comprehensive global system of protection and registry for GIs. Perhaps the most telling of these was the behaviour displayed by the European Union in 2005 following the decision against them by the Dispute Panel set at the request of the United States (Australia also filed a similar request). Although it would be cumbersome to enter into the details of that request (see WTO, 2005), one of the main arguments of the United States was that the European Union, through its implementation of protection to geographical indications (Council Regulation 2081/92, see EU, 1992), failed to obey Article 3 of TRIPS, which specifically requires that members 'shall accord to the nationals of other Members treatment no less favourable than that it accords to its own nationals with regard to the protection of intellectual property'. The Dispute Panel found in its report that the United States had made a *prima facie* case for its arguments, and that report was approved without changes by the Dispute Settlement Body of the WTO. The European Union did not appeal to that ruling and swiftly adopted a new regulation (Council Regulation 510/2006, see EU 2006) that incorporated all changes ensuing from it. Those changes benefitted of course all countries and not just the United States and Australia. As a matter of fact the first Protected Geographical Indication (PGI) granted by the Commission of the

European Communities to a country outside the European Union was given to *Café de Colombia* in 2007 (EU 2007).

1.4 Geographical Indications, development and international trade

The well-known relation between economic development and international trade takes a special meaning when dealing with GIs. There are at least two reasons for this, respectively related with traditional knowledge and with biodiversity.

The first has to do with the avenues that developing countries could use to take advantage of the fruits of globalization. Some developing countries, notably China and other East Asian countries, thanks to a virtuous coincidence of good policies carried out at a favourable period of the world economy, have benefitted enormously from the growth of international trade and the redeployment of large components of manufacturing away from industrial countries. Other countries, mostly in Africa and Latin America, are struggling to find ways to share in this trade-led growth of the world economy. Exports of primary goods and agricultural commodities have clear developmental limitations due to their low labour content and the fragile terms of trade they imply. One response to this apparent impasse comes from innovation and its application to the development of new products or services that would find demand in international markets. The conventional sort of innovation, relying on new technologies and requiring a substantial scientific and industrial base, at least in the medium term, and barring the transfer of technology from other countries, is out of reach to most developing countries. Many of them, though, possess a wealth of traditional knowledge that is either forgotten or confined to limited communities. Casual observation, and the experience of developed countries such as Italy, Japan or France, indicates that large parts of that knowledge could serve as sources of innovation to develop new products or services adapted to modern tastes and customs. Confining our observation to traditional knowledge that is related to foodstuffs it is reasonable to expect that sort of innovation to give rise, in particular, to new GIs from developing countries. If we extend the scope of GIs to other products the door is open for a host of new products and services. Many of these have already found acceptance among tourists from other countries but that incipient demand could only grow if two important conditions were to be met. One is an entrepreneurial effort of innovation, in terms of presentation, packaging, and other elements, to make those goods acceptable to a wider public; the other is the branding and protection necessary to enable them to obtain a higher price in international markets. The former relies on local entrepreneurship and propitious public policies, the latter on an extension of the global system of GIs to these products. As for the extension of the concept of GIs to traditional knowledge there has been some movement within the World Trade Organization to that effect, at least since the preparations in 1999 for the ill-fated Third WTO Ministerial Conference in Seattle. Several WTO members, especially from Latin America, pressed for the amendment of the TRIPS to include other forms of intellectual property such as traditional knowledge. As quoted in Pugatch (2004, pp. 161–2) a joint communication by Bolivia, Colombia, Ecuador, Nicaragua and Peru stressed that 'the entire modern evolution of intellectual property has been framed by principles and systems which have tended to leave aside a large sector of human creativity, namely the traditional knowledge possessed by local and indigenous communities.' Eventually these views made their way into the Doha Declaration whose paragraph 19 instructs the TRIPS Council to include into its work programme consideration of the relations between the TRIPS, specifically its Article 27.3(b), and traditional knowledge and folklore (WTO, 2001). Unfortunately, as made clear by the recent communication from Director-General Pascal Lamy (WTO, 2011), there has been no more progress on these issues than on other points of the Doha Development Agenda.

The second issue, biodiversity, is of high relevance for many developing countries. Biopiracy has become a big issue, especially for those countries lacking the entrepreneurial capacity or the global reach to take advantage of the riches in their territories. A well-known case is that of the tropical fruit *Cupuaçu*, found in abundance in the Amazon region of Brazil and even now little exploited in that country despite its very attractive flavour and appealing health properties. In 2002 a Brazilian manufacturer of cupuaçu-flavoured chocolate discovered that, to be allowed to export that product to Japan using the name of the fruit, it would have to pay licensing rights to Asahi Foods, a large Japanese food processor and distributor who had registered trademarks for the name in Japan, the United States and the European Union the preceding year. The news became a scandal in Brazil and eventually the patents were cancelled (see Piedade, 2008). The Doha Declaration also instructed the TRIPS Council to examine the relations between the TRIPS and the Convention on Biological Diversity (CBD). It is not surprising that there has been no progress on that line of work at the TRIPS Council given that, as pointed out by many observers, the

Convention on Biological Diversity and the TRIPS are fundamentally in conflict.

1.5 Looking ahead: some concluding remarks

As globalization, fuelled by advances in technology and communications, follows its course, several emerging trends are bound to increasingly highlight the importance of GIs and their role in international trade.

First let us consider the relationship of GIs with luxury products. The consumption of many products carrying GIs, particularly those from European countries, evokes a sense of 'luxury'. This is due not only to the fact that their prices are usually higher than those of similar generic products but also to their relative scarcity and to the clever branding that producers have cultivated through long periods of time. Especially in the case when those products are imported that sort of consumption is perceived as being exclusive of an elite. Access to luxury consumption is, however, undergoing important changes. In what observers of these trends have called 'democratization of luxury' or 'massification of luxury' (see, for instance, Mortelmans, 2005) vast segments of the public are becoming able and willing to consume those goods. The phenomenon is not only limited to developed countries but is also taking place in developing countries, especially the large emerging economies of Brazil, China and India. According to Atsmon et al. (2011), the share of China in the world luxury market, estimated in 2010 at 10 per cent, is expected to grow to 20 per cent by 2015. That will make China overtake Japan and become the largest luxury world market. Despite the fact that food and beverages constitute a relatively small segment within the luxury goods sector this trend implies that the demand for GIs is set for further growth. As the existing GIs have, by their very nature, a limited supply, the natural way to satisfy that demand will be for new GIs to appear, both from developed and developing countries.

A second trend contributing to the increase in demand for GIs relates to the ongoing 'internationalization' of food products. More and more food products reach consumer markets at the end of an international production chain that is almost as complex as that of manufactured products. This trend raises important and worrying issues concerning the effects on consumers of defects or failures in the production chain. These sorts of food safety anxieties have the potential of driving more affluent consumers away from standard food products towards more personalized and location-specific food products, in particular towards GIs.

References

Atsmon, Y. et al (2011) 'Understanding China's Love for Luxury', McKinsey Consumer & Shopping Insights, May, http://www.mckinsey.com/locations/greaterchina/InsightsChina_LuxuryGoods.pdf, date accessed 24 December 2011.

Bérard, L. (2005) 'Les Produits du Terroir entre Cultures et Règlements', 16 June, presented in the cycle of conferences *Cafés-Débats à Marciac*, http://www.agrobiosciences.org/IMG/pdf/Produits_de_terroir1.pdf, date accessed 10 December 2011.

Daley, D. (2008) 'Canada's Treatment of Geographical Indications: Compliant or Defiant? An International Perspective', in Y. Gendreau (ed.) *An Emerging Intellectual Property Paradigm – Perspectives from Canada*, Queen Mary Studies in Intellectual Property (Cheltenham: Edward Elgar).

European Court of Justice, 'Case C-132/05 Commission v Germany, judgment of 26/02/2008', http://curia.europa.eu/juris/liste.jsf?language=en&jur=C,T,F&num=C-132/05&td=ALL, date accessed 10 December 2011.

European Union (EU) (1992) 'Council Regulation (EEC) 2081/92 of 14 July 1992 on the Protection of Geographical Indications and Designations of Origin for Agricultural Products and Foodstuffs', http://eur-lex.europa.eu/LexUriServ/LexUriServ.do?uri=CELEX:31992R2081:EN:NOT, date accessed 24 December 2011.

European Union (EU) (2006) 'Council Regulation (EC) 510/2006 of 20 March 2006 on the Protection of Geographical Indications and Designations of Origin for Agricultural Products and Foodstuffs', http://eur-lex.europa.eu/LexUriServ/LexUriServ.do?uri=CELEX:32006R0510:EN:NOT, date accessed 24 December 2011.

European Union (EU) (2007) 'Commission Regulation (EC) 1050/2007', *Official Journal of the European Union*, 13 September.

Fink, C. and K. Maskus (2006) 'The Debate on Geographical Indications in the WTO', in R. Newfarmer (ed.), *Trade, Doha, and Development: A Window into the Issues* (Washington, DC: The World Bank).

Frayssignes, J. (2010) 'System IV: Roquefort Cheese (France)', in R. Barham and B. Sylvander, *Labels of Origin for Food: Local Development, Global Recognition* (Wallingford, Oxon: CABI Publishing).

Gamboa Vilela, P. (2011) 'Las Denominaciones de Origen en el Perú', presented at the 'Worldwide Symposium on Geographical Indications, WIPO/GEO/LIM/11', World Intellectual Property Organisation, Lima, 22–4 June 2011.

Moore, M. (2002) 'The Doha Development Agenda: Reflections on the Road Ahead', *Asia-Pacific Review*, 9(1).

Mortelmans, D. (2005) 'Sign Values in Processes of Distinction: The Concept of Luxury', *Semiotics*, 157(1/4), 497–520.

Piedade, F.L. (2008) 'Biopiratataria e Direito Ambiental: Estudo de Caso do Cupuaçu', Master's Thesis, 'Luiz de Queiroz' Higher Agricultural School, University of Sao Paulo, Piracicaba.

Pugatch, M.P. (2004) *The International Political Economy of Intellectual Property Rights*, New Horizons in Intellectual Property (Cheltenham: Edward Elgar).

Schwab, S. (2011) 'After Doha: Why the Negotiations Are Doomed and What We Should Do About It', *Foreign Affairs*, May/June.

Taplin, R. (2008) 'Japanese Intellectual Property and Employee Rights to Compensation', *Asia Pacific Business Journal*, 14(3), 363–78.

United States Patent and Trademark Office (USPTO) (2011) 'Geographical Indication Protection in the United States', http://www.uspto.gov/ip/global/geographical/protection/index.jsp, date accessed 24 December 2011.

World Trade Organization (WTO) (2001) 'Ministerial Declaration', WT/MIN(01)/DEC/1, 20 November, http://www.wto.org/english/thewto_e/minist_e/min01_e/mindecl_e.pdf, date accessed 24 December 2011.

World Trade Organization (WTO) (2005) 'Dispute DS174', *EC – Trademarks and Geographical Indications*, 15 March, http://wto.org/english/tratop_e/dispu_e/cases_e/ds174_e.htm, date accessed 24 December 2011.

World Trade Organization (WTO) (2011) 'Report by the Director General', WT/GC/W/633, 21 April, http://docsonline.wto.org/imrd/directdoc.asp?DDFDocuments/t/WT/GC/W633.doc, date accessed 24 December 2011.

2
Are Food Markets Special Markets?

Philippe Steiner

The aim of this chapter is to examine the notion of a *special market* which can be linked to Karl Polanyi's conception of fictitious commodities. The framework employed here is that of economic sociology, a domain I define as studies which seek to inscribe economic facts within social facts, such that on a regular basis concrete research *simultaneously* takes account of self-interested behaviour and other social relations.

The first part begins with Polanyi's conception, and then seeks to demonstrate that food markets must be understood as special markets insofar as fictitious commodities are sold in such markets. The second part deals in particular with the way in which contemporary economic sociology concerns itself with markets. It is then suggested in conclusion that the study of agrofood markets is an essential path for the understanding of current transformations in respect of the commoditization of new fictitious commodities related to health (biomarkets) and to knowledge (knowledge markets).

2.1 Social markets and fictitious commodities

The market is a social mechanism facilitating the provision to individuals of the resources that they need without requiring intervention on the part of a central authority, or of a behavioural norm originating in ethics, politics, aesthetics or religion; and understood as such its emergence can be located in the eighteenth century. It is a *social mechanism* in the sense employed in contemporary sociology (Hedström and Swedberg, 1998), since one can there find formative mechanisms relating to expectations (respect for contractual rules, legitimacy of self-interested behaviour, and so on), individual behaviour (bidding) and, finally, procedures for the aggregation of individual behaviours. Central to this mechanism is individual behaviour based upon a simple principle: the self-interest of individuals leads to the increase of supply and the decrease of demand when the price of a good rises and, inversely, to a decrease of supply and an increase of demand when the price falls.

At the same time a market is a political *apparatus* (*dispositif*). Michel Foucault (2001, p. 299) defined this term as an agency constituted by heterogeneous elements such as texts, laws, regulations, architectural forms, individuals, objects, through which those whose task it is to 'lead' others achieve one of their ends: guaranteeing the food security of a population. It is a *political* apparatus in that it defines a mode of existence of individuals in society, a general and generalizable mode of interaction, of hierarchy and legitimation. The market defines a way of relating those who govern to those who are governed; it incorporates the governed through their self-interest and does the work of 'harmonizing' these interests. One can go further and treat the market as an apparatus that imposes an asceticism on those who participate in it (of gain pursued for its own sake, as an end in itself) an asceticism that leads to an *ethos* and a specific life conduct, that of optimization or of efficiency as the ultimate values.

The particular nature of a special market must be distinguished from what can be called the social construction of the market, for a standard or normal market is also susceptible to a social construction. We refer to 'special markets' when the adjustment of price and quantity escapes simple regulation by self-interested behaviour. The typical case of a special market is the labour market, whether because of rigidities in the downward flexibility of nominal wages, or because of the incomplete nature of the labour contract, or because of informational asymmetries. The financial market is likewise a good example of a special market since in this market (which defines the way in which society relates itself to the future) uncertainty is associated with phenomena of belief that develop and which can give rise to 'sun spot' equilibria, that is, any kind of equilibrium upon which the beliefs of market participants happen to converge.

2.1.1 Polanyi and fictitious commodities

According to Polanyi, a commodity is a fictitious commodity when it has not been produced for the purpose of sale in the market:

> The crucial point is this: labor, land, and money are essential elements of industry; they also must be organized in markets; in fact, these markets form an absolutely vital part of the economic system.

> But labor, land, and money are obviously *not* commodities; the postulates that anything that is bought and sold must have been produced for sale is emphatically untrue in regard to them. [...] Labor is only another name for a human activity which goes with life itself, which in its turn is not produced for sale but for entirely different reasons, nor can that activity be detached from the rest of life, be stored or mobilized; land is another name for nature, which is not produced by man; actual money, finally, is merely a token of purchasing power which, as a rule, is not produced at all, but comes into being through the banking or the state finance. None of them is produced for sale. The commodity description of labor, land and money is entirely fictitious. (Polanyi, 1944, pp. 75–6)

What Polanyi identifies here is the fact that certain goods are produced *for* the market and distributed *by* a self-regulating market, while others are only involved in this latter phase, as are in fact fictitious commodities. By extension, one could call a fictitious market a market in which a *fictitious commodity* is exchanged. Such fictitious markets form one class among special markets.

Polanyi's idea has resonated with economic sociologists, but one has to be cautious in dealing with his rhetoric. First of all one should not be misled by the term 'fiction', since fictitious does not mean false. Many areas of contemporary society rest upon fictions without any particular problem; and sometimes these fictions are created to avoid the commodity fiction in Polanyi's sense. A prime example is that which provides for the transfer of resources at the moment their owner dies intestate, a fiction according to which a father or mother loves all his or her children equally and in conformity with which the French 1804 Civil Code established the principle of egalitarian inheritance. A second example is that of organ donation. So that organs can be grafted for therapeutic purposes while avoiding the commercialization of healthy organs from persons living or dead, French law introduced the fiction of presumed consent. This presumes all French citizens with legal capacity, unless they have indicated otherwise while living, to have a natural bond with citizens who are ill and they may, because of this fact, without explicit declaration nor authorization by immediate relatives, be declared 'donors' and their healthy organs removed.[1] These fictions are one of the forms with which 'institutions think', to use Mary Douglas's phrase (1986), and there is no reason to condemn the self-regulating market for making use of such means.

Such fictions are rarely pushed to their ultimate consequences since there is a more or less stable equilibrium between different interests (of individuals, families, society). Any fiction pushed to the limit of its possibilities risks running into serious problems with respect to social justice and according to the legal adage: *summa jus, summa injuria*. Hence presumed consent is de facto related to a request made to the families, and if there is a refusal to make the donation surgeons terminate the process *contra legem*. All the same, equalitarian inheritance includes a corrective, since French law sets aside one part of the patrimony (the disposable part, equal at least to one quarter of the total patrimony) which the owner may dispose of at will.

The second problem that Polanyi's text raises is that of the definition of a *fictitious* commodity. If the good has not been produced as a commodity to be bought and sold on the market gainfully, then this good can only enter the market in the form of a fictitious commodity. This definition follows from the substantivist vision of the economy that Polanyi put forward (1977, pp. 19–34) but in practice there are a number of difficulties. The first of these is that the disconnection between the goal pursued by the producer and that of a trader seeking gain creates problems, there being an evident risk that the number of fictitious and special goods with be subject to inflation. Could it be said that the unrefined art market is a special market because the sketches, pictures and sculptures made by seriously disturbed mental patients are torn from their original context and made the objects of speculation with a view to gain? A second problem relates to the nature of the phenomenon characterized as production. Polanyi responds to this indirectly, emphasizing the role of the machine. By this he refers to the *industrial production* of goods without which a self-regulating market capable of invading and overturning the conditions of life in commercial society could not exist. From this angle, the formula immediately makes sense: the soil and individuals are not produced in the same way that shoes or frozen food is made with the help of machines to be then distributed, thanks to the social mechanism of the market.

But why then place so much importance on production by machine? This definition presumes that human beings can make themselves sovereign over nature by virtue of the fact that milk, flesh and animal labour can be unproblemmatically transformed into commodities. But does this mean that a heart taken from a person in a state of brain death is a product, and that it is therefore a real commodity that can be distributed through the market, because a system of machines is necessary – those that maintain the vital function of organs in a dead body, those that make encephalograms, those which establish the compatibility of blood – to procure a human organ for therapeutic purposes? I do not think that Polanyi would have agreed with such a formulation. Machine production is insufficient to define a commodity as non-fictive; there is therefore something else behind this definition of fictitious commodities and special markets.

2.1.2 Fictitious commodities and biopolitics

Fictitious commodities mark the fact that the market latches on to life, the life of the mass of individuals upon which the functioning of the market depends. The fictitious commodity is a Polanyian formulation that can be linked to Foucault's biopolitics (1977, 1978) – the subsequent phase being the commodification of life itself, the *zoe* of Giorgio Agamben (1995), and no longer only the *bios* (life qualified by its political dimension).

The self-regulating market is one form of biopolitics, and special markets are those that substantively realize this form of politics. It is also not just by chance that Foucault, when interested in the market, dealt with the grain market (Foucault 1978). Biopolitics has two aspects: on the one hand it is founded upon the market, making self-interested behaviour a means of governing individuals; on the other, it is founded upon the statistical techniques of the management of the health of populations. Market *and* public health are two faces of the same political form. In this sense the agrofood market is a special market since it subordinates human life to the market inasmuch as grain, the good that secures life *and* health, is nonetheless treated as a commodity which moves according to the information conveyed by price. Grain is certainly a commodity produced for and distributed by the market, but it is a fictitious commodity because it touches directly upon life.

If this definition of fictitious commodity is adopted, whereby the market is the heart of the modern form of politics since the eighteenth century, then the *prime fictitious commodity* is neither labour, nor money, nor land: it is *grain*. The grain market is also the market for flour and for bread, which means that the agricultural product (grain) cannot be apprehended independently of the process of distribution and industrial transformation through which it passes.[2] The markets for grain and bread experience a major disruption. One shifts from the market of encounter – Polanyi's marketplace – to the self-regulating market, where the market is ubiquitous, which is to say nowhere, invisible to the eyes of populations used to going in person to a marketplace stocked by local producers. This disruption to the system of expectations and actions is reinforced by a significant organizational modification: police, that is, local administration, has to protect the merchant from 'popular emotion', instead of performing its traditional role of protecting the population from the cupidity of merchants. Following on from the work of the English social historian Edward Thompson (1971), it is possible to link the commercialization of grain with market uprisings throughout the eighteenth century, in Spain, in France, in Great Britain – attacks on grain convoys, pillaging the granaries of bakers, traders and millers.

The economists of the time knew that the grain market was the site where expectations and beliefs form. These expectations rendered the grain market unstable as soon as the population, rightly or wrongly, become worried about their existence. The reactions by populations are more than simply the reactions of starving people, as Thompson's studies showed. A sense of justice played a part; or something more than this if one believes Adam Smith, who compares such sentiments to religious faith:

> The laws concerning corn may every where be compared to the law concerning religion. The people feel themselves so much interested in what relates either to their subsistence in this life, or to their happiness in a life to come, that government must yield to their prejudices, and, in order to preserve the public tranquillity, establish that system they approve of. (Smith, 1776, I, p. 539)

The grain market involves strong social representations; in this sense, the agrofood market is a special market.

2.2 The economic sociology of agrofood markets

How might economic sociology deal with special markets, extending the framework established by Polanyi? Any such treatment has to take into account the social characteristics of market mediations through which individuals relate to the purchase of their food.

2.2.1 Commercial rationalization and alimentary fear

The development of the town increased the distance between the individual and nutrition, between man and nature. Madeleine Ferrières (2002) has traced the social representations which have since the thirteenth century been linked to 'alimentary fear' – regulations, edicts, laws which municipal authorities or even guilds, an urban institution if there is one – all of which are created to reassure the feeder who has become a consumer by virtue of the distance that urbanization created with regard to the feeder's source of nutrition (ibid., chapters 1–3). The transformations induced by urbanization in purchasing behaviour, consumption and the preparation of food remain an important variable of the globalization process and the transformation of agrofood industries and the problems of food security (Pinstrup-Andersen and Pandya-Lorch, 1995; Fischler, 2001, chapter 1; Stanziani, 2005).

The distancing of the consumer from his source of nutrition is a dimension of the process of rationalization that Max Weber addressed in his famous lecture on 'Science as a Vocation'.[3] The rationalization which facilitated the development of science and technology meant increasing remoteness in the practical mastery of the environment. This distancing was compensated by the belief that, if enough time were taken to bring together sufficient knowledge, rational explanations could be found for the connection of cause to effect. It is also of significance that Weber posited an opposition between his hearers in the lecture hall and an Indian or a Hottentot *in their respective relationships to the means of procuring their food*: the former through the market, and the latter thanks their mastery of instruments with which they produced their daily food.[4]

In the course of this 'cognitive pauperization' of consumer quality standards play an important role, as the work of Alessandro Stanziani (2005) on food quality has shown. These standards protect the consumer by imposing processing procedures and quality norms, the absence of which is deemed fraudulent. The phenomenon fits well with the logic of security described by Foucault, although it should also be emphasized that Stanziani shows that two different modalities are at work. In some cases (butter and wine) it is the market order which takes the lead in the protection of the consumer, since this order is assumed to be a product of interested behaviours in relation to food quality, and to which scientific apparata allow a clear response in case of any suspicion of fraud; in other cases (milk and meat) it is the other way around, and the administration comes first since scientific expertise is less certain, but also because the problems of hygiene and of public health are here directly at stake.

Even in markets whose norms arise from these legal frameworks the competitive market creates social abstraction by eliminating the marketplace in which agents actually meet. It also creates a cognitive abstraction by distancing the consumer from the production process, and does so in a way that is ever more forceful as the path taken by production is extended. This work of social and cognitive abstraction produced by the market as an institution is managed only by the degree of abstraction with which we think of the market and the apparata there in play. Under normal conditions, where we calmly recognize (or believe we recognize) that the rationalization process effects practical command of a globalized market, these apparata provide food of a level of quality for which we are also able to pay. This is based upon the practical reality of a long-established *ethos*, whereby the masses of individuals making up modern society should not have to treat the food market as a problematic institution. When this normal regime is shattered by the circulation of information, whether true or false, which undermines this belief in food security, then an anxious regime arises, which can lead eventually to alimentary fear. In this sense the agrofood market is also a *special market* because it is imbued with powerful representations linked to the conditions securing the life of individuals, and because the market creates at the same time the structural conditions – cognitive and practical distancing – for the production and diffusion of alimentary fear.

2.2.2 Market representations and market standards

The agricultural market is characterized by powerful representations relating the individual to the socialized character of the goods which that individual (literally) consumes; and economic sociology directs its attention to the nature of the goods so consumed (in respect of nutrition that is healthy, actually nourishing and balanced) why such products might change from being repugnant to edible, served up to the rich or to the poor and so forth. At this level the sociology of taste and food (Fischler, 2001) can be used, the agrofood market being considered from this downstream perspective, a perspective thought to be all-determining by specialists in this market.

But this level is in need of completion. These social representations are institutions in the Durkheimian sense, so we have to consider their particular genesis as well as their mode of functioning. This amounts to stating that economic sociology cannot concern itself only with describing, or even explaining, how social representations regarding food and agrofood products are created. While such description or explanation is in itself an important achievement, we have to go further. We have to demonstrate how these social representations play a role on the actual functioning of this or that branch of the agrofood business (cattle in respect of the BSE crisis, poultry in respect of avian flu). This means that we must study the social structure of supply and demand.

On the demand side we need to consider 'alimentary fear', placing due emphasis on the role of the media, which plays an essential part here. There are organizational vectors that are less apparent, but which are as important as the media. Local authorities can intervene at the root of the alimentary fear and prevent this or that product from being included in the menus of those collectivities for which they are responsible (Allaire, 2005, p. 950). These prescriptions apply on a small scale a precautionary principle that conforms to a mechanism described by Sophie Dubuisson-Quellier (1999), where for example the local mayor intervenes with respect to the provider (the catering firm supplying schools) so that he might indicate to those responsible (parents) for 'clients' (children) that he takes his responsibility for public health seriously. The prescribing agent seeks to cover himself with respect to his electorate (parents) from any legal or political risk arising from such a circumstance. In the same way, it is necessary to take account of managers linked along supermarket chain – for the agrofood sector the vital wholesale and retail chain – for an understanding of how 'demand' takes shape in a particular market regime, a regime that Olivier Favereau (1989) has called an 'organization market'. In short, the social underpinning of demand has to be studied while at the same time taking account of the social structure that serves as a substantive support to the way in which individuals deal with their food.

On the supply side, organization markets have been studied in respect of the way in which such organizations establish relationships between themselves and so form a branch (Dubuisson-Quellier and Neuville, 2003), or again how norms and standards are developed which enable market managers to reduce transaction costs and help them respond to downstream conditions, in other words, the demands of supermarket buyers, relaying the demands of final consumers. So that legal norms can be established there is a need to standardize existing standard procedures for scientific evaluation, since without such standardization it is not possible to eliminate duplication of expertise nor reduce uncertainty. Normalization insures the quality of the product by setting the thresholds below which the product is rejected; and traceability allows the product to be tracked right through the chain and permits identification of the relevant link if the quality norm is not achieved. We also have to take account of the complement to this tracking of the normed product, which is to be found at the intersection of the sociology of economic law and of organizational sociology. As the work of Stanziani clearly shows, the definition of a norm associated with a form of traceability – accounting for instance (Stanziani, 2005, chapter 15) – means that in the event of any problem traceability functions to allocate *responsibility*. This is something to which a great deal of importance should be attached, alongside scientific expertise and those 'hybrid forums' in which market managers and professionals, public authorities and consumers join together to produce standards, since this question of responsibility is related to the key representations that characterise the agrofood market.

The two sides of the market are not independent. If the domination of production by commerce seems currently to be the rule, the fact remains that the very classical disjunction between producer and trader is transformed by strategies by some producers to approach the client by using labelling that characterizes a product by place of origin and form of production although commercialization had enforced a process of standardization for economic purposes (Dubuisson-Quellier, 2003; Dubuisson-Quellier and Lamine, 2004). Moreover, the political dimension that consumption has assumed in the northern countries, where a concern for environmental protection and sustainable development has brought the weight of final demand felt to bear on all branches, especially in cases where non-governmental organizations have been able to influence the decisions of transnational firms (Wilkinson, 2006). In this case it is possible to trace out a connection between actual or potential decisions of activist consumers and production, mediated by social movements motivated by an ultimate value which is, as Smith suggested, not in itself religious, but concerned with the protection of the planet, a new laicized ultimate value with wide implications.

Lastly, these representations have a *quantitative* expression. The study done by Maurice Halbwachs (1912) on working-class purchasing behaviour in the early twentieth century helps to clarify this important point for contemporary economic sociology. According to Halbwachs, the commercial relationship to food is characterized by its frequency when compared to the purchase of clothing or shelter – and in spite of changes over the course of the century, this hierarchy remains valid. As a result, Halbwachs argues that there is less of a distance between the consumer and his or her food than there is in the case of other goods. Does this run counter to the Weberian argument? Not at all. Halbwachs is talking of a reduced distance with respect to the couple price–quality, because the frequent consumer of a product has a numerical representation of what this costs under normal conditions (the shop that he uses, at particular period of time, and so on).[5] But this same consumer is helpless when faced with the product itself, confronted with the 'complex service' which the product has become (Allaire, 2005, p. 950). Familiarity bears upon the price–quality couple, but quality itself remains obscure to the consumer. There is an illustration of this problem in an anecdote reported by Michèle de La Pradelle's ethnography of the Carpentras market. A stallholder, a butcher, had received from his supplier trays of *croustillons* [spare ribs] at a lower price than usual (4 Francs instead of 7 Francs). He decided to pass this on to his clientele, but faced some unexpected reactions. Pradelle reports the stallholder's story as follows:

> The first customer that arrived and who usually took a complete tray or sometimes two, I said to her: 'Well, today you'll get a bargain'. I had still not marked up the prices, she said to me: 'That's good, I'll take two trays today.' When she saw the price, it was almost half of what I normally charge, she suddenly stopped and said to me, 'What is this all about?' So I explained the cut in price. 'Are they fresh?' So I said yes, you can see, I reached them almost to her nose. 'Oh, give me some sausages instead!'

In this example quality remains quite obscure for the customer even though she is a regular buyer of the product; it is the normal price 'which becomes in some way part of its existence' (Halbwachs, 1912, p. 404) that serves as the point of reference. In this verbal exchange between seller and customer it is possible to see that any disturbance to the relation of quality to price has effects that can perhaps be apprehended quantitatively: the amount sold of the commodity whose price–quality relation has been altered, the sale of alternative products at the same price. It might be conjectured that the mechanism also works when alimentary fear affects quality, which modifies the 'natural' relation of quality and price, and one could investigate the evolution of prices and quantities that allow these social representations to be quantified, including in this the case of modern alimentary fears.[6] If a fall in price is under normal conditions the sign of a risk, as can be seen from the case reported from Carpentras market, is it any different in the event of alimentary fear? What becomes the new 'natural' indicator under such a regime? How does it play its part in sustaining the branch, maintaining an adequate level of remuneration, at least for the time being, to the producer and to the chain of distributors between the producer and the consumer? How, and when, does the initial 'natural' indicator become restored?

These are some of the problems that the economic sociologist can pose, and thanks to which the notion of a special market, here applied to the agrofood market, can become a more important object than it still is for contemporary economic sociology.

2.3 Conclusion

The final surprise is that agrofood markets are too often absent from the renewal of economic sociology while being at the same subject to a markedly interdisciplinary approach. An economic sociologist open to work in this area quickly feels at home, that the domain is after all very familiar. It seems therefore that even a moderate research effort would give these markets the place in the framework of contemporary economic sociology which they deserve.

Beyond, it is essential to give food markets a definite place in modern thinking on the sociology of markets, since these markets touch on the core of social life – the relation of men and women to the natural and the living world – in modern society. Wheat in the eighteenth century, then meat and milk in the nineteenth, sugar, today soya – these are markets in which the fictitious commodity fully plays its role and calls for renewed reflection in responding to the problems posed by the extension of the society of markets. There is no need to create a new fictitious commodity – food – but to acknowledge the fact that food being at the crossroads between two fictitious commodities – nature and human life – it falls in the province of Polanyi's analysis. This means that the functioning of food markets requires a significant amount of social phenomena that must be taken into account according to the embeddedness/disembeddeness conceptualization; this also means that such markets should be considered in a comparative way, in view of what is done in the case of the pricing of nature[7] or in the case of the pricing of body parts.[8] Finally, this means that the study of these markets entails to bear in mind the social and political consequences of the process of commodification of food and how specific market devices made this process possible.

Notes

1. This point is elaborated in greater detail in Steiner (2010).
2. One is not therefore obliged to break entirely with Polanyi; the importance given to the machine, while no longer as central as he said, is paramount.
3. 'Thus the growing process of intellectualization and rationalization does *not* imply a growing understanding of the conditions under which we live. It means something quite different. It is the knowledge or the conviction that if *only we wished* to understand them we *could* do so at any time. It means that in principle, then, we are not ruled by mysterious, unpredictable forces, but that, on the contrary, we can in principle *control everything by means of calculation*' (Weber, 2004, pp. 12–13).

4. The passage preceding the well-known definition of scientific and technological rationalization stated the idea in the following way: 'When we spend money, I would wager that even if there are political economists present in the lecture room, almost every one of them would have a different answer ready to the question of how money manages thing so that you can sometimes buy a lot for it and sometimes only a little. The savage knows how to obtain his daily food and what institutions enable him to do so' (2004, p. 12).
5. The consumers drawn from the general public in David Miller's 1998 study of the ethnography of supermarket purchase were largely ignorant of prices, apart from those for bread and milk, which they purchased frequently.
6. That can also work in reverse, as Claude Fischler reports (2001, p. 201) in connection with a TV programme on the 'French paradox' which had an important impact in the United States on purchasing behaviour in connection with red wine.
7. See, for example, Marion Fourcade's analysis of the discrepancies in national procedures when it comes to valuing nature after an ecological disaster (Fourcade, 2011).
8. This is already at work in the case of Iran in which a legal and regulated market for kidneys exists since the end of the 1980s. Furthermore, there are many proposals coming from economists, legal scientists, bioethicists and surgeons in favour of such biomarkets (see Steiner, 2010, chapters 6 and 7).

References

Agamben, G. (1995) *Homo Sacer*. French translation: *Le pouvoir souverain et la vie nue* (Paris: Seuil).

Allaire, G. (2005) 'Des secteurs aux normes. Les "peurs alimentaires" et la régulation du "modèle anthropogénétique"', *Économie et sociétés*, 27(5), 939–54.

Benbouzid, D. et al. (1995) 'La sécurité alimentaire considérée du point de vue de la santé', *Économie et sociétés*, 22–3(3–4), 37–50.

Douglas, M. (1986) *How Institutions Think* (New York: Syracuse University Press).

Dubuisson-Quellier, S. (1999) 'Le prestataire, le client et le consommateur. Sociologie d'une relation marchande', *Revue française de sociologie*, 40(4), 671–88.

Dubuisson-Quellier, S. (2003) 'Confiance et qualité des produits alimentaires: une approche par la sociologie des relations marchandes', *Sociologie du travail*, 45(1), 95–111.

Dubuisson-Quellier, S. and C. Lamine (2004) 'Faire le marché autrement. L'abonnement à un panier de fruits et de légumes comme forme d'engagement politique des consommateurs', *Sciences de la société*, 62, 145–67.

Dubuisson-Quellier, S. and J.-P. Neuville (eds) (2003) *Juger pour échanger* (Paris: Éditions de l'Ehess).

Favereau, O. (1989) 'Marché interne, marché externe', *Revue économique*, 40(2), 273–328.

Ferrières, M. (2002) *Histoire des peurs alimentaires. Du Moyen Âge à l'aube du 20ème siècle* (Paris: Seuil).

Fischler, C. (2001) *L'Homnivore. Le goût, la cuisine et le corps* (Paris: Odile Jacob).

Foucault, M. (1977) *Il faut défendre la société* (Paris: Gallimard-Seuil, 1997).

Foucault, M. (1978) *Sécurité, territoire, population* (Paris: Gallimard-Seuil, 2004).
Fourcade, M. (2011) 'Price and Prejudice: On Economics and the Enchantment (and Disenchantment) of Nature', in J. Beckert and P. Aspers (eds), *The Worth of Goods* (Oxford: Oxford University Press), pp. 41–62.
Halbwachs, M. (1912) *La classe ouvrière et les niveaux de vie* (Paris and New York: Gordon and Breach, 1970)
d'Hauteville, F. and R. Green (2000) 'Internationalisation de la distribution: la logistique comme source d'avantages concurrentiel?', *Économie et sociétés*, 24(10–11), 187–98.
Hedström, P. and R. Swedberg (1998) *Social Mechanisms. An Approach to Social Theory* (Cambridge: Cambridge University Press).
Kaplan, S. (1976) *Bread, Politics and Political Economy in the Reign of Louis XV* (Ithaca: Cornell university Press).
Kracht, U. (1995) 'Short and Long-Term Food Security', *Économie et sociétés*, 22–3(3–4), 67–75.
de La Pradelle, M. (1996) *Les vendredis de Carpentras. Faire son marché en Provence ou ailleurs* (Paris: Fayard).
Micheletti, M. (2004) 'Le consumérisme politique. Une nouvelle forme de gouvernance transnationale?', *Sciences de la société*, 62, 118–42.
Miller, D. (1998) *A Theory of Shopping* (Ithaca, NY: Cornell University Press).
Padilla, M. and G. Le Bihan (1997) 'La dynamique internationale de la consommation alimentaire', *Économie et sociétés*, 23(9), 11–25.
Pinstrup-Andersen, P. and R. Pandya-Lorch (1995) 'The Supply Side of Global Food Security', *Économie et sociétés*, 22–3(3–4), 17–36.
Polanyi, K. (1944) *The Great Transformation: The Political and Economic Origins of Our Time* (Boston, MA: Beacon Press, 2001).
Polanyi, K. (1977) *The Livelihood of Man* (New York: Academic Press).
Pouch, T. and C. de Lorgeril (2004) 'La dynamique des échanges de produits agroalimentaires (1967–2000)', *Économie et sociétés*, 26, 507–29.
Rastoin, J.-L. and G. Ghersi (2000) 'La mondialisation des échanges agroalimentaires', *Économie et sociétés*, 24(10–11), 161–85.
Rio, Y. (2000) 'Le concept de filière dans un contexte de mondialisation', *Économie et sociétés*, 24(10–11), 213–21.
Smith, A. (1776) *An Inquiry Into the Nature and Causes of the Wealth of Nations* (Indianapolis: Liberty Press, 1981).
Stanziani, A. (ed.) (2003) *La qualité des produits en France (xviiie–xixe siècle)* (Paris: Belin).
Stanziani, A. (2005) *Histoire de la qualité alimentaire xixe–xxe siècle* (Paris: Seuil).
Steiner, P. (2010) *La transplantation d'organes: un commerce nouveau entre les êtres humains* (Paris: Gallimard).
Sylvander, B. (2004) 'Crédibilité et flexibilité de la certification: le cas de l'agriculture biologique', *Économie et sociétés*, 26(3), 471–86.
Thompson, E.P. (1971) 'The Moral Economy of the English Crowd in the Eighteenth Century', *Past and Present*, 50, 76–136.
Weber, M. (1919) *The Vocation Lectures* (Indianapolis: Hackett, 2004).
Wilkinson, J. (2006) 'The Mingling of Markets, Movements and Menus: the Renegotiation of Rural Space by NGOs, Social Movements and Traditional Actors', paper presented in the workshop 'Globalisation: Social and Cultural Dynamics', Rio de Janeiro.

3

Standardization vs Products of Origins: What Kinds of Agricultural Products Have the Potential to Become a Protected Geographical Indication?

Louis Augustin-Jean

The diverging perception related to Geographical Indications (GIs) in Europe and the United States represents a different kind of understanding of food quality along the two shores of the Atlantic. It demonstrates that quality is a social construct with various meanings across time and cultures (see the chapters by Steiner and Allaire in this volume), while it also reflects the power relations within the market and the importance of the 'architecture of the market' (Fligstein, 2001).

The painful negotiations at the World Trade Organization (WTO) remind us of the importance of these statements, which are corroborated by historical evidence. For example, the redesign of the market structures of the Burgundy wines during the 1920s and 1930s and the related shift of power between the traders (the *négociants*) and producers began with a redefinition of quality. This redefinition, built around the notion of *terroir*, allowed producers to gain more profits, to the detriment of the *négociants* (Laferté, 2006; Boyer, 2006; Boyer et al., 2007).

The same study also showed the forces behind this evolution. The operationalization of economic, but also political and cultural, networks explains the success of the 'challengers' (the producers) in reshaping the market and imposing the change (in a perfect illustration of the pioneering work of Granovetter, 1985). Similarly, a journey through history with Sidney Mintz tells us how the same product (sugar) has changed other the years – this energetic food has successively served as a medicine, a product of mass consumption, and now a product responsible for sickness and obesity (Mintz, 1985). From these examples, one can see that quality is subjective as elegantly summarized by Laferté: 'In 1910,

God would probably be satisfied with a "cut wine". But in 1939, he does not want it anymore. The wine blessed by God, is the AOC [Appellation d'Origine Contrôlée]' (Laferté, 2006, p. 241).

As can be inferred from these introductory notes, the analysis of GIs is usually framed by the theoretical discussion over this subjective nature of (food) quality. If it is an important aspect,[1] it does not capture the whole perspective because in focusing on the changing nature of quality, the discussion ignores the process of the creation of a commodity and, in relation to it, the way in which markets are created. In other words, the analysis of GIs usually focuses on market structures, their evolution, and the reshaping of qualities, but not the creation of the market and the commodities themselves. Nevertheless, the understanding of how the market 'operates by turning "things" into goods' (Gerard et al., 2010, p. 2) is important because it helps to explain how commodities are constructed and, in turn, casts some light on the different natures of mass consumption goods and geographical indications, as well as on their different degrees of acceptance. It also provides some reasons for the current difficulties in lowering the gap between the European and American positions in relation to the concept of geographical indications.

In order to answer this question, the first two parts of this chapter bridge the two theoretical debates over the 'social construction of the markets' and commodification. While markets and commodities cannot exist separately, it is surprising that there is so little academic literature (with the major exception of Polanyi, 1944) on the topic. Still, this is an important issue, not only in relation to the purpose of this chapter, but, more generally, for understanding the way markets are functioning. In the third part, I shall examine how this theoretical construction justifies the existence of a different cognitive knowledge of commodities for WTO negotiators, as well as for citizens located in different parts of the world, whose cognitive knowledge is evolutive.

3.1 The social construction of the market

Since the seminal works of Granovetter (1973, 1985) and Geertz (1978), research on the 'social construction of the market' has developed steadily. While, during the 1980s, priority was given to case studies (leading to a plurality of theoretical perspectives), in more recent years, efforts have been made to provide a more unified analytical framework, so most specialists now agree on the conditions of the existence of markets, which is a core element of the theory (Coriat and Weinstein, 2005;

Allaire, 2009; François, 2008). This section aims not to revise this large amount of literature,[2] but to present some key points of the structures of the markets and indicate their role in the 'commodification' of (agricultural) products – a topic often been left aside by these different scholarship traditions.[3] Hence, the objective is not only to analyse 'concrete markets' (including their organization and performances), but to also propose a normative perspective of their emergence and extension.

Generally speaking, researchers of the social construction of the markets start by showing that a neoclassical understanding of markets is useful, but insufficient (Steiner, 2008). This comment is easily illustrated by providing one of the clearer definitions of neoclassical markets by Roger Guesnerie:[4]

> According to Guesnerie, a market is a coordination device in which: a) the agents pursue their own interest and to this end perform economic calculations which can be seen as an operation of optimisation and/or maximization; b) the agents generally have divergent interests, which lead them to engage in c) transactions which resolve the conflict by defining a price. Consequently, to use Guesnerie's words, 'a market opposes buyers and sellers, and the price which resolve this conflict are the input but also, in a sense, the outcome of the agents' economic calculation'. (Callon, 1998, p. 3)

Such kind of definition frames human actions in a way that is helpful to the construction of models. To employ an analogy, if a map is not territory, it displays useful indications for individuals in their travels. But, and this is one reason for the limitation of the previous definition, there are different maps for different uses – hiking, travelling by car or foot, and so on. Similarly, the theoretical framework of markets needs to be adapted for different analytical objects. Thus, Guesnerie's definition can be enlarged to specify the concrete conditions of the existence of markets and to encompass its links with economic or social conditions. Based on the existing literature, Coriat and Weinstein (2005) probably provided the most concise analytical framework for the 'social construction of markets'.

In a preliminary statement, the two authors indicated that exchanges usually do not occur between two isolated individuals – a notion shared by most sociologists of markets. Markets have a permanent structure with a host of specific institutions and regulations, leaving room for the flow of information (Coriat and Weinstein, 2005). Thus, since markets are no longer (or not mainly) an impersonal structure in which buyers and sellers solve their inherent conflicts by setting prices (like in Guesnerie's definition), their structures and performances can be studied. After this preliminary remark, the authors proceeded in two steps: first, they established the conditions for market transactions to exist; second, they pinpointed the fact that while transactions are necessary, they are not sufficient to the existence of markets: other prerequisites need to be stated.

Thus, according to Coriat and Weinstein, for transactions to occur, three conditions are necessary: (1) a good definition and general agreement over ownership rights; (2) a mechanism that guarantees a respect for these rights. In most societies, this mechanism is controlled by the state. More importantly, the way these ownership rights are protected and recognized is a reflection of the power relations that exist within the market and beyond (which may lead to an 'asymmetry of exchange'). The market is like a political device, not the neutral instrument presented in the neoclassical tradition; and (3) a good definition of the object that is going to be traded. This definition is also a (social) construction and requires that the respective rights and obligations of sellers and buyers are precisely described – which is not always the case – as well as a certainty over the quality of the good to be exchanged. For example, uncertainty over quality may, in the worst case, prevent a realization of the exchange that would occur (Akerlof, 1970). In fact, this third condition can be seen as insufficient because the word 'object' is not precise enough (even if it includes services). As I will detail below, not all objects are suitable for sale in a market, even when they are supposed to be perfectly defined. What is socially marketable depends on history and culture, and many objects (in the large sense) are not produced for the market (Steiner, 2009 and 2010).[5]

In the second step, the authors noticed that 'transactions' (even monetary transactions) do not equate to 'markets', which require repeated and multiple transactions incorporated into a specific institutional framework. 'Speaking of a market presumes bringing together a group of transactions held to be similar' (Coriat and Weinstein, 2005, p. 2). The situation is, in reality, more complex because transactions are increasingly individualized: 'the individualization of transactions and products has become one of the major dimensions of competition' (Coriat and Weinstein, 2005, p. 2; see also Karpik, 2010). Consequently, the market is unified or even created by a common set of rules and regulations (or procedures and devices). The construction of the market is social and political, while the development of the rules and regulations, as well as their stabilization (which Fligstein (2001) has defined as a 'field'), is also the reflection of the power relations among the main actors in that market (such relations are not only related to economic competition, as suggested by Fligstein, but are political and social as well). In particular, the market needs either a specific location (such as the stock market or wet market) or to be unified by complex sets of instruments, institutional devices, and so on, that link producers to consumers. Examples proliferate in which a change in the institutional setting of a given market has also led to a change in the 'equilibrium price' (Garcia-Parpet, 2007; McMillan, 2002). To give a typical example, McMillan, while trying to demonstrate that markets are 'natural', showed how the price of rare books dropped with the development of the internet. In fact, the internet, while putting more buyers in touch with more sellers, changed the organization of the market and the equilibrium price (McMillan, 2002, p. 4) – but increased the asymmetry of information.

In short, this definition incorporates the definition of property rights and their guarantee, the definition of the object to exchange – the combination of the two provides the conditions of exchanges – and the aggregation of transactions. The consequences are multiple in the framework of this chapter. First, as already indicated, goods need to be commoditized: since the eighteenth century, more products have been sold in the market, but this operation of commodification is not neutral. Second, the clause of the aggregation of transactions implies the existence of an equivalence system, as some product's qualities may not be exactly the same but need to be considered similar. This equivalence process is also cultural and may lead to various interpretations. Third, since different 'architectures of the market' can give birth to different prices, there are also different equilibrium prices (a consequence that is never analyzed by neoclassical theorists). Thus, as Fligstein (2001) indicated, competition is not only over prices, but also over the social construction of the market, which explains the change in the wine market that was presented in the introduction (Laferté, 2006). Consequently, markets are either created by the apparition of new commodities (but not necessarily new goods) or by the deconstruction and reconstruction of markets. These three propositions will be studied with regards to geographical indications in section 3.3, but before that, it is necessary to examine the definition of a commodity and the commodification process.

3.2 The social construction of a commodity

Over the last few years, steep increases in food prices have prompted economists and policy makers to renew their interest in commodities.

For example, during its French presidency, the G20 re-emphasized the need to control instability and curb the prices of 'commodities'.[6] But these commodities are, at best, only weakly defined, including by people whose job is specifically to study their price evolution – economists. As a characteristic example, in an anthology that gathers 31 of the most influential articles on the topic, the two editors did not even provide, in their general introduction, a basic definition of a commodity (Greenaway and Morgan, 1999). In addition, the definition of economists, when provided, contains a semantic slip that changes its nature entirely. In this section, I shall examine the primary meaning of a commodity, while its definition by market operators and the consequences of it will be the topic of discussion in the next section.

The notion of a commodity has been, for the most part, conceptualized and made operational by sociologists and anthropologists who understand commodification in its cultural dimension (Polanyi, 1944; Appadurai, 1986; Haugerud et al., 2000; Steiner, 2009, 2010). The general introduction of Stone et al. can be seen as a useful starting point to grasp the concept. Quoting Kopitoff (1986, p. 64), they emphasized that, 'certain things and rights to things are produced, exist and can be seen to circulate through the economic system as they are being exchanged for other things, usually in exchange for money' (cited in Stone et al., 2000, p. 5). The authors saw this definition as an extension of the earlier analysis of Polanyi, who defined a commodity as a good produced for the market (see also Rothman, 2000, p. 164 and Steiner in this volume).

As will be detailed later, a great advantage of the two definitions and, particularly, that of Polanyi, is that they show how markets and commodities are two sides of the same coin – a reality that is often forgotten by economic sociologists and anthropologists who study the commodification process, including those who have referred to Polanyi's work. But, as this author already understood, the analysis of the 'construction of the market' cannot be complete without one of the 'construction of commodities'.[7] This statement is not as trivial as it seems and important consequences will be drawn below.

Nevertheless, Polanyi's definition remains incomplete because it considers existing commodities, but not the process by which goods are turned into commodities (Rothman, 2000, p. 164). In other words, it does not allow one to know 'why out of the total range of things available in a society are only some considered appropriate for marking as commodities, and why is the same thing treated as a commodity at one time and not another?' (Stone et al., 2000, p. 5). Or, to put it differently, not everything qualifies as a commodity and the problem is to define the conditions of commodification. This is an important question for this chapter because the development of a new geographical indication is also a process of creating a new commodity (commodification) – but unfortunately, a definitive answer, as the discussion below will show, is out or reach.

One possible way to approach this problem would be to rely on the traditional Marxist differentiation between use-value and exchange-value.[8] Nevertheless, in this case, this differentiation introduced a tautology, of which Stone et al. are well aware (ibid., pp. 5–7).[9] In fact, the only logical explanation for the build-up of a commodity is to introduce elements of culture and history,[10] as previously illustrated by Zelizer (1983). The implication is that it becomes nearly impossible to draw upon a general theory, since the commodification may be different for each good, or, at best, can have differentiated patterns for different categories of goods.

To illustrate the role of culture in the transformation of goods into commodities (or, more precisely, the process by which the use-value of goods acquire an exchange-value to become commodities), two characteristic examples will be detailed. Additionally, these examples reinforce the idea developed by Mintz in his study of sugar (1985), which argued that commodities have a changing nature. In that sense, the 'requalification' of existing commodities, geographically and temporally, and its consequences have to also be considered. The two elements are related and, at times, difficult to separate.

The first example has a strong symbolic value because it concerns the 'qualification' and, in connection, the possible 'commodification' of human beings (Steiner, 2009, 2010).[11] In his sociological study of organ transplants, Philippe Steiner showed how the idea of a 'human being as a resource' could not have been put forward in such a large scale without changing the perceptions that humans have about themselves. He then carefully described the cultural and historical steps by which these new perceptions could be created, while the topic was not closed once and for all.

The first step lies in technological improvements in medicine (a technological invention in the Schumpeterian sense of the term) that allowed organs to be transformed into potential resources. That new 'functionality' gives a 'use-value' to organs and blood; it is a necessary condition in the process of commodification, but not a sufficient one. The invention has to be turned into an innovation and the 'object' needs to acquire an 'exchange value' – with the final possibility (rejected by many) of establishing a 'bio-market'. In other words, the technical and 'industrial' capability to transfer blood or organs to other bodies is a necessary condition, but not a sufficient one, and existing technological capabilities do not equal a general acceptance of the creation of a market.

Thus, the development of the technology and its consequences for the creation of a 'bio-market' have called for a discussion of the conditions of using such a technology. This is of special importance when innovations can affect human health or, in this specific case, the very notion of human being. It should be said that these discussions are affected by cultural factors, as well as by existing social and economic forces. The law plays a role of intermediary between a culture and an economic system, as Steiner and, before him, Emile Durkheim (Steiner, 2009, p. 496) noticed, but in turn, a judicial system is a reflection of a compromise between social, economic, and political forces, and of the system of justification that reinforces the position of each group (Boltanski and Thévenot, 2006). In this respect, the way genetically modified (GM) organisms have been accepted in the United States and mostly rejected in the European Union is a perfect illustration: the judicial fiction that considers GM and non-GM products as 'substantially equivalent' through lobbying by manufacturers was not accepted by European consumers.[12] As I will detail in section 3.3, that divergent perspective is the same kind as the one on GIs and is linked to a cultural understanding of the notion of a commodity.

In the case of organ transplants, a compromise is also difficult to reach because it involves a conceptual redefinition of fundamental notions such as human beings, persons, bodies, or corps, as well as their integration, through a 'judicial fiction' (in the words of Steiner, 2009, p. 499) into the law system. At present, the perceived 'sacred nature' of a human being still prevents the trading of organs for therapeutic reasons in most countries (and thus, has not resulted in the emergence of a market), even though some progress towards the creation of an exchange-value (what the author called a 'social trade without payment') has been made through cultural evolution and its inscription in the system of law.[13]

The first consequence that can be drawn from these comments is that there is no clear separation between a good and a commodity, and between market exchanges and non-market exchanges, but there is the existence of continua. Second, the relationships between the emergence of a new commodity, its definition, and the creation of its market are quite complicated. The market cannot exist without a proper definition of the quality of a good, as discussed in section 3.1, but also, more fundamentally, without an agreement over its intrinsic nature that is shared by at least a group of people. Directly or indirectly, consumers (and citizens), like the other agencies in a value chain, participate in the commodification process, with the result being the acceptance of a 'good' into the 'market sphere'. In this way, the construction of a market for a product implies the participation of people and its 'politicization' to a greater extent than indicated by Fligstein (2001).

Nevertheless, even if consumers (citizens) have a say in the commodification process, it does not mean that they are in control of the extension of the market. Polanyi already stated this point, and the current economic crisis fully reminds us of the danger of the overextension of the market and of the weak control citizens have over it. In addition, the previous analysis hardly indicated what criteria people use to judge certain goods as acceptable commodities, but not others. It also gave little indication of how they participated in the creation of these commodities – two questions that this article cannot fully answer, and would certainly require more theoretical research,[14] even though the second example provides piecemeal information on them. But before I move on to it, there are two additional points I want to make.

First, as mentioned earlier, the construction of a commodity, as well as its definition, should be shared by a 'certain number of people'. In the previous example, this group can be equated with the nation because, despite discordant voices, this definition is accepted (or, at least, not rejected) by a majority of citizens. It has a sound legal base and a set of formal rules and regulations. Nevertheless, when these rules are only informal and shared by market participants, the size of the group can be more fluctuant and difficult to circumscribe. Even though the informal market for blood and organs is booming as a result of limited supplies and large demand, a better example of such a market may be the drug market, which has very strict rules and regulations – although informal – shared among its participants.[15] Their acceptance of these rules and regulations (including the definition of the products and their quality) are necessary; otherwise, the result would be the collapse of the market itself (Akerlof, 1970). This analysis, to some extent, already anticipates section 3.3 of this chapter because it is difficult, by definition, to separate market structures and the commodification – while this last notion already includes the concept of quality. In practice, these three notions are intrinsically embedded into each other, but remain different (see section 3.3). In addition, the system of rules and regulations (both formal and informal) specifies the institutional setting of the market and its performance (Coriat and Weinstein, 2005) because 'institutions matter' (North, 1990).

The second point insists on a theme that has already been briefly introduced: the cultural process at work in the build-up of a commodity. As indicated earlier, the 'sacred nature' of human beings has prevented (so far) the full commodification of organs, such as kidneys, in *most* societies. The legislation on the topic is the result of a compromise that permits the 'transfer' of organs to other people, but not their full marketization. This compromise is not shared by all countries, is prone to future evolution, and is contested by some. As Philippe Steiner stressed twice in the same article, Iran has legalized a market for kidneys between unrelated people (Steiner, 2009, pp. 501, 513). Even though Iran is, thus far, the only country that has done so, the door is open to the commodification of organs, which is advocated by some economists and medical doctors in the United States and beyond. As indicated earlier, a modification of the perception related to human nature can lead to the commodification of organs (the relaxation of the condition of the 'sacred nature' of the human being), but it does not say much about the criteria people use to judge which goods should become commodities and how such criteria can change: this is clearly related to social and cultural evolutions and the answer to this question differs from that for different goods and cultures.

While this example concerned an ongoing process of commodification, the next one concerns the reconstruction of the commodification and marketization in ancient Mesopotamia – a process that, far from being natural, took two millennia: 'goods that in the fourth millennium were received and distributed by the palace entered a commodity situation, as did goods collected and produced by the state to exchange for work in the third and early second millennia. As a result, a system of exchange was institutionalized, in which a class of traders (...) rather than the primary producers, became the agents for circulating subsistence goods, thus commoditizing them' (Rothman, 2000, p. 175). As can be inferred from this citation, the creation of a commodity and, related to it, the creation of its market, did not directly link consumers and producers, but was the product of the intervention of a new specialized class of middlemen and entrepreneurs: the traders. Consequently, the author isolated four components in the process of commodification, among which the following two are the most important for the purposes of this chapter: '(1) members of a society see classes of goods culturally marked as commodities, as distinct from non-commodity goods; (2) these classes of goods are *created in a commodity situation outside the barter or reciprocal exchange system of primary producers* with its emphasis on use-value' (ibid., pp. 174–5; my emphasis). In other words, according to the author, historical evidence does not support the traditional standpoint of economists that the monetary market stemmed from bartering. On the contrary, it was the outcome of the actions of entrepreneurs who became professional operators in that market. Therefore, since its early existence, the market has been a matter of professionals and was institutionalized. Then, the standpoint of neoclassical economists can be seen, at best, as a useful theoretical construction/abstraction that was not confirmed by historical evidence, at least not in all cases (see section 3.1).

Finally, it should be noted that the research of Rothman supported the previous analysis. First, it showed how culture can turn a 'good' into a 'commodity' (and eventually can be reverted to a 'good'), while the impact of market forces remained important (in this case, demand certainly played the major role).[16] Second, and more interestingly, commodification depends on the way goods are valorized by a society (Zelizer, 1983). This process extends beyond the places where goods are effectively produced. In their introductory chapter, Stone et al. indicated that 'things' have different use-values in different societies; for example, a carnation has nearly no use-value for a Kenyan farmer, but plenty for a Dutch consumer (Stone et al. 2000, p. 5), which means that carnations are only produced in Kenya for their exchange-value.[17] Similarly, in the example of Tinawon rice (see Chapter 9 in this volume), its use-value in Ifugao Province and the United States differs because, among other reasons, it incorporates different cultural values. In addition, the exchange value of Tinawon rice has changed in the Philippines after its introduction to the United States (before that, it was zero).

In conclusion, if Polanyi's classic definition (extended by Kopitoff) is to be kept, several consequences can be drawn. The obvious one is that the construction of a market cannot be effective without the construction of its commodity. But then, the question of why certain goods are commodities at certain times and in certain places (Stone et al.) cannot be answered without the introduction of culture. If the involvement of culture only displaces the problems, it also has important implications.

First, even though use-value and exchange-value are different concepts (not everything is for sale), the commodification process is not separated from the existence of a use-value (by definition). But this use-value can be determined at a very distant location from the production place of the good (the example of a carnation is a case in point). Second, if consumers (or citizens) cannot weigh in on the spread of a market, they at least have a role in the acceptance or rejection of certain commodities and they are fully integrated into the commodity chain. Culture here is instrumental because the response given by consumers/citizens can significantly differ across societies: GM food in the United States and Europe; organs in Iran and the rest of the world; life insurance during different periods in the United States' history; and so on. Third, the involvement of consumers and citizens in the build-up of commodities implies that a significant number of them have shared values. Consequently, a good is codified as a commodity by means of the legal system and/or by the introduction of informal rules and regulations (in the case of the drug trade). This codification is also an important step in the definition of a good's quality, which, therefore, is susceptible to changes over time and places. It is also an important element in the creation of a market because it imposes a certain level of institutionalization, which is provoked by the existence of professional market operators (that is, institutional entrepreneurs). Thus, because of these two parameters (codification and the existence of operators), markets cannot exist without specific rules (Callon, 1998) that can apply to individual goods or a bunch of goods. How this theoretical framework applies to the creation of geographical indications is the topic of section 3.3.

3.3 The process of constructing and deconstructing commodities

While markets and commodities are two related concepts, commodification is not a sufficient condition for markets to exist. If commodification permits exchanges to occur, then the aggregation of transactions of a similar nature is the condition of existence for markets (see section 3.1). Thus, the system of codification introduced in section 3.2 must permit the grouping of goods that are not rigorously identical, but are considered to be 'substantially identical'. Differently stated, codification should erase differences and enhance similarities at the price of a 'simplification' of quality. The details of this transformation are not trivial and involve a shift from the definition of a commodity by sociologists and anthropologists to one by economists and 'market analysts'. Interestingly enough, this shift mainly relates to this aggregation of goods of different qualities, or, in other words, their standardization:

> A first approach allows us to differentiate commodities, *trivialized and standardised* products for which prices fluctuate according to the brutal law of the market, from *specific* or value added products for which the logic of price fixing is much more subtle. (Habert, 2002, p. 13, my emphasis)[18]

Similarly, the *Business Dictionary Online* defines a commodity as 'a *reasonably homogeneous* good or material, bought and sold freely as an article of commerce. Commodities include agricultural products, fuels, and metals and are traded in *bulk* on a commodity exchange or spot market.'[19]

In this definition, the words 'reasonably' and 'bulk' seem to be especially important. The first implies that goods are not fully homogeneous, which imposes a specific system of aggregation in order to be able to consider them equivalent and sold 'in bulk' in a market. Garcia-Parpet (2007), in her article on the 'social construction of a perfect market', documented the way in which this aggregation was possible for strawberry growers in Sologne (France). Quoting an undergraduate textbook on economics, she first recalled the four conditions for the existence of perfect competition. The second condition is of special interest to us, as it states that 'the product is homogenous. This means *it should have the same significance for all concerned,* and that it should be identifiable without considering the seller' (Garcia-Parpet, 2007, p. 26, my emphasis). The second sentence shows that the aggregation of goods into the same category is not a natural process, but a construction – a codification that has an important cultural component. This point is illustrated further by the author:

> The technical staff and members of the Chambre d'Agriculture [of Loir-et-Cher] (...) were interested in (...) enabling growers to match the quality and appearance of the strawberries grown in the major producing areas in France. To achieve this, certain producers and technical staff launched a campaign and edited brochures describing the '13 commandments' for good strawberry growing. These were intended to reduce the number of varieties grown, to stop the practice of mixing different varieties in the same tray, and to impose some uniformity on the method of packaging. (Garcia-Parpet, 2007, p. 30)

In recognition of these efforts, a label of quality was awarded for the 'Strawberries from Sologne' in 1976. This label meant that these strawberries were not a product to be sold in bulk (so, not a commodity in the sense that is analysed here), but the example still highlighted interesting aspects of this aggregation process. First, the build-up of a homogeneous product, far from being natural, was the result of a strong political and collective action. This process was done at the expense of the diversity of the product and through a reduction of its qualities. Second, as indicated by the author, the label, 'Strawberries from Sologne', was established with a direct reference to existing strawberry standards in other parts of France. Thus, while the reference to the region might indicate an evolution towards a GI, in fact, it is just an indication of a 'standard quality' (of a higher grade). In other words, the indication of a geographical entity does not equate to the valorization of a tradition, a specific know-how, or product, but rather the erasing of local specificities and an effort towards standardization.

This same process is found, albeit in a more extreme form, in the construction of commodities and futures markets, which need to deal with standardized and mass products, thereby erasing existing differences. The previous section discussed the changing nature of commodities in different geographical and temporal settings. Nevertheless, the condition of aggregation has the opposite effect, while the creation of spot and futures markets denies these geographical, historical, and, even more radically, cultural elements. For example, futures contracts establish a correspondence between goods produced at different periods of time. Historical thickness is thus replaced by the yield of the contract, a rate that reflects the equivalence between the desire of the operators to dispose of a good today or sometime in the 'future' (Hugon, 1991).

Therefore, far from the advertisement showing a buyer in Latin America personally selecting the best quality coffee for herself, traders in the spot and futures markets essentially communicate with numbers. These 'devices' give them the information they need to make market decisions in relation to this standardized, industrial product.[20] Thus, the decision-making process is different when the coffee is bought by direct contact or in the commodities market. It is also guided by different principles and norms based on 'tradition' and personal interactions in the first instance and on industrial tools and market situations in the second one (Boltanski and Thévenot, 2006; Nicolas and Valceschini, 1995). It must also be said that the product and its quality are intrinsically different in the two instances because they are judged by different principles.[21]

Like the 'strawberries from Sologne', the definition of a commodity (in fact, the establishment of its 'industrial', measurable quality) is the result of a political process in which the actors compete to impose their standards (Fligstein, 2001; Augustin-Jean, 2010). Still, the process is imperfect (or unfinished?) because it somehow fails to establish a complete uniformity: on one hand, the market takes into account some cultural differences (for example, the use of different measurement units); on the other hand, goods are still differentiated – for wheat, one can cite: the No. 2 Soft Red Winter in Chicago (for which its futures contract was created in 1877 and is now the most traded wheat futures in the world), the Hard Red Spring in Kansas City (created in 1876), the wheat (with no further indications) in Argentina (created in 1991), and so on (Habert, 2002, p. 128).

In short, the establishment of commodity markets corresponds to a process of aggregating different (qualities of) goods. The result is to erase significant differences and provide a mass and standard product (a notion that is embodied in the notion of a commodity, as developed by professionals and economists). The extension of a market is made possible by eliminating some important components of a product that have a use-value and possibly an exchange-value. Geography and space, which are necessary components in the process of commodification, are, at different degrees, evacuated during the construction of worldwide markets: the globalization phenomenon does not easily accommodate notions such as *terroir*, know-how, traditions, and so on – all notions that are integrated into the concept of geographical indications. This 'dequalification', which is equivalent to a loss of memory, is also a cultural process.

The futures markets for commodities are only an extreme form of global markets. Despite the tendency towards standardization and measurable criteria when the size of a market increases, the 'dequalification' process has its opponents. The establishment of markets for commodities, with their long history and leaders and challengers, also has a political component. Overall, the usefulness and existence of such global markets is generally not called into question (what is at stake tends to be the limitation of their volatility), but their universality as the overarching form of market organization is contested.

More precisely, the competition between dominant players and challengers, which has found an arena in the WTO, concerns not only the architecture of the market, but also, more fundamentally, the different conceptions of a commodity. In other words, even a basic agreement over the equivalence of wheat or rice produced in different regions can be challenged, as the commodification of the Tinawon rice will show (see Chapter 10). In this respect, the case of wine is of special interest, not only because it has a strong cultural value, but also because a possible evolution will be to treat it as a mass product with different grades. The reference to the vine (*cépage*) tends to make the product more uniform and standardized, with the 'adequacy of technological wines to the taste of the customers' (Boyer et al., 2007, 19, Table 7) – or, more exactly, the taste of new global customers who do not share the same elements of culture and do not perceive this 'dequalification', in comparison to the more traditional wine consumers (and producers) of Southern Europe. Given such a new cognitive knowledge (Allaire, 2004) and referential, what is at stake here is no longer the creation of the new commodity, but its reinvention through its requalification.

Therefore, for the tenets of geographical indications, the aggregation of different goods (or quality) into a single category and its related loss of physical, cultural, immaterial, even genetic 'capital' can be perceived as negative. They indeed have difficulties explaining the pattern of commodification for geographical indications, while the referential is not shared by their counterparts. As indicated by Hélène Ilbert in Chapter 5, the codification of *terroir* and its incorporation into the French system of law date back to 1919 and is the product of a long evolution. Nonetheless, there are also motives for more positive feelings because what has been aggregated or ignored can also be differentiated again or reincorporated (apart from the loss of genetic heritage). Thus, it is possible to emphasize the unique characteristics of these commodities including their history, know-how, tradition, and so on. While the globalization movement is contested by the reaffirmation of cultures and diversity, the requalification of commodities and the development of geographical indications could be part of such an evolution. In fact, the large increase in the number of GIs indicates a trend towards the disassembly of mass products and the reaffirmation of cultures.

Again, the attitude of consumers, especially in developed countries, is decisive, as they have to at least accept, or eventually be in search of this diversification. The recent food crises have helped them rethink their consumption modes and become more active consumers, including in their search for more differentiated and traditional products (among them GIs). Even in the United States, a significant number of people are now looking for products of origin, which can come from very distant places and for a great diversity of commodities.

Thus, even for the typical 'commodities' that are sold in bulk, there may be a possibility of differentiation: the 'sel de Guérande', sold in the gourmet market in France and overseas, while not technically a GI, indicates, for a daily commodity like salt, a pattern of differentiation.[22] Nevertheless, the necessary innovation (in the sense of Schumpeter) of re-enhancing differences cannot be held for any kind of product anywhere. On one hand, the development of too many GIs for the same product category would tend to smooth over existing differences and lead to a continuum from a 'lower' grade to a higher one – achieving, in a way, the reconstruction of mass commodities that GIs were supposed to challenge. The number of GIs that cannot find their way into their national or international markets and only have little extra value compared to generic products may be seen as indicators of this trend.

On the other hand, the process of deconstructing commodities and the valorization of their differences is not possible everywhere or for any kind of production because these differences could be seen as too slim or difficult to confer monetary advantages. Nevertheless, even for some of the most widely-traded agricultural commodities like sugar (or other by-products of the sugar cane like gur or Khandsari) or salt, there are possibilities for disaggregation and 'valuing the unique' (Karpik).

3.4 Conclusion

In conclusion, the condition of the aggregation of transactions in the creation of a market also implies the aggregation of goods that are not strictly identical. That provokes a codification process that leads to the erasure of cultural specificities and homogenization. The final form of this process is the creation of futures markets, in which all the particularities of the commodities disappear to be replaced by technical criteria expressed by numbers. With the development of global markets and global consumers, there is a possibility that this pattern will gain all type of commodities, including the most culturally valued such as wine. On the other hand, the contestation of globalization and the re-emphasis of culture open the door to the de-homogenization of certain commodities. A renewed interest in geographical indications is inscribed in this movement. Nevertheless, the cognitive knowledge necessary for grasping the nature of these two conceptions of a commodity is not shared by everyone, which leads to misunderstandings, for instance, during international negotiations.

But even when this misunderstanding is avoided, it does not necessarily smooth over the negotiation process: the definition of commodities that is accepted by market operators has huge implications on the competition regime. For example, new wine producers from the New World, who do not benefit from the reputation and history/tradition of their European counterparts, and their consumers, who have difficulties 'reading' the complicated European classification, have sought a new definition of a commodity and promoted what Boyer called 'technological wines'. As Laferté noted, this strategy of changing the definition of a commodity in order to change the market structure is exactly the one adopted by winemakers from Bourgogne during the 1930s (Laferté, 2006, p. 245). Similarly, the USA rejects Japan's claim to limit the use of 'Wagyu beef' to Japanese cattle born and raised in Japan (see Augustin-Jean and Sekine in this volume). Therefore, global competition can be established not only in terms of price, between territories, or through the establishment of standards, but, even more fundamentally, through the definition of commodities. In that case, the fixing of standards and the competition between territories are only part of a system that directly touches upon the process of commodification.

Notes

1. For the study of the construction of quality in agro-food products, see Nicolas and Valceschini (1995) and Allaire and Boyer (1995). For a more recent economic sociological approach to understanding food quality, see Allaire (2009) and in this volume.
2. P. François recently presented the different approaches of the 'sociology of markets' and their theoretical foundations in textbook (François, 2008). A more concise analysis can be found in Steiner (2008).
3. This presentation will mainly rely on the work of Coriat and Weinstein (2005). The political elements of markets and their role for regulating competition are well detailed in Fligstein (2001). Several important theoretical works related to markets or networks have been collected by Swedberg (1994). On networks, beside the classic presentation of Granovetter (1985), readers can refer to Powell (1990). Concerning the analysis of existing markets, see the fascinating study of Abolafia (1996) on the New York Stock Exchange. See also Garcia-Parpet (2007) for the creation of a 'neoclassical' strawberry market in Sologne (France) and its social and cultural consequences. For an example in Asia, see Augustin-Jean (2009, 2010) on the sugar market in Guangxi province (China).
4. It is interesting to note that most undergraduate textbooks in economics do not clearly define markets. Similarly, Douglass North noticed as early as 1977 that 'it is a peculiar fact that the literature on economics (...) contains so little discussion of the central institution that underlies neoclassical economics – the market' (North, cited by Callon, 1998, p. 1).
5. This is already a simplification. In fact, 'on a large number of markets, the exchange does not concern well-defined products but rather, groups of rights and obligations which are often very badly specified' (Coriat and Weinstein, 2005, p. 2). Without even mentioning services or financial products, the increasingly complexity of goods fully supports this remark. In fact, the analysis should be of the commodification of rights, not 'goods' or 'objects'. Nevertheless, this degree of complexity is not justified in the framework of this chapter and will not be developed further.
6. See, for example, the website of the G20-G8, 'Why discuss volatility price at the G20?', http://www.g20-g8.com/g8-g20/g20/english/priorities-for-france/the-priorities-of-the-french-presidency/sheets/commodity-price-volatility.353.html, date accessed 29 October 2011.
7. The definition of a commodity is often given indirectly in many works on the economic sociology tradition. For example, François, in his over 300-page volume dedicated to the 'sociology of markets', did not include a single section on commodities. The theme of a commodity was only analyzed

indirectly in the definition of 'quality'. The article of Allaire (2009) also treated a commodity as it pertains to the definition of quality.

8. In fact, Zhuangzi, a Chinese philosopher, already introduced the distinction between use-value and exchange-value, although very differently from Karl Marx: 'In Sung, there was a man who was skilled in making a salve to prevent chapped hand, and generation after generation, his family made a living by bleaching silk in water. A traveller heard about the salve and offered to buy the prescription for a hundred measures of gold. The man called everyone to a family council. "For generations we've been bleaching silk and we've never made more than a few measures of gold," he said. "Now we can make a hundred measures in one morning (...)." The traveller got the salve and introduced it to the king of Wu who was having trouble with the state of Yüeh. The king put the man in charge of his troops, and that winter, they fought a naval battle with the men of Yüeh and gave them a bad beating. A portion of the conquered territory was awarded to the man as a fief. The salve has the power to prevent chapped hands in either case; but one man used it to get a fief while the other never got beyond silk bleaching – because they used it in a different way' (Watson, 1968, pp. 34–5). The differences between a 'use-value' and an 'exchange value' are well stated, but not as clear-cut as in the Marxian tradition. In addition, according to Zhuangzi, markets and governments are not fully separated – an element that still prevails today. That calls for deep theoretical and historical research not only on the development of markets in Asia, following the path set by William Skinner (1964), but, more fundamentally, on the process of creating the institution of the market. I would like to thank Dr Cheung Hei-Yee for bringing this citation to my attention.
9. Guthman (2002) tried another way, but that also came to an impasse. While her purpose was to 'examine the conversion of tastes into commodities (as well as the reverse)' (Guthman, 2002, p. 296), her analysis, in the absence of a proper definition of a commodity, shifted to one of the Marxian cycle of 'money transformed into commodity and back to money again' (ibid., 297). If this article allowed her to raise important points in relation to organic food, she could not really answer her primary question, which involved the evolution of the use-value of a good to an exchange-value, as I will develop later. In other words, things can have a use-value (including 'taste'), but no exchange value, and thus, are not considered commodities. Curiously enough, Guthman did not refer to this Marxian concept or to the work of Appadurai (1986).
10. Indeed, the general definition of Stone et al. (2000) did not allow them to answer completely their own question of why goods can be commodities at some times but not others. Nevertheless, the cultural elements embodied in their definition may be considered a step in that direction: 'A commodity is any good that can be exchanged for other goods. Commodities existed in pre-capitalist economies, *are culturally defined and molded, and are embedded in political and social systems* which they both reflect and help to shape.' (Stone et al., 2000, p. 9, my emphasis)
11. Of course, this example is very particular because humans are, by definition, not 'produced' for the market. So, their eventual 'commodification' poses a debate, which is exactly why the example is especially interesting.
12. Many have noticed the inconsistency of the judicial apparatus in the United States in relation to GM food. On one hand, GM food is considered

'substantially equivalent' to non-GM food. On the other hand, GM organisms are protected and cannot be utilized without paying a licence fee.

13. Referring again to Polanyi (and to note 11), it could be said that even though human beings are not produced for the market, the 'extraction' of organs from corpses and their 'preparation' for transplant can be seen as a preliminary step of producing a new commodity for the market. In other words, a passage from invention to innovation would also involve the development of a new commodity that is created for the market by the innovative process. This interpretation is, of course, highly conjectural.
14. The classic work of Bourdieu on distinction (1984) is informative in explaining some of the processes by which people choose already existing commodities. Similarly, Karpik (2010) detailed the use of 'judgment devices' in making choices to acquire unique products. Boltanski and Thévenot (2006) also illustrated the decision-making process and its justification. All these works are useful, but are only part of the answer.
15. I would like to thank Professor Neantro Saavedra-Rivano for drawing my attention to this example.
16. This was not always the case. The case study of Viviana Zelizer (1983) on the introduction of life insurance in the United States showed its first rejection by American consumers on the grounds that life and death were only in the hands of God before they finally accepted it. In that case, the stimuli came from the supply side.
17. See also the quote from Zhuangzi in note 8.
18. My translation. To be precise, in this citation, the French word 'marchandises' was translated as 'commodities'. In addition, in the previous section of his book, Habert gave four attributes to commodities: (1) they should be 'a primary product'; (2) a 'uniform product'; (3) a 'mass product'; and (4) a 'market product' that can easily fit with the rule of supply and demand (Habert, 2002, p. 12).
19. Online Business Dictionary, *Commodity*, http://www.businessdictionary.com/definition/commomdity.html, date accessed 21 November 2011 (my emphasis).
20. For example, in the case of wheat in the French futures market, the numbers indicate the weight (kg/hl), the humidity rate, the percentage of broken grains, sprouted grains, and impurities (Habert, 2002, p. 15, note 2). Whether the wheat is produced by farmer A or farmer B or in different countries does not matter. In the case of coffee, the same cannot be said if the product is sold by personal interaction, as illustrated by the previous discussion.
21. The theoretical discussion on quality will not be developed further in this chapter. Interested readers can refer to the chapters of Allaire and Steiner in this volume.
22. The salt museum in Tokyo presents the diversity of this commodity, which is usually sold in bulk as a mass product. This diversity does not only concern the technical criteria themselves, but also their method of production and reminds us of the cultural process of salt production.

References

Abolafia, M. (1996) *Making Markets: Opportunism and Restraint on Wall Street* (Cambridge, MA: Harvard University Press).

Akerlof, G. (1970) 'The Markets for "Lemons": Qualitative Uncertainty and the Market Mechanism', *Quarterly Journal of Economics*, 84, 488–500.

Allaire, G. (2004) 'Quality in Economics: a Cognitive Perspective', in M. Harvey, A. McMeekin and A. Warde (eds), *Qualities of Food* (Manchester: Manchester University Press), pp. 61–93.

Allaire, G. (2009) 'Economics of Conventions and the New Economic Sociology and our Understanding of Food Quality and New Food Markets and Trade Institutions. What are markets that pure economics does not know?' in the 27th International Conference of Agricultural Economists (IAAE), Plenary Session 5 'The New Landscape and the Need for an Extension to the Agricultural Economics Toolkit', Beijing, China, August.

Allaire, G. and R. Boyer (eds) (1995) *La grande transformation de l'agriculture* (Paris: INRA/Economica).

Appadurai, A. (ed.) (1986) *The Social Life of Things: Commodities in Cultural Perspectives* (Cambridge: Cambridge University Press).

Augustin-Jean, L. (2009) 'Which Market Economy for China? The Decision Making Process and Bureaucratic Networks in the Sugar Market in Guangxi Province', *Canadian Journal of Development Studies*, 28(3–4), 567–88.

Augustin-Jean, L. (2010) 'The "Social Construction of the Market" in a Transitional Economy. The Sugar Industry in China in the Context of Globalization', *Economic Sociology – The European Electronic Newsletter*, 11 (3), 33–42.

Boltanski, L. and L. Thévenot (2006) *On Justification: Economies of Worth* (Princeton, NJ: Princeton University Press).

Bourdieu, P. (1984) *Distinction: a Social Critique of the Judgement of Taste* (Cambridge, MA: Harvard University Press).

Boyer, R. (2006) 'Postface: Comment changes les modes de regulation sectoriels', in G. Laferté, *La Bourgogne et ses vins: image d'origine contrôlée* (Paris: Belin), pp. 251–62.

Boyer, R., D. Boyer and G. Laferté (2007) 'La connexion des réseaux comme facteurs de changement institutionnel: l'exemple des vins de Bourgogne', *Paris School of Economics*, Working Paper no. 2007-42.

Callon, M. (1998) 'Introduction: the Embeddedness of Economic Markets in Economics', in M. Callon (ed.), *The Laws of the Markets* (Oxford: Blackwell).

Coriat, B. and O. Weinstein (2005) 'The Social Construction of the Markets', *Issues in Regulation Theory*, 53, September, 1–4.

Fligstein, N. (2001) *The Architecture of Markets: An Economic Sociology of Twenty-first-century Capitalist Societies* (Princeton, NJ: Princeton University Press).

François, P. (2008) *Sociologie des Marchés* (Paris: Armand Colin).

G20-G8 (not dated) "Why Discuss Volatility Price at the G20?", http://www.g20-g8.com/g8-g20/g20/english/priorities-for-france/the-priorities-of-the-french-presidency/sheets/commodity-price-volatility.353.html, date accessed 29 October 2011.

Garcia-Parpet, M.F. (2007) 'The Social Construction of a Perfect Market: The Strawberry Auction at Fontaines-en-Sologne', in D. MacKenzie, F. Muniesa and L. Siu (eds), *Do Economist Make Markets? On the Performativity of Economics* (Princeton, NJ: Princeton University Press), pp. 20–53.

Geertz, C. (1978) 'The Bazaar Economy: Information and Search in Peasant Marketing', *American Economic Review*, 68(2), 28–32.

Gerard, F., A. Alpha, R. Beaujeu, J.M. Broussard, L. Levard, E. Maitre d'hotel, H. Rouille d'orfeuil, N. Bricas, B. Daviron, and F. Galtier (2010) 'Managing Food Price Volatility for Food Security and Development', GREMA.

Granovetter, M. (1973) 'The Strength of the Weak Ties', *American Journal of Sociology*, 78(6), 1360–80.

Granovetter, M. (1985) 'Economic Action and Social Structure: the Problem of Embeddedness', *American Journal of Sociology*, 91(3), 481–510.

Greenaway, D. and C.W. Morgan (eds) (1999) *The Economics of Commodity Markets* (Cheltenham: Edward Elgar).

Guthman, J. (2002) 'Commodified Meanings, Meaningful Commodities: Re-thinking Production–Consumption Links through the Organic System of Provision', *Sociologia Ruralis*, 42(4), 295–311.

Habert, N. (2002) *Les marchés à terme agricoles* (Paris: Ellipses).

Haugerud, A., M.P. Stone and P.D. Little (eds), *Commodities and Globalization. Anthropological Perspectives* (Lanham, MD: Rowman & Littlefield Publishers).

Hugon, P. (1991) 'L'économie du développement, le temps et l'histoire', *Revue Economique*, 42(2), 339–66.

Karpik, L. (2010) *Valuing the Unique: The Economics of Singularities* (Princeton, NJ: Princeton University Press).

Laferté, G. (2006) *La Bourgogne et ses vins: image d'origine contrôlée* (Paris: Belin).

McMillan, J. (2002) *Reinventing the Bazaar: A Natural History of Markets* (New York: W. W. Norton).

Mintz, S. (1985) *Sweetness and Power: The Place of Sugar in Modern History* (New York: Viking-Penguin).

Nicolas, F. and E. Valceschini (eds) (1995) *Agroalimentaire: une économie de la qualité* (Paris: INRA/Economica).

North, D.C. (1977) 'Markets and Other Allocation System in History: The Challenge of Karl Polanyi', *Journal of European Economic History*, 6, 703–16.

North, D.C. (1990) *Institutions, Institutional Change and Economic Performance* (Cambridge: Cambridge University Press).

Online Business Dictionary (2011) *Commodity*, http://www.businessdictionary.com/definition/commomdity.html, date accessed 21 November 2011.

Polanyi, K. (1944) *The Great Transformation: The Political and Economic Origins of Our Time* (Boston, MA: Beacon Press).

Powell, W.W. (1990) 'Neither Market nor Hierarchy: Networks Forms of Organization', *Research in Organizational Behavior*, 12, 295–336.

Rothman, M.S. (2000) 'The Commoditization of Goods and the Rise of State in Ancient Mesopotamia', in A. Haugerud, M. P. Stone and P. D. Little (eds), *Commodities ad Globalization: Anthropological Perspectives* (Lanham, MD: Rowman & Littlefield Publishers), pp. 163–78.

Skinner, G.W. (1964) 'Marketing and Social Structure in Rural China, Part 1', *Journal of Asian Studies* 24(1), 3–44.

Stanziani, A. (2005) *Histoire de la qualité alimentaire (XIXe–XXe siècle)* (Paris: Editions du Seuil).

Steiner, P. (2008) *La Sociologie Economique* (Paris: Coll. Repères, La Découverte).

Steiner, P. (2009) 'La marchandisation de l'humain et de la personne', in P. Steiner and F. Vatin, *Traité de sociologie économique* (Paris: Quadrige, PUF).

Steiner, P. (2010) *La transplantation d'organes: un commerce entre êtres humains* (Paris: Gallimard).

Stone, P. et al. (2000) 'Commodities and Globalization: Anthropological Perspectives', in A. Haugerud, M.P. Stone and P.D. Little (eds), *Commodities and Globalization. Anthropological Perspectives* (Lanham, MD: Rowman & Littlefield Publishers), pp. 1–31.

Swedberg, R. (1994) 'Markets as Social Structures', in N.J. Smelser and R. Swedberg (eds), *The Handbook of Economic Sociology* (Princeton: Princeton University Press), pp. 255–83.

Watson, B. (ed.) (1968) *The Complete Works of Chuang Tzu* (New York: Columbia University Press).

Zelizer, V.A. (1983) *Morals and Markets: The Development of Life Insurance in the United States* (New Brunswick: Transaction Books).

4
The Multidimensional Definition of Quality

Gilles Allaire

4.1 Introduction

Since the 1990s, the developing global economy has experienced important changes in market structures and governance regimes, meaning the ways of competition and of coordination within economic actors, entrepreneurs, professions, civil organizations, the states, and local governments. Trade liberalization and the decline of institutional prices in the agrofood sectors were major driving forces leading to a change in the competition regime. Contractual regulation by voluntary standards partly substitutes state regulation within the agrofood economy. Principal features of this change we consider here encompass: (i) the internationalization of food provision systems; (ii) a 'quality turn' or 'services turn' in commodities markets; (iii) a dematerialization of the food production process both upstream with the patenting of genes and downstream with the promotion of intangible qualities as related to modes of production, circulation or delivery; (iv) the multiplication of market quality standards and of standard setting organizations (SSOs); (v) and, finally, a de-corporatization of agrofood chains. This evolution gave opportunities for affirming various policies related to food qualities, both in developed and emergent countries, and for developing local multi-actor initiatives. The regional level in general, in Asia, Europe or Latin America (at both the supranational level and the provincial or regional level inside European or Latin America countries), plays a key role in designing, managing or supporting these policies and initiatives embedded in global production networks, mobilizing varieties of stakeholders. It is in this global perspective we position the reflexion on the multidimensional dimension of quality.

While mainstream economics offers a normative view of consumption function related to quality variety along the lines of Lancaster (1979), we follow in this chapter an institutionalist approach of the markets and a global (or cultural) approach of the worlds of food consumption, in which we position quality issues. Market institutions include property rights, governance structures, conceptions of market competition and of quality control, and rules of exchange (Fligstein, 1996). Prevailing quality standards relate to these different institutions (Allaire, 2010). The coevolution of these implies the circulation of common representations, or conventions structuring the market orders and the universe of qualities. For the circulation of quality conceptions social movements are key intermediaries, in particular in periods of changing the market rules. In recent decades both quantitative developments in international trade development and multinational agreements have also exerted pressure to change the rules controlling quality.

Quality in the usual sense is not any property of a good, but a relation in which means and aims are confronted. An expression about quality is a judgement; it refers to a hierarchy of values, civic or personal, but according to customs and social routines. Thus quality in the world of commodities is under the control of both public (controversial) doctrines and (fallible) public norms and market standards. In the following sections we consider, successively, quality, as judgements, as institutions, and in markets.

4.2 Quality as judgements

There are multiple domains in which quality judgements can be stated. Considering food, domains or dimensions of quality encompass: convenience in respect of food preparation (industrial processing or home cooking), hygiene, freshness, the capacity to nourish and preserve health, the capacity to procure enjoyment, as well as the social and ecological implications of the modes of food production, processing, delivery and consumption. In all cases *a quality judgement is an assessment regarding a system of resources*. A quality judgement is related to an end and it assesses or qualifies a set of resources (or means) for achieving it.

What we call a quality judgement is a public expression of the quality of the things which lives with us. Many, if not all things and also many situations provide individuals with experiences, emotions and thoughts. *Quality judgements are expressions in various public arenas of experience-based knowledge put in relation with values*. They are social judgements resulting of social forms of inquiry (Dewey, 1939). Food qualities obviously relates to human values. They are expressed throughout many kinds of narratives; into community values and ethics, into popular knowledge, into media opinions, into pieces of scientific theories, and into social routines (de facto rules) and law (formal rules).

4.2.1 Intrinsic and extrinsic dimensions of quality

The multiple dimensions of quality can be classified into two main types: the *intrinsic* ones, which refer to physical properties of a good or to the material infrastructure of a service; and the *extrinsic* ones, which refer to processes of production or use and the transaction in which a given good or service is involved. Thus, there are two modalities of quality assessment, the first concerning the *properties* of an entity and the second the *outcomes* of it functioning as resource. In both cases, as properties or as outcomes, the quality is assessed in respect of a particular end, and it reflects expectations. The first case refers to corporeal, material or tangible, qualities; the second to incorporeal qualities institutionalized as intellectual property rights related to trade, and to intangible qualities sanctioned by reputation.

The assessment of the outcomes of the services delivered by a given resource can be powered from two perspectives – an individualistic and hedonistic perspective, and a civic or community one. The hedonistic perspective includes the relevance of material properties regarding personal goals and the satisfaction of altruist expectations regarding the social dimension of intangible qualities (which are on the basis of responsible behaviours). That is, in respect of health or education, private or public services can be valued by an individual in relation to the personal benefits s/he perceived as well as from public aims by which s/he is concerned, public health or knowledge diffusion. To evaluate public policies both dimensions are relevant. Both individuals and the society are concerned by the public or moral dimensions of quality judgement. In the food sector, in the same manner, intangible qualities are related to hedonic aspects of the buying choice or of the use of particular products, distinguished by transcendent resources, as the origin or the label organic (Allaire and Wolf, 2004) as well as to public values, such as environmental or social justice awareness or cultural values, which may be community-specific. For example, Geographical Indications (GIs), beyond taste value, are matters of cultural heritages, be they local or considered parts of the global heritage. In total, quality judgements have three dimensions, hedonic in corresponding with the good life, cultural and moral in corresponding with community-based values, and public in relation to policies.

Corporeal qualities relate to *efficiency*; what matters here is the capacity of an entity regarding its known properties to perform expected services; for example, in the case of food: nutritional or hygiene efficiency; and, for agricultural raw products: the ability to be processed efficiently.

Incorporeal qualities are publicly circulating imageries relating to an entity or a situation. They correspond to qualitative hierarchies created *by judgements integrating a principle of distinction and a principle of superiority*. Geographical Indications (GIs) are a perfect example of incorporeal quality schemes: the principle of distinction is not the origin per se but in a particular relation with the characteristics or the reputation of product by this way distinguished;[1] the principle of superiority refers to cultural or social hierarchies, ranging from cuisine cultures to common heritages. In this regard GIs are part of the heritages not only of specific industries or of local communities of producers, but also of social groups mixing consumers – connoisseurs – and producers or processors, and generally local elites. GIs producers are aware of this patrimonial feature of their activity in which they are committed and not mere performers. Incorporeal quality for GIs is instituted as intellectual property rights. Policies add several dimensions to the social assessment of GI systems,[2] including the support of rural economies in less favoured areas, territorial planning, the sectoral control of supply (Sylvander et al., 2006) and, more recently, the provision of ecological services or the conservation of local or indigenous knowledge (Allaire and Thévenod-Mottet, 2009; Rangnekar, 2004).

Economists generally consider the distinction by the origin to be a 'horizontal' one – a matter of individual preferences and not market segmentation based on hierarchical criteria. However, to segment markets quality standards such as GIs are in fact combined with some hierarchical criteria, and the GI-labelled food generally receives a premium price, indicating some reputation for superiority in the market. When a specific market exists for a GI, this means the intellectual property right has acquired a market value. When the market goes past the local, the GI quality features are always associated with hierarchical criteria in line with the consumers' supposed demand for quality. We learn from the market experience that a GI system has to maintain some coherence to comfort the link of the product reputation with quality criteria. Thus, the strategic issue for the stakeholders turns out to be managing the collective reputation as a common resource.

4.2.2 Social valuation of qualities

Intangible qualities refer to social values. As extrinsic qualities they correspond to qualitative hierarchies generated *by judgements based on principles of social or moral superiority*. When GI producers make claims to provide ecological services, as, for example, in the area of biodiversity conservation, they link the production system with an intangible quality domain, provided the conservation of biodiversity is socially valued and instituted as a public policy objective. In the same manner, organic food or fair trade products are referring to principles of moral or political superiority valuing intangible qualities. But intangible quality is generally at stake in all operations of norm setting; all types of norm provider and standard setting organization are motivated by the idea that norms and standards do good (Brunsson and Jacobsson, 2000). All norms, however, have some intangible component and often fail to make the future world a better place. Intangible quality judgements refer, in the words of Commons (1934), to 'reasonable values' and to the 'principle of futurity', social consensus for reasonable collective behaviours, issued from socially assessed customs and from the common law principles.

By their nature quality judgements are uncertain statements, for the valued attributes are known imperfectly, and for the relation with an end expressed by a judgement over a system of resources will occur in the future, and thus is itself uncertain and not always assured by experience. Uncertainty about intrinsic characteristics comes with measurement errors. In fact, only relevant characteristics for a quality domain (which are according to a state of knowledge) are measured or observed. New events can introduce suspicion on quality-prevailing conceptions, when, for instance, the unknown and even unconceivable 'prion' becomes the attribute of mad 'cows'. Uncertainty in the case of extrinsic qualities is dependent on social knowledge and the evolution of quality conceptions.

Inquiry processes in the domains of quality are permanent in various ways and involve various stakeholders. *Quality forums* bring together experts and lay people (Callon, 1999). Quality assessments going through mediated social debates are then inscribed in quality doctrines and theories and in market quality standards (Busch, 2000). Standards serve to link incorporeal quality with observable criteria (the standard specifications) or to guarantee the mode of production (the use or non-use of specified resources) or the recognition of social rights such as workers' rights, thereby serving to align the means and the end in the view of intangible qualities. Standards function with control procedures, implying various types of certifying competences, by the exchangers themselves, by participative or administrative bodies or commercial third parties. Certifying bodies deliver certificates of conformity with the standard specifications. Certificates are not quality judgements, which are embedded in the doctrines or theories which justify the specifications, but certificates attest some form of quality control. Certificates and doctrines are two forms of quality publicness.

Quality judgements feed the reputation of things and of resource systems. Incorporeal and intangible qualities value relies on collective reputation. Reputation is developing and thus threatened in several places and its dynamics involves several institutional levels. From cultural debates and connoisseurs' chronicles to public accountability pressures which increase when the market becomes bigger. Collective reputation failures generate quality crises. Quality knowledge and quality orders are threatened by quality crises which develop at the institutional level.[3]

4.3 Quality as institutions

Corporeal or intrinsic qualities are controlled by technical standards while incorporeal qualities are signalled by signs and generally controlled by intellectual property rights (collective or private), and the intangible ones are promoted by social movements. Although the reliance on a quality standard is what matters in the momentum of an act of buying, this function of coordination is effective in a context of transaction where common interpretations of the simple knowledge transmitted by the standard are present. This dimension of coordination of the exchange participants corresponds to the notion of 'quality conventions', as developed by Eymard-Duvernay (1989). The variety of quality conceptions according to socio-cultural contexts (captured by comparative studies) reveals the conventional aspects of the quality standards. Conceptions of the qualities, their inscriptions in norms, and the organization of control procedures vary according to institutional *quality regimes*.

For a given market to exist (to emerge and develop) it is necessary to have the following: (i) conceptions of the production methods; and (ii) conceptions of the use of the product or service as resource. They are shared conceptions, and they are rooted in broad social experiences. We label these conceptual frameworks 'doctrines'; they are collective, in the sense that they are contestable. They include popular knowledge, professional competencies, product culture, and scientific texts. They relate to communities and public values and moral or aesthetic principles (Allaire, 2004).

4.3.1 Institutionalization of quality

At the societal level, food doctrines are embedded in sets of cultural, political and moral values (Zelizer, 1978, 1994). There are various ways in which societies consider human values; in particular, according to how social responsibility is allocated; what we call 'responsibility regime', which vary according to time and space. We call 'quality regimes' both the prevailing conceptions in a period of time and place for a domain of resource, and the structural tendencies in the corresponding society which interact with institutional change we refer as change in quality regimes. This change concerns market institutional organizations and the competences that make quality doctrines coherent and effective. In a given regime, standards are confronted on markets and doctrines are confronted in quality forums (Allaire, 2010).

Let us give an example that corresponds to a modern regime. It is currently a mandatory rule to include 'nutritional facts' on food packaging – measurements of nutritional content according to a specified methodology and for specified aggregates (for example, lipids and protein) or particular nutrients (such as vitamins). Whatever the type of control procedure (mandatory rule and administrative control or private standard and third-party certification), the specifications of the standard do not say why nutritional facts matter and why it is a public affair (if it is a mandatory rule) or a reputational and accountability stake (if it a private standard). Such knowledge (in other terms, the institutional support) is implicit. The standard setter considers this knowledge as generic and universal – in the case of food all households and all individuals when shopping in a supermarket are supposedly concerned by nutritional facts labelling. The conception of the significant facts varies, however, according to nutrition theories. For several decades vitamins have become a matter of concern due to their role in health and child growth, and such knowledge has become popularized and taken for granted by every modern moms. Recently the weight of salt in food became a significant nutritional fact in developed countries, and subject to public health regulation and labelling initiatives, due to its denunciation as an obesity factor. At the same time that the control of the quantity of salt as generic component of industrial food became a criterion for quality regarding health, voluntary food labels added another type of information and value in identifying salts of specific origins.

Pure economic approaches find it difficult to accommodate the increasing complexity of quality market settings and conflicting knowledge about quality, which have become a structural feature of contemporary food markets (Allaire, 2004). As pointed out by Nelson (1970), in a paper which continues to inspire that literature, goods can be distinguished on the basis of how they convey information to the consumer: *'search goods'* which exhibit directly their characteristics to the consumer in search are opposed to *'experience goods'* of which the property are revealed only by the act of consumption. Varying with the type of attributes of the good and the type of transaction, these distinctions do not lead to fixed types of goods. As a result of education, the consumers associate characteristics exhibited in place of the transaction with previous experiences. In many cases, individual experience is insufficient to assess the product or service qualities. Consumers benefit from knowledge acquired by others, experts and connoisseurs, and are confronted with private or public signalling initiatives, included mandatory labels. Finally, if the product information were complete and comprehensively formalized, 'search goods' would correspond to all of the standardized goods and services; standards allow for a large expansion in transparent markets. By contrast, intermediaries compete to label product properties and outcomes; and the informative effectiveness of a given label is conditioned but, threatened by the plurality of the signs coming with. A perfect specification of products by quality standards clashes with irreducible measurement errors (Barzel, 1982) and with unknown properties at the present (Lupton, 2005).

A third category of knowledge attributes attached to goods is generally distinguished in the recent food economics literature: the so-called 'credence attributes', denoting such features as are important to the consumer, but which the consumer cannot discover by consumption experiences. The agrofood industry 'quality turn' may be related to the developing opinion in the specialized literature that food markets feature this type of attribute. The qualities covering credence attributes are extrinsic ones. They do not refer to direct properties of the product or the service as materiality, but to contextual conditions and consequences of the transaction, meaning the implication of the modes of production, of delivery and of uses of the object of the transaction in a domain of assessment (see above). In such a perspective, what is given as a 'product' quality we call intangible (such as organic food) is related to a specific transaction considered from the point of view of the outcomes associated with the series of processes making this specific product to exist. And thus the product is assessed by the consumer as generally is a service.

A service is valued from the quality of its performance; but what is expected by a service buyer beyond the service achievement is its outcomes (that is, beyond the accuracy of the diagnosis and the pertinence of the prescription, who consults a physician is indeed expecting better health, which particularly cannot be measured without errors). The economic issue emerged from the fact that the consumer has to rely on intermediaries to appreciate the effectiveness of services related with intangible qualities. Experts providing 'repair services' (either the physician or the mechanic) can act in a fraudulent manner (Darby and Karni, 1973). This issue has been extended by economists to the analysis of the development of food certification schemes. There are, in fact, two different issues: one related to the tools and the procedures of observation or of calculation mobilized by prescription or certification experts; the other regarding the effectiveness of the services expected from qualified resources. The first uncertainty can be controlled by private or public assurance quality schemes, which cover a wide spectrum of the intangible qualities of food; they include those linked to food safety or to nutritional properties, those related to geographical indication, sustainable farming or animal welfare, those providing consumers with information regarding the labour conditions or other social characteristics of the production process. Certainly different market governance structures may induce non-fraudulent behaviours by experts certifying standard specifications or promoting its use. But the credence issue will not be wholly controlled by market governance mechanisms. It includes the relevance of public quality doctrines, introducing institutional trust issue, and the possibility of quality crisis. What is thus in cause is the relation between the resource the quality of which is qualified and social effective outcomes.

Products carrying intangible qualities can be termed 'products-services'; they account for both intrinsic and extrinsic qualities. This is the case for GIs, organic food and fair trade. Beyond the personal satisfaction procured by the taste of food or some altruistic feeling, the service provided is the outcomes which the advocates of these types of alternative food are claiming; the credence issue is in that expectation (saving a community heritage or the planet, achieving social solidarity), which cannot be verified by experience, but which is supported by social inquiries in several forms, including governmental and non-governmental research. To summarize, following the example of organic food, the current market standards and associated certification procedures guarantee specific means used in the production process, the consumer expects one or both of the two benefits: to experience better taste or personal health as outcome, or to contribute to the 'saving of the planet'. The individual rationale for such action can be care for our children or altruistic behaviour. Individuals buying organic food are generally also advocates of individual responsibility for the 'saving of the planet', and for public regulation and support in support for their aims. Social debates related to organic agriculture and its performances in various domains led to the formulation or the critique of public policies.

Intangible qualities are indeed common attributes of food, in relation to social concerns. In current times, animal welfare and environmental concerns, but also food safety issues like the use of antibiotics as growth promoters or the use of hormones, or local food concerns are becoming new public values making up intangible quality candidates to segment markets. GMOs advocacy claims for their role in the mitigation of hunger, something that is contested by opponents; but for both reasons GMOs are endowed with intangible qualities. In usual buying, the buyer-consumer suspends quality questions s/he could have; as stated by Andersen and Philipsen (1998), 'without the application of biases and highly simplifying heuristics, consumers would simply have to make a radical reduction of the scope of their consumption'.

A distinction has to be made between measurable characteristics on the one hand, about which individuals may lack information due to the cost of private or public investigation and spreading out or due to labelling failures and on the other hand, global features or intangible quality attributes which cannot be identified according to measurement procedure. The issue of credence appears when we consider that measurable or observable and thus certifiable characteristics do not abstract the whole significance of the quality valuation. While the cost of investigation of product intrinsic properties is lessened by reference sharing and public information, socialization of the experience of the users is limited by its personal and contextual character. Credence involves a reliance on intermediaries to identify extrinsic characteristics. According to Tirole (1988), markets for credence goods are made possible by supplying consumers with 'a substitute for the information and trust they lack'. We call this type of substitute a *sign*. The credence issue extends to the public policies controlling food attributes. Good science, good codes of practice in industries and services, and good regulation are more or less implicitly supposed for the success of the trust substitution and the functioning of credence markets. But, with 'credence goods' we are confronted with several conceptions of quality, although the current mainstream literature generally addresses isolated food credence attributes and assimilates them to levels of quality, retaining a Lancasterian consumption perspective (credence attributes are in this account considered as objective and separable characteristics). Nevertheless the notion of credence introduces a particular type of knowledge by linking identifiable characteristics (signs) with qualities that cannot be assessed; thus, the normative view is confronted by fuzzy goods (Allaire, 2004). Provisioning signs with trust is what professions, experts, and influential media and elites are doing through their interventions in quality forums. Uncertain costs springing from the incompleteness of the quality specifications, intermediaries receive incentives to supply producers, consumers and various stakeholders with relevant knowledge. All claim for intangible quality being contestable, credence crises are component of the institutional scene (Allaire, 2010).

4.3.2 Quality regimes and quality turn debate

There is an abundant sociological literature on the so-called 'quality turn' in agrofood innovation systems in the late twentieth century. This turn appeared first as corresponding to the emergence and development of alternative agrofood networks, such as organic food provision circuits, strategies to valorize local food products or to promote 'fair trade', as well as to quality assurance schemes, which were developing rapidly under state, collective and private initiatives, both in B2B (business to business) relations and in final consumption markets. Goodman (2004) criticized the 'alternative food networks' vision not only for the limited extent of these alternatives, but also for missing the theoretical link between innovation in production models and food consumption behaviours. One point at issue in this debate is the identification of the innovative actors: some authors stress the emergence of alternatives as corresponding to a new 'social compact', others see them as limited 'niche markets', while others stress a general change in food chains corresponding to the reversal of their governance shifting from upstream industries to downstream food service providers. The phrase 'quality turn' is an insufficient qualification of the turn in prevalent quality doctrines and in the market organization at that time, although it corresponds to a transformation in the role of standards.

The so-called 'quality turn' extended the reach of market segmentation to intangible qualities which are now integrated into the referencing system (mainstreaming). Alternatives were presented as in line with responsible attitudes both from sellers and buyers and with responsible collective concerns with sustainable development. The dominant actors in food provision systems (professional farms, processing and retail leaders) have entered the dance, and today they are also dominant with respect to the significant changes linked with the development of food services, which concern the logic of innovation and market institutions. Multinational firms produce organic food, and large processing firms including co-ops extend the range of their products and differentiate their participation in markets. Supermarkets, for their part, contribute to enlarging alternative circuits (organic, fair trade, origin labelled products and so on). Although they are extending worldwide, for the past two decades supermarkets in developed countries have been confronted with a decline in the rhythm of expansion of their market share. As a result, competition and concentration, have developed at the international level and includes differentiation within types of store and services. On the consumption side these so-called 'alternative' foods impact food representations beyond their market position. The diversification of 'products-services' (see above) corresponds with a new demand from the individuals for personal care services substituting for the household-based regime of care. In comparison with the previous industrial regime of quality combined with household economy, the new quality regime reveals the immaterial and intangible qualities of goods and gives market consumers some capacities to exert social responsibility.

This change corresponds to a shift in economic driving forces from industry to retail services in the food chains. It corresponds to the involvement of new actors in the food products-services design, along with the traditional actors of food industrialization. Thus the quality turn stresses strategies that differ from the industrial way of adding service to products (prepared food products); not only through integrating social, moral, and sacred values in holistic quality conceptions, but also in transforming market governance structures and quality hierarchies. Today, the turn is not limited to the so-called 'alternative networks'; the differentiation of food by quality standards concerns the whole system of food production and provision, it includes the development of food services and product-service hybrids. Professional, industrial and public strategies which develop quality schemes and labels indicate the generality of the issue.

4.3.3 Governance structures and competition regime

In a market view, social services corresponding to intangible qualities are considered 'public goods'; market premium is contributing to the provision of such public goods, but in a proportion which is insufficient in the regard of the advocates of alternative food networks. In particular, organic food producers and organic markets benefit from public subsidy and institutional support in many countries. GI systems also benefit from public support. In parallel, market accountability constraints are increasing.

Current agricultural and food policies involve stakeholders – consumers, ecologists, local governments, taxpayers and non-governmental organizations (NGOs) – situated outside the professional spheres. Quality standard setting is therefore a process that is negotiated both inside and outside the region of production, with consumers and other parties. Such a change does not necessarily mean a complete reversal in the leadership of market governance structures. Quality struggles open market opportunities for incumbent entrepreneurs as well as newcomers and also multiply the number of market segments. The change involves a shift from policies elaborated by administrative bodies with professional experts (nutritionists or agronomists) to the formulation of policies which have a higher claim to being 'science based' and which are developed both by public agencies and by coalitions of private firms or collective networks, but which are challenged by ethics-based quality doctrines.

The competition regime is shifting from a stage characterized by fixed market rules to one in which rules are in flux. The level towards which competition is shifting is focused not only on setting new standards but also on integrating new concerns into market conceptions. This level is structured by quality forums. The change in the governance structures of markets and in coordination/competition among actors in food chains gives rise to several types of forums where product specifications and modes of production or of delivery standards are debated and negotiated among various types of actors, private or governmental, scientific experts and NGO representatives, whether experts or laypeople. A quality forum is a network, including moral entrepreneurs, policy makers, various knowledge sources, as well as firms and coalitions of firms, constituting a cognitive framework for quality controversies, for example regarding environmental and health impacts of production activities and/or the social consequences of the diffusion of the use of products. Its functioning depends on a legal framework allowing standards to be set and implemented. Quality forums include standards-setting organizations, influential media and social movements. They develop at different scales and separate out as well as integrate domains of quality conceptions. Producers, processors and retail firms as well as various collectives have strategic resources at stake within quality forums and engage in strategic behaviour known as forum shopping. This type of competition regime may be called a 'media regime', in which movements of opinion play a key role. The new standardization regime which relates product codification with intangible qualities is characterized by several levels of fallible coordination: (i) international agreements subsequent to the setting-up of the WTO, but which remain incomplete; (ii) multi-actor initiatives to set up global norms (for example, 'sustainable' soya, palm oil, and cocoa roundtables) which tend to constitute market entry conditions; (iii) and by the renewal of marketing strategies at the various stages of agrofood chains.

4.4 Quality in markets and policies

Quality is present in market settings with the two faces of quality standards, specifications or codes of practices and justification doctrines. Market standards are compromises, in terms of knowledge and in terms of distribution of control power within stakeholders. They are promoted and put in critical examination in several market areas and social arenas. Fundamentally, they are the expression of strategies to manage by setting the rules of the game radical tensions springing from intangible quality perspectives. In this section we principally consider GI markets.

4.4.1 Markets as compromises

GI systems are submitted to two contradictory logics. One is the maintaining of the traditional design seen as heritage and the true basis of the collective reputation, while the other is by contrast the need for innovation to maintain a high collective reputation when market conditions are changing; for example, PDO (Protected Denomination of Origin) cheese producers which want to persist in using local breeds milk have to set up a collective scheme for breed selection. In both directions, to maintain tradition and to manage innovation, it is necessary to have co-operative rules, and finally the social organization of producers and of the market chain affects the GI characteristics. Thus, the quality scheme is controlling a trade-off between local routines based practices and innovation. Organic food chains face the same type of trade-off – on one hand the principle of the use of local resources and on the other the trend towards the specialization of both farms and production zones.

As noted by Jahn et al. (2004), there is a 'trade-off between generality and effectiveness in certification systems'. It is a problem of certification cost which augments, even exponentially, when the variables to control are numerous or involve high investment, while in reducing the selection constraint the heterogeneity of examined and certified goods can augment until nullifying the significance and the differential value of a class of goods. But the issue is twofold. First the efficiency of the procedure of certification is dependent upon the trade-off solution in minimizing investigation costs. Second, certification is in itself a process of identifying classes of good (qualification), even if the certification body is not the standard setter. The delivery of a certificate closes the question of the nature of a good in giving a name that has a general application, if it has significance; for example, in the phrase 'certified organic', one important thing is the class organic (credence to organic) and the other is that it is certified (credence to the institutional system). What allows the closure is an (open) list of specifications that costs to be acquired and measured, but that gives to the standard its effectiveness if this list makes sufficiently distinct the class. This last problem is that of designing the standard, which is not the same efficiency problem. For instance: in general, GIs are heterogeneous. To safeguard the reputation and the value of a given GI, agreements have to be reached on the criteria to differentiate levels of quality inside the GI (the ageing, particular components or techniques). But not just any property or variable can play this role. It has to be named. To be able to segment a GI market a quality criterion has to make sense in the quality doctrine, to find its role in the GI narrative. Not any procedure of segmentation and then of certification can rely on perfectly decomposable argumentation and method while any generality introduces potential organizational slack. Thus, while a quality standard represent institutional balance in segmenting markets, the institutional arrangement is threatened by movements in critical opinion. Standard failures do not generalize in stabilized markets beyond individual cases. But quality crises can extend to large sectors, when existing standards are facing emergent concerns. For example, the 'Mad Cow crisis', in Europe, began with the revealing of a critical emergent property of certain 'mad' cows and of the fact that there was no way of knowing which ones were infected. The globalization of markets increases the scope of quality crises.

We have seen the intangible dimension of quality in relation to social, political and ethical values and principles; a dimension which is intricately expressed by standards and doctrines. The diffusion of standards within markets is conditioned by the private user utility of such coordination instruments. Their collective and public dimensions are constructed in forums in which standard-setting organizations and stakeholders participate, and by networks mobilized around moral projects; processes in which standards become instruments for collective strategies or public policies. When standards become providers of public goods, stakeholders/users and not only purchasers/consumers emerge onto the stage. Accountability, as mentioned above, introduces social movements into market forums. When an intangible quality standard functions, the common quality representation assimilates the specifications and the standard heuristic, giving it both its strength and its fallibility.

4.4.2 The multiplication of standards and quality claims problem

The multiplication of standards is both a marketing objective and a problem; the issue being one of complementarities, tensions, and the separation of quality domains. Segmentation failures are not direct consequences of the number of standards per se, but the consequence of a lack of integration or, inversely, of separation between intangible quality claims. A standard does not just have a signification, it is also in relation to a conception of quality. For example, when the USA established a federal standard for organic food, in 2000, in the first release there was no separation between organic food and GMOs; it was only inscribed in the standard for the final release after a substantial campaign.

Considering the market aspects of the complementarity within intangible quality standards, Siner-GI researchers (see Allaire, 2008) have presented three alternative economic scenarios with respect to the position of GI identifiers as marketing tools: Convergence, Divergence, and Plurality. To define Plurality, we hypothesize the consistency of quality judgements, while in the real world the plurality of quality standards fuels no negligible tensions. This hypothesis is confronted with: (1) the hypothesis of the unification of stakeholders' representations and strategies, requiring some convergence of national competition laws, trademark systems and GI protection doctrines; and (2) the hypothesis of consumers which do not place significant value on GI as a quality sign. Each scenario concerns both the future of GIs (different conceptions of GIs) and the future of the relationship between GIs and other quality standards. The first scenario is based on the idea that GI refers to a particular convention of quality, which can translate as a whole in different contexts. Convergence refers to the vision of the nature of GIs and of their link with desirable agricultural practices. In this perspective, the challenge for a convergent GI doctrine in terms of social value is to achieve a shift from a cultural position to one related to the new concerns for healthy, local, natural food, biodiversity, and the preservation of social heritage. The second considered scenario (Divergence) corresponds to the hypothesis of a weakening of the prescriptive type of GI standard. Empirical studies show various situations regarding the success of GI systems. In some cases, the quality reputation can suffer from scaling up, whether this stems from the incapability of the GI system to maintain collective quality control, or from the unreadable nature of the quality signalling system. Thus, in this scenario, private standards and various signs claiming some link to the notion of origin can therefore challenge the European PDO/PGI or other GI signalling systems. Collective initiatives revalorizing places of production, and the link between consumption and places and seasons, can contribute to the weakening of GI signs, by confusing the standards for origin products. There are several competing rationales underpinning the logic of this second scenario. The third scenario (Plurality) assumes permanence in the diversity of GI forums. In contrast to the first and second scenarios, the diversity of the GI products and signs in this scenario is not considered to be an obstacle to the recognition of qualities by market actors, the diversity being assumed to be integrated within a pluralistic signalling system, where quality domains are clearly separated or associated. The role of global quality forums regarding what can be expected from family agriculture, geographical indications or organic farming is in structuring such quality knowledge systems, from which competitors get arguments (Allaire and Sylvander, 2011).

The consideration of collective and public objectives associated with standards leads to a distinction between 'neutral' standards and standards that are influenced by intangible quality schemes and in line with public policy (Allaire and Thévenod-Mottet, 2009). Neutral GI standards can be associated with a conception of Intellectual Property Rights (IPRs) as 'neutral rights as they do not care about quality nor protection of the consumers, but rather aim only at encouraging people to invent, create, trade and nothing else' (Hermitte, 2001). Neutral GIs are protected through judicial procedures related to unfair competition or the misleading of consumers. Responsible (non-neutral) GI standards include controlled criteria related to methods of production, biological resources, and so on. The notions of *neutrality* versus *responsibility* characterize the codes of practice, which may be of any nature, level of detail, focus, and so on, and the doctrine which supports the diffusion of the standard and its inclusion in public policies. Neutral GI standards leave the biodiversity issues to other voluntary public or private standards (such as organic, fair trade, and various green labels). The non-neutral character of the GI standard depends both on the collective rules characterizing a particular GI and also the legal framework under consideration. Conventions on the qualification of typical qualities are central to the process of discriminating within modes of production as regard social and cultural values involving public concerns. There are possible gaps between claims for responsibility and the real implications of standards. When the standard succeeds in becoming diffused, however, generally collective rules sustain the collective reputation benefiting from the standard. To a greater or lesser extent, specific qualities relate to particular natural and cultural resources which need common investments for their maintenance as is the case, for example, for animal breeds.

4.5 Conclusion

This chapter has considered successively quality, as judgements, as institutions, and in markets, particularly with regard to GI markets. Quality judgement values a system of resources. We have distinguished corporeal or intrinsic, and incorporeal and intangible extrinsic dimensions of quality, according to the principle of valuation. In the institutional sphere, quality is under the control both of public controversial doctrines and also of fallible public norms and market standards. Corporeal qualities are controlled by technical standards while incorporeal qualities are controlled by intellectual property rights, and the intangible ones by social movements. These prompt debates about the linkages between the different aspects of the intangible qualities of food: safety, environment, fair trade, and so on, including labelling of origin. Seen in this light market standards are compromises promoted and put under critical examination in several marketplaces and social arenas.

In the current trade regime, GIs are confronted in quality forums with new social concerns and values, from biodiversity to food security. How intangible qualities combine in effective markets varies according to polities.

Notes

1. The TRIPS agreement (a component of the 1994 WTO framework) states: 'Geographical indications are, for the purposes of this Agreement, indications which identify a good as originating in the territory of a Member, or a region or locality in that territory, where a given quality, reputation or other characteristic of the good is essentially attributable to its geographical origin.' By this definition GIs are identifiers of a type of goods. Nevertheless how origin matters in the processes of products qualification is still a question in debate (Allaire et al., 2011). There is some ambiguity whether the origin is responsible

for 'a given quality' on which the reputation is based or if we are only dealing with the existence of reputation (which is a restricted interpretation).
2. According to the research project Siner-GI: 'The GI system is the set of actors who are effectively engaged in creating value and improving the strategic marketing position of the GI product by individual or organized collective action, and those who are engaged in the activation and reproduction of those local resources (natural resources, knowledge, social capital) which make the GI product specific.'
3. It is the same for financial markets, which are a particular type of dematerialized quality market.

References

Allaire, G. (2004) 'Quality in Economics: a Cognitive Perspective', in M. Harvey, A. McMeekin and A. Warde (eds), *Qualities of Food* (Manchester: Manchester University Press), pp. 61–93.

Allaire, G. (2008) 'Strengthening International Research on Geographical Indications: from Research Foundation to Consistent Policy' (STREP SINER-GI, SSPE-CT-2005-006522), final activity report, http://www.origin-food.org/, date accessed 15 November 2011.

Allaire, G. (2010) 'Applying Economic Sociology to Understand the Meaning of "Quality" in Food Markets', *Agricultural Economics*, 41, supplement, 167–80.

Allaire, G. (2011) 'La rhétorique du terroir', in C. Delfosse (ed.), *Le terroir dans tous ses états* (Paris: La boutique de l'histoire, éditeur, coll. mondes ruraux contemporains), pp. 75–100.

Allaire, G., F. Casabianca and E. Thévenod-Mottet (2011) 'The Geographical Origin: A Complex Feature for Agro-food Products', in B. Sylvander and E. Barham (eds), *Geographical Indications and Globalization in Agro-food Supply Chains* (Wallingford, Oxon: CABI Books), pp. 1–12.

Allaire, G. and B. Sylvander (2011) 'Globalization and Geographical Indications', in B. Sylvander and E. Barham (eds), *Geographical Indications and Globalization in Agro-food Supply Chains* (Wallingford, Oxon: CABI Books), pp. 106–21.

Allaire, G. and E. Thévenod-Mottet (2009) 'Diversity in Typicity: How Geographical Indications Could Become an International Standard', Colloque international 'Localiser les produits: une voie durable au service de la diversité naturelle et culturelle des Suds?', organisé par l'Unesco/Mab, l'IRD, le CIRAD, le MNHN, Paris, UNESCO, 9–11 June.

Allaire, G. and S. Wolf (2004) 'Cognitive Representations and Institutional Hybridity in Agrofood Systems of Innovation', *Science, Technology and Human Values*, 29(4), 431–58.

Andersen, E.S. and K. Philipsen (1998) 'The Evolution of Credence Goods in Customer Markets: Exchanging "Pigs in Pokes"'. Paper presented at the DRUID Winter Seminar, Middelfart, 8–10 January.

Barzel, Y. (1982) 'Measurement Costs and the Organization of Markets', *Journal of Law and Economics*, 25, 27–48.

Brunsson, N. and B. Jacobsson (2000) *A World of Standards* (Oxford: Oxford University Press).

Busch, L. (2000) 'The Moral Economy of Grades and Standards', *Journal of Rural Studies*, 16, 273–83.

Callon, M. (1999) 'The Role of Lay People in the Production and Dissemination of Scientific Knowledge', *Science, Technology and Society*, 1999, 4(1), 81–94.
Commons, J.R. (1934) *Institutional Economics – Its Place in Political Economy* (New York: Macmillan).
Darby, M. and E. Karni ([1973) 'Free Competition and the Optimal Amount of Fraud', *Journal of Law and Economics*, 16, 67–88.
Dewey, J. (1939) 'Theory of Valuation', in *International Encyclopedia of Unified Sciences*, vol. II, no. 4 (Chicago: University of Chicago Press).
Eymard-Duvernay, F. (1989) 'Conventions de qualité et pluralité des formes de coordination', *Revue Economique*, 40(2), 329–59.
Fligstein, N. (1996) 'Markets as Politics: a Political Cultural Approach to Market Institutions', *American Sociological Review*, 61, 656–73.
Goodman, D. (2004) 'Rural Europe Redux? Reflections on Alternative Agro-Food Networks and Paradigm Change', *Sociologia Ruralis* 44(1), 3–16.
Hermitte, M.-A. (2001) 'Les appellations d'origine dans la genèse des droits de la propriété intellectuelle', in P. Moity-Maïzi et al. (eds), *Systèmes agroalimentaires localises, Études et Recherches sur les Systèmes Agraires et le Développement*, no. 32 (Montpellier: INRA-CIRAD-CNEARC), pp. 195–206.
Jahn, G., M. Schramm, and A. Spiller (2004) 'Differentiation of Certification Standards: The Trade-off between Generality and Effectiveness in Certification Systems', http://www.ifama.org/conferences/2004Conference/Papers/Jahn 1024.pdf, date accessed August 2010.
Lancaster, K.J. (1979) *Variety, Equity and Efficiency* (New York: Columbia University Press).
Lupton, S, (2005) 'Shared Quality Uncertainty and the Introduction of Indeterminate Goods', *Cambridge Journal of Economics*, 29(3), 399–421.
Nelson, P. (1970) 'Information and Consumer Behaviour', *Journal of Political Economy*, 78(2), 311–29.
Ostrom, E. and X. Basurto (2011) 'Crafting Analytical Tools to Study Institutional Change', *JOIE*, 7(3), 317–43.
Rangnekar, D. (2004) 'The Socio-Economics of Geographical Indications, a Review of Empirical Evidence from Europe', *UNCTAD/ICTSD Capacity Building Project on Intellectual Property Rights and Sustainable Development* (8).
Sylvander, B., G. Allaire, G. Belletti, A. Marescotti, E. Thevenod-Mottet, D. Barjolle and A. Tregear (2006) 'Les dispositifs français et européens de protection de la qualité et de l'origine dans le contexte de l'OMC: justifications générales et contextes nationaux', *Revue canadienne des sciences régionales*, 29(1), 43–54.
Tirole, J. (1988) *The Theory of Industrial Organization* (Cambridge, MA: MIT Press).
Wilkinson, J. (2006) 'The Mingling of Markets, Movements and Menus: the Renegotiation of Rural Space by NGOs, Social movements and Traditional Actors', International Workshop: Globalisation: Social and Cultural Dynamics, Rio de Janeiro.
Zelizer, V.A. (1978) 'Human Values and the Market: The Case of Life Insurance and Death in 19th Century America', *American Journal of Sociology*, 84, 591–610.
Zelizer, V.A. (1994) *The Social Meaning of Money* (New York: Basic Books).

5
Products with Denominations of Origin and Intellectual Property Rights – the International Bargaining Process

Hélène Ilbert

This work is focused on the identification of the practices and discourses related to geographical indications. Analysis of the places that generate affiliation and the laws covering defence of the protection of 'origin' names is based on the recording of the trajectories, dispersals and upsets that occur under the impact of globalization. The increasing complexity of the globalization movement characterized by the speed of interconnections (Rosa, 2010), the 'archipelagos' of social relations (Appadurai, 1996) and increased pressure from markets and innovations generates a need to regulate or even ward off fears of systemic risks (Beck, 2003). Coordination by standards and 'soft power' highlights institutions rather than economic activity itself.

Both historical and critical, this chapter addresses the frameworks that institute the geographical indications that we consider as indicators of shifts in the origin and quality regime at the global scale. Without any question of correcting the regime, our work considers the relations between discourses and practice, between the knowledge and the people who organize and distribute the principles, standards and rules by generating and reinterpreting them. The question of truth is raised in terms of truthfulness – knowledge and the play of verity – the play of power – legitimacy awarded at a given moment by law, standards and governmentality – and the play of relation to the subject – subjectivity and the experience of oneself (Foucault, 1971). By addressing the reconstruction of the links that demarcate the need to protect reputed goods, the analysis is centred on the regimes of truthfulness of intellectual property rights and especially geographical indications awarded and supported by institutions with their principles, standards, rules and procedures (Krasner, 1983) that give them legitimacy and priority.

Unlike those schools that attempt to eliminate information asymmetry to establish coordination evaluated according to the degree of rationality of the stakeholders (Schelling, 1960; Axelrod, 1986), the analysis here is focused on explaining the conditions of emergence and the dissemination of statements and practices that form the condition for the emergence and dissemination of zones of intellectual property rights. The individual is addressed in his intersubjective dimension and not in a behaviourist or cognitivist perspective.

The first part of this chapter is devoted to the two main historical foundations of geographical indications at the global level. The first is the collective action of French winegrowers in the nineteenth century and the second concerns the coordination between states involved in the defence of the rules of the Trade-Related Aspects of Intellectual Property Rights (TRIPS) agreement of the World Trade Organization (WTO). This pathway shows the shifting of the balances of power: in 2006, following an injunction from the WTO, the European Union, the cradle of 'appellations d'origine', had to undertake reforms applicable to all the member countries that in particular submitted producers to external controls.

The second part examines the dissemination of geographical indications at the international level and the national reinterpretations that have been made since the 1990s hinge period. The producers' association OriGIn, founded to exert pressure on geographical indications at the WTO, is symptomatic of the institutional gridding that is now being consolidated. The developing countries argue that they own heritage resources, such as biological materials or traditional knowledge, that could correct imbalances with the high-technology countries: formalization of local know-how, prior informed consent, access and benefit – sharing and technology transfer design a shift in the geographical indication use; the chain is anchored in the European Union which distributes the doctrine of standards law for geographical indications while coupling it with the rules of free trade and quality and origin policy. Bilateral cooperation and soft law often go further than the rules of common law.

The final part addresses the question of power. Geographical indications and the brands form a historical node. Governments are not neutral players; they are also players in competitiveness and intervene to prevent the brand values of companies from being called into question by the system of geographical indications and heritage value. In conclusion, access to knowledge and know-how and their transfer modes are driven by the search for economic rent. What about the human question of public uses and free transfer of knowledge?

5.1 The historical trajectory of Geographical Indications: a normative legal foundation constructed in the twentieth century

The first establishment of geographical indications, then referred to as *'appellations d'origine'*, resulted from the collective action of French winegrowers at the beginning of the twentieth century. Strikes, lawsuits and conflicts resulted in the legal recognition of the link between a name, a *terroir* and cultivation and cultural practices (Bérard and Marchenay, 2007).

By achieving recognition of the origin of a wine, growers called on the courts to delimit production areas or *terroirs* benefiting from protection against usurpation. The Republican pact for the defence of *terroirs* became established (Jacquet, 2008). Legal arbitration supported by the political and economic body led to a social arrangement concerning the right to *appellations d'origine*. Once delimited and awarded, farmers can use this right that gives them a monopoly for the use of the name. This exclusion function is exerted on any third party who wishes to use an appellation indicating a reputed product from a specific place. Governments ensure this (Audier, 1993).

The creation of national bodies such as the *Institut National des Appellations d'Origine* (INAO) in France in 1935 and then the international conventions and agreements managed by multilateral bodies such as the World Intellectual Property Organization in 1967 contributed to the establishment of a body of regulations. Protection gained increasing importance in world trade and the legal measures became increasingly complex (Olszak, 2001).

The second focus for the construction of geographical indications took shape in the regularity of the negotiations and conformity of the intellectual property rights incorporated in world trade regulations. Indeed, from 1995 onwards, when the setting up of the World Trade Organization became effective, the term 'geographical indication' established correspondences between intellectual property law and trade regulation at the global level. The old institutional arrangement formed at the beginning of the twentieth century by the collective action of winegrowers is being reinterpreted nearly a century later by states involved on the one hand in implementing rules of free trade and on the other in the defence of their national preferences. The national delegations handling negotiations are seeking points of convergence to reduce barriers to trade while claiming the validity of their domestic choices. Using as a base the political consensus of the opening up of economies that forms the foundation of the Bretton Woods institutions, a new technico-political consensus obtained during the GATT negotiations materialized as the conformity of national measures to the principles, rules and procedures of the TRIPS agreement: the harmonization of legal systems is conducted according to the principles of non-discrimination, the 'most-favoured nation' concept and reciprocity. The determination to remove both tariff and non-tariff trade barriers is applied to intellectual property rights in trade (Barton et al., 2002, 2006). National positions are the subject of compromises that can be either internal (interministerial, social forums, links with inter-branch bodies) or external (multilateral negotiations governed by an agenda, rules of discussion and application). This second focus for the establishment of geographical indications that are in the category of intellectual property rights related to trade proceeds according to a calendar, procedures of multilateral negotiations and sanctions applied by the Dispute Settlement Body. Standards law has gained powers enabling sanctions at the international level under the influence of international lobbies (Ryan, 1998).

A single definition of geographical indications valid for 154 member states was thus achieved in 1995. The TRIPS agreement defines the terms. Since the launching of the Doha cycle of negotiations in 2001, the conditions for the implementation of this body of rules has come up against the question of the voluntary or obligatory nature of the system of registration of geographical indications; one uses the notion of base of consultable information while the other expresses the undertaking of the states to effectively guarantee the information notified (Arhel, 2007). At the level of states, two opposition 'fronts' – the United States and the European Union – show how difficult it is to achieve the convergence of national preferences. Supported by Australia and other New World countries, the United States opposes the community proposals backed by the 'friends of geographical indications', suspecting the latter of pursuing protectionist policies disguised by the imposition of a system of notification and effective registration that would form a new barrier to entry (Ilbert and Petit, 2009). At the same time, the complaint by the United States against the European Union brought before the Dispute Settlement Body (DSB) of the WTO calls into question the European legal model. Indeed, if it were generalized, the EU's constrictive notification and registration system would oblige third countries to provide protection equivalent to that in the EU. Whence the allegation of discrimination between member countries with regard to the non respect of the most-favoured nation principle (ibid.). It could endanger private rights, and in particular trademark rights, that are law-based in the United States. The *Lanham* Law administered by the Patent and Trademark Office protects trademarks alone, including certification marks, which is the system closest to that of denominations of origin (Barham, 2010). By virtue of the most-favoured nation principles and the national treatment clause that regulate global trade, the special group appointed by the DSB required adjustments to be made to the European Council regulation (2081/92) on designations of origin. In conformity with the decisions taken by the special group, the European Union changed the regulation in 2006 (EC Regulation 510/2006) and its implementing rules in 2006 (EC Regulation 1898/2006) (Ilbert and Petit, 2009). The revisions to the text and corresponding practice included opening to producers in third countries and controls by private third party certification bodies. Indeed, a major objection concerned 'the additional obstacle' that third countries would run up against if their national authorities had to perform control tasks. Public authorities cannot be constrained to internalize these functions as specified by the conclusions of the WTO Special Group (WTO, 2003b; Ilbert, 2005). As a result, the European Union members countries have undertaken domestic reforms since 2006 to transfer to private agencies the power to verify that the specifications of designated origins are effectively followed: auto-controls by the profession are twinned with controls performed by private certification bodies.

The body of references used as a measuring stick by politicians is that of free trade: the standards aspect of the former European designations of origin must adapt to the injunctions of the Dispute Settlement Body by matching global trade disciplines.

5.2 Dissemination of geographical indications at the international scale and national interpretations: the 1990s hinge point

As there was no strict international register with effective legal protection, private and public stakeholders in search of forms of protection of reputation goods became organized as they sought to extend the scope of law to cover geographical indications.

5.2.1 oriGIn

Without prejudice to the true power of oriGIn – the Organization for an International Geographical Indications Network – its role as a pressure group lies at the interface between several currents and this organization is symptomatic of the institutional grid created between producers and institutions on the global level. The association groups farming professionals of various sizes and is at the crossroads of the forces that operate to defend the internationalization of geographical indications, whether in developing countries or in the European Union. Created in 2003 during the dispute between the United States and the European Union, its founder members are inter-branch associations and producers' groups in the European Union and its associates are producers or groups in 24 countries. Over the years it has gradually became more international, first in its mode of internal governance as it is chaired in turn by representatives of producers' organizations based in Europe and then in Latin America (Guatemala and Mexico). It also has a broad opening in terms of the number of members and affiliated countries: in 2006 its members comprised 150 professionals, including 40 producers' associations working with geographic indications. In 2011, it reported that it had 200 professional organisations and two million GI producers in 40 countries around the world (oriGIn, 2011c). In line with the corporatist movements of winegrowers in Europe at the beginning of the twentieth century, producers in different parts of the world have united to establish an institutional structure to claim the right of protection of goods of reputation, but this time on an international scale.

Actions are conducted at different levels of decision-making. Pressure is exerted first at the level of WTO negotiators. The Vice-Director-General of WTO, a delegation from World Intellectual Property Organization (WIPO) and the European Commissioner for Trade were invited to the constituent assembly of oriGIn. The association obtained the possibility of organizing a round table discussion on geographical indications within the framework of the WTO annual public symposium in 2004. It also gained the status of permanent observer at the WIPO in 2004, giving it a high level of information about the technical assistance programmes set up by WIPO and the legal options that might play a role in protection. Finally, it acts at the level of the European Commission and the national authorities of countries such as Switzerland, Mexico, Brazil and China (Hannachi, 2008). As its headquarters are in Geneva, the association can deploy permanent action on WTO delegations, the WIPO and the European Commission. It has asked to be an observer at the European Counterfeiting and Pirating Observatory since 2011 and is demanding the creation of a specialized EU agency to handle registrations and requests for opposition and is offering to list the protected geographical origins in the world (oriGIn, 2011a). Indeed, the inter-branch associations are seeking to become more effective.

This international network now has a permanent office in China and representatives in 40 countries around the world. It encourages countries to adopt specific legislation and seeks to broaden the circle of countries that are favourable for geographical indications at the international level. The pressure group addresses the field of international politics and also provides services among members. Each of these undertakes to disseminate information about the positive role of geographical indications and to report cases of usurpation. Partnerships are formed between producers: *Viande séchée du Valais* (Switzerland) and *Oignon violet de Galmi* (Niger), *Plateau de Phurua* wine (Thailand), *Roquefort* cheese (France) *Parmigiano Reggiano* (Italy) and *Longjing* tea (China) have joined forces to share their experiences. The network also provides technical assistance to developing countries that require expertise, especially with regard to unfair competition practices. This consists of regular provision of specialized information to all members of the network (via a specialized professional journal) while exerting pressure within the international field of the WTO.

The oriGIn association federates allies and thus operates as a vector for initiatives aimed at achieving better protection. Its actions are relayed in Europe by professional organizations such as the European Association of Geographical Indications (AREPO) and the European Federation of Origin Wines (EFOW) that play a political role as regards member states to defend geographical indications by preparing amendments for draft reports.

For producers, economic intelligence is focused on the consolidation of international areas that are harmonized to reduce risks of counterfeiting. Its aim is to correct market failures by setting up the conditions for a regulated market that is harmonized by effective protection standards. The main international target is that of increasing the number of countries equipped with strict legal infrastructure to validate the protection of reputed names.

5.2.2 Developing countries: the Woof

The question of developing countries is that of claiming the recognition of sovereign rights to resources and to identify the potential of products with high value-added by protecting names in order to gain anteriority with regard to companies that may wish to appropriate local know-how. With few goods of reputation, they undertook policies for the recognition of these rights during the 1990s hinge period (SOLAGRAL, 1993; Ilbert et al., 2000). After leading the *Megadivers* within the framework of negotiations on biodiversity at the end of the

1990s, they steered the 'GI Friends' group and the 'Hundred group' at the WTO at the beginning of the 2000s. The governments of developing countries with rich biodiversity intervened to obtain recognition of the rules that could protect their national resources at the international level. They demanded sovereign rights for their biological resources, rights for native populations and *sui generis* intellectual property rights. For it to be possible to award these rights, traditions are considered as forms of innovation: the contractualization of knowledge, linked to the conservation and exploitation of resources, should encourage transfers of technology or direct investments abroad and thus make it possible to balance historical losses by the progress made by the high technology countries (SOLAGRAL, 1999). This offensive protection policy steered by governments is aimed at reducing the imbalance with the high-technology countries that protect innovations through the use of patents. In economic terms, the growth of trade and of the markets for intellectual property rights is considered to lead to transactions that are theoretically beneficial for the local populations (Aubertin et al., 2007). In practice, it results in applications for the extension of protection for the recognition of local know-how and geographical indications. Technical committees meet at WIPO to decide on the legal founding of the criteria of utility and industrial application of know-how, examining in particular the problem of the status of genetic resources and the law as regards traditional resources (Dutfield, 2000).

Bodies of so-called *sui generis* law are becoming established in numerous countries. 'Basmati' rice, 'Neem' and 'Thaumatine' are emblematic of these procedures conducted by traditional indigenous communities and relayed at the national and multilateral level in particular within the framework of the Biodiversity Convention. The issue is that of protecting traditional resources and limiting abusive patent application practices (Posey and Dutfield, 1997). Recognition of the anteriority of rights involves the codification of native practices supervised by NGOs, territorial or national bodies or international development programmes: inventories, databases, sector studies, specifications, territorial delimitations, technical agricultural, commercial and legal studies and research and cooperation programmes participate in the dissemination of forms of protection. The awarding of heritage status to nature and the cultural diversity of rationalities and practices set up intersecting global to local dynamics (Cormier-Salem et al., 2002; Louafi and Roussel, 2005). Geographical indications participate in the dynamics by delimiting and giving value to local know-how and ancestral practices. Considered as tools that can enhance the 'virtuous circle' of development, they generate the multiplication of practices of formalization of know-how with a view to the reserved use of a name said to be reputed. This is shown by the numerous guides covering geographical indications published by international cooperation or teaching organizations such as the FAO and the International Trade Centre and by national and regional organizations.

Identity, environmental or economic values that are considered to be propitious for rural development, eco-tourism, landscape conservation and the development of income-generating activities contribute to form a set of objectives and practices that are positive for geographical indications. The latter are presented as a means for developing countries to differentiate their products, to safeguard against falls in price and to guarantee forms of redistribution throughout the chain. This function of long-term rural development and aid in the formation of social organization and territorial dynamics is highlighted in the research conducted by Dolphin and then by SINER-GI (Sylvander, 2004).

The combined effects of actions for the conservation of reputed names, the management of territories and their heritage resources and population consolidates the choice of opting for GIs. While being a tool for legal protection focused on the defence of a system of notification and registration extended to products other than wines and spirits and extended to as large a number of countries as possible, the geographical indication system is a tool for protecting a bio-cultural heritage, a lever for market access and a vector for socioeconomic development. In some cases, it is an integral part of development programmes and induces numerous practices of delimitation and formalization of knowledge and know-how, as in the recent experience of the development of GIs within the framework of the 'Maroc Vert' plan (Conseil Général du Développement Agricole, 2010).

By forming alliances with producers in developing countries that defend GIs at the international level, OriGIn is becoming linked with the policies of developing countries that are in favour of the sharing of profits, economic transfer and the use of know-how and traditions, a counterpart to innovations in the high-technology countries.

5.2.3 The European Union – the chain

The European Union forms the chain. By seeking to internationalize its system of protection of geographical indications, it exerts centrifugal and centripetal forces that accelerate the dissemination of this indication of origin.

Geographical indications were seen as being strategic in the new European quality policy launched in the early 1990s. The quality package and the regulations of application form a horizontal pattern that is independent of product type (Berlottier, 2009). This new international competition regime systematically associates quality and origin (Allaire, 2009). The reform of the Common Agricultural Policy (2013–20) currently being drafted combines attention on strengthening the law of European geographical indication (PGO/PGI/TSG) and a concern for sustainable development. Emphasis is laid on questions of food safety in terms of the quality of foodstuffs, protection of the environment, traceability and labels. Without waiting for the outcome of multilateral negotiations, the European Commission is organizing the recognition by the largest possible number of countries of laws covering protection by geographical indications, while remaining in conformity with the rules concerning the openness of economies.

The dissemination movement is formalized by bilateral and regional trade agreements and cooperation agreements whose number is increasing and that often go further than multilateral rights (Morin, 2003). These agreements specify the position of geographical indications in the jurisdictions of partner countries. The European Union first consolidates protection levels with trade partners where usurpation risks are greatest. The first step was the agreement between the EU and the USA in 1983 for mutual recognition of their protection systems. But the USA added restriction to geographical indications by requiring the removal of any reference to a positive list that could become a constraint (Audier and Commission Européenne, 2000). Proceeding step by step, the EU performed negotiations with its other trade partners to fix procedures that made it possible to subordinate trade to national registration of geographical indications. Thus bilateral agreements such as that ratified in 1994 between the EU and Australia specify transition periods for certain wine appellations that have still not been set. The same applies to the agreement with South Africa in 2001 and with Chile in 2002. The latter is a reference agreement for the protection of European geographical indications as it requires the removal of existing usurpations, the recognition of traditional names and the creation of positive lists of oenological practices. The obligations are based on national treatment and the most-favoured nation (EC, 2002). Treatment is thus in conformity with international law covering world trade. It combines rules for the opening of markets and a strengthening of intellectual property rights, with specification of the implementation conditions. Regional cooperation programmes as in the Mediterranean encourage the setting up of legal and practical frameworks for the delimitation of *terroirs* and the identification of potential products, without forgetting aid for the drafting of specifications. This technical cooperation stemming from European know-how – especially French and Italian – is relayed by research and training institutes in Turkey and materialised mainly in Morocco, Tunisia, Algeria and Lebanon (Tekelioglu et al., 2009).

In parallel with the dissemination of the discourses and practices related to geographical indications outside the European Union, there is a trend for attraction towards the EU created partly by the opening of the European register to the rest of the world following an injunction by the WTO and partly by the European policy quality package. Applications come from producers in third countries. Following the recognition of Colombian Coffee in 2006, the European Union and China agreed on the reciprocal protection of some ten reputed geographical indications. The drafting of the lists of foods and agrofood products and the setting up of procedures for the assessment of the reciprocal importance of these products for each trade partner, whether in volume or value, set the terms of the agreement (oriGIn, 2011b).

Bilateral and cooperation agreements specify and conduct the technical assistance programmes that strengthen the intellectual property regime on trade principles of reciprocity. On the Doha cycle time scale in which the two points on the agenda of the delegations are suspended – the constrictive notification and registrations system and the scope of protection – the institutional gridding of cooperation hands out the doctrine of standards law covering intellectual property coupled with free trade disciplines.

The conditions of transactions are specified by compromises on exchanges of information, application of the rules and modes of cooperation. The maintaining of *terroirs* and landscapes as environmental services, remuneration functions and the clarification of relations with consumers are highlighted. Rules concerning labelling, the simplification of registration and control are detailed. Special measures are planned to prevent irregularities and fraud. Ad hoc committees supervise conformity with market rules. The prevention of 'free riding' is a shared concern, but the criteria for exclusion and modes of application are the subject of many conflicts of interests.

5.3 The power of symbolic conflicts

5.3.1 Geographical Indications: an international legal order that is limited at the global scale

Of the 1,032 GIs registered in 2001, only a few names like *Parmegiano Reggiano* and Parma Ham are on the small list of GIs registered in Europe that are likely to have export commercial value (Appendix 1). They are an integral part of economic development policies and assume collective action organized at several levels (Fanti, 2007). These goods of reputation combine protection by origin and by private brand by establishing strategic alliances that ensure legibility, exclusivity and reputation.

The other names are often little known and raise problems of legibility at the international level. For example, the applications for registration in 2009 by EU countries were as follows: *Montes De Toledo, Aglio di Voghiera, Traditionally Farmed Gloucestershire Old Spot Pork, Spressa delle Guidicarie, Csabai Kolbasz, Gyulai Paroskolbasz, Tettnanger Hopfen, Pintadeau de la Drôme, Hopfen aus der Hallertau, Tarta de Santiago, Partheno Eleolado Selino Kritis, Castana de Galicia* and *Canestrato di Moliterno*.

The value of PDO and PGI production in the European Union in 2008 was estimated at €14.8 billion (oriGIn, 2010a). The including of spirits would take the total to more than €20 billion, but the data vary according to source as some authors mention figures as high as €50 billion. Depending on whether the top or the bottom of this range is considered, the market accounts for 2 to 3 per cent of the total market for '*terroir*' products in Europe. The Mediterranean countries account for more than 70 per cent by value of this total as this is where more of the geographical indications are found. Spain, Italy and France have a dominant position and concentrate export markets with a number of star products with international fame. The market as a whole is thus small in comparison with the mass markets (Ilbert, 2009).

With regard to the attractive nature of the European range, few third countries have effectively registered geographical indications. Colombian Coffee is followed by six Chinese geographical indications and, the latest, '*Darjeeling tea*' from India.

Few applications from outside the EU have been made or published on the EU register: eight from Asian countries and two from Turkey and Morocco. Protection applies to the names of emblematic products such as Argan and Darjeeling. In both cases the cultural character is twinned with confrontation with the anteriority of private brands steered by groups well versed in the international mechanisms of defence of financial rights.

5.3.2 Rivalry between brands and Geographical Indications: a historic problem

Balances of power between the defence of brand value and heritage value are asymmetrical and spotlighted by complex economic and legal evaluations that result in tensions of varying acuteness. Historically, the authorities handling competition have taken decisions on a case-by-case

Table 5.1 Application and registration by third countries on the EU register

	Country	Name	Status	Date in force	Application date
ASIA					
	China				
		Jinxiang Da Suan	**Registered**	**01/11/2011**	**16/07/2007**
		Longjing cha	**Registered**	**11/05/2011**	**16/07/2007**
		Guanxi Mi You	**Registered**	**11/05/2011**	**16/07/2007**
		Shaanxi ping guo	**Registered**	**11/05/2011**	**16/07/2007**
		Lixian Ma Shan Yao	**Registered**	**11/05/2011**	**16/07/2007**
		Longkou Fen Si	**Registered**	**30/10/2010**	**16/07/2007**
		Zhenjiang Xiang Cu	Published	22/09/2010	16/07/2007
		Dongshan Bai Lu Sun	Application	16/07/2007	16/07/2007
		Pinggu Da Tao	Application	16/07/2007	16/07/2007
		Yancheng Long Xia	Application	16/07/2007	16/07/2007
	Thailand	Khao Hom Mali Thung	Published	29/06/2010	20/11/2008
		Doi Tung Coffee	Application	27/05/2010	27/05/2010
		Doi Chaang Coffee	Application	27/05/2010	27/05/2010
	India	*Darjeeling*	**Registered**	**21/10/2011**	**12/11/2007**
		Kangra Tea	Application	25/01/2008	25/01/2008
	Vietnam	*Phu Quoc*	Application	26/08/2009	26/08/2009
MED.					
	Turkey	*Aydin ncir*	Application	24/08/2010	2/08/2010
		Antep Bklavasi	Application	10/07/2009	10/07/2009
	Morocco	*Argane*	Application	14/10/2011	14/10/2011

Source: UE Database on latest registered/published/applied designations http://ec.europa.eu/agriculture/quality/door/October 2011.

basis of abusive monopole practices such as the buying-merging of brands with portfolio effects (Valceschini and Blanchemanche, 2003) or agreements between inter-branch designation of origin groups with a club and control effect (Marette, 2003). Assessment of the instrumentalization of market rules is complex as collective strategies and forms of contractual organization make it possible to differentiate products on the market continue to evolve. Distinctive signs are played against each other when they are supposed to fulfil different functions as the private brand follows company marketing strategies whereas the public law geographical indication enables groups of producers to protect a name related to a *terroir* and to human factors (Appendix 2).

At the WTO, the balance in rights between the owners of brands and geographical indications is the subject of fastidious legal techniques focused mainly on the possibilities of the translation of an origin name. In the conclusions of the WTO dispute, translations were limited so that the registration of a geographical indication did not award a positive right to use the name in another non-registered language version.

In practice, the Budweiser company is pleased with the political and legal results obtained. The question was that of preventing the Czech Republic, which joined the European Union in 2004, from claiming the rights of the Czech firm Budvar in all the official languages in Europe and especially in English and German, because this would give 'Budweiser', which would affect the rights of the American company Anheuser-Busch, the holder of the brand. The arguments were anchored in a long series of legal procedures that started with a simple story of immigration: a Czech migrant called Anheuser Busch who was acquainted with the local know-how of Czech breweries registered 'Budweiser' as a private brand in 1878. With anteriority over the Budvar company that did not register the name until 1895, Anheuser-Busch had since been attacked by his country of origin with regard to the right to use the translation of the name of the town Budejovice: the Czech Republic sought to forbid the use of the brand name 'Budweiser' or 'Bud' by the American company for many years. Several provisional agreements were reached and since 2008 the Anheuser-Busch company has imported Czech beer to the United States, but rivalries still remain.

Today, after numerous court hearings and appeals, Anheuser-Busch cannot sell its beer under the name 'Budweiser' but as 'Bud' in Germany, Austria, France, Portugal and Switzerland and in June 2011 the cancellation of the brand 'Budweiser' was obtained in Italy (oriGIn, 2011a). In conformity with the principle of territoriality and the anteriority of rights, some European governments have chosen to limit the use of the brand 'Budweiser' in translation.

Governments, who both guard the law and are stakeholders in competitiveness, defend the commercial, legal and political positions that can protect companies that are national economic 'stars'. While the Czech company sought to gain a position on the world market, the American company sought high-level interventions to position itself on the international market. It received support from US government policy that intervened with regard to market rules at a multilateral level (WTO panel) to limit the right to translate geographical indications. In response to this, certain European governments used the right of geographical indications to the exclusive use of their name, in turn limiting the rights of brands to translation.

In a free market, governments intervene so that the world trade rules facilitate the positioning of reputations goods designed according to their national collective preferences. The race for legitimacy for the extension of legal protection in time, scope and effectiveness mobilizes high-level diplomacy with legal, economic and political competences. The legal procedures and interventions at various political decision levels are continuous. Socioeconomic compromises involve specialized language and legal procedures: oppositions, court hearing aggravating rivalry for the use of a reputed name without bodies of law being able to legitimize a point of balance between brands and geographical indications. The United States took the question of geographical indications to the WTO Dispute Settlement Body above all because Europe had clearly failed to open its market and because the protection of geographical indications should not affect the rights of owners of brands, according to the Secretary of Trade Robert B. Zoellick in 2005 during the conclusion of the WTO panel on geographical indications (Mills and Moorjani, 2004).

While the arguments concerning doctrine are procedural, they also refer to political and economic issues and even cultural and social aspects. Thus a complaint was made recently by the Champagne inter-branch committee with a request for a domain name usurped by a third party (champagne.co) should be transferred to them. But procedures to denounce cybersquatting that are regulated by the Internet Corporation for Assigned Names and Numbers (ICANN) only have measures for company brands and not for geographical indications. As the inter-branch body is not a company that owns a commercial brand, the complaint was refused by the WIPO Arbitration and Mediation Centre. Only stakeholders that own brands are taken into consideration (Saez, 2011).

This restrictive legal interpretation of the right of protection to company brands alone has contributed to the calling into question of the European designated origin regime. It creates a procedural legal vacuum for inter-branch associations that hold geographical indications and is resulting in other legitimization actions. Although the definition of geographical indication was accepted within the framework of the bargaining process between states during the Uruguay Round of global negotiations that resulted in the TRIPS in 1995, warfare between holders of signs is in fact getting worse. Transaction costs are high and require technical knowledge, political know-how leading to legal action of the complaint type, appeals and cases at a global scale. Only a few have the level of information required to inflect the formation of rights and take recourse to the courts.

5.3.3 The universe of brands and the market power of brand values

Long-recognized brands are based on solid institutional gridding giving brand rights effectiveness and flexibility at the international scale. The international brand system facilitates the obtaining of a renewal or international registration. A single application is made to a national intellectual property bureau and there are then links between the national protection of the registered names and those of the 84 countries that are members of the Madrid system. The system records procedures, provides information about the parties involved and services to clients, such as the issuing of certificates and the management of brand portfolios.

The use of brands and their reputation effect corresponds to the strategies of companies capable of investing and defending their brands at the international scale (legibility, reputation, fidelity). A brand is a company asset and an instrument for competitive positioning. It is incorporated in the accounting, management, marketing and legal and financial administration of a company and is the source of creation of value.

It was estimated that 16.4 million brands existed world-wide in 2007 with a growth rate of 1.6 per cent per year. A third are held by US and Japanese companies, followed by the European countries. A total of 43 per cent of trademarks registered in the USA are protected in other countries of the world (WIPO, 2009).

Interbrand considers that the Top 100 most reputed brands have a total worth of $2,000 thousand million. The value of a brand, an intangible asset, is linked to the life of the company, to its investment choices, its transmission and communication strategies – in short, its ability to add value to its own value. Anchored in relations with consumers and shareholders, the calculation methods used to estimate the value of brands for ranking purposes sum up the quantitative data linked to earnings and the qualitative data corresponding to the value expected. Variation in the estimates of the value of brands is explained in particular by the monetary retranscription of parameters such as consumers' opinions, the strength of protection, its geographical scope and its fame.

Processed products, beverages and fast food head the list of brands. The value of the Coca-Cola brand has escaped market variations in the last five years and gives it a position in the world top ten brands. The American brand Budweiser, purchased by the Belgian group InBev in 2008 (Ermenier, 2009), is in 45th position in the Top 100 with a value bracket of between $16 and 12 thousand million according to 2011 estimates. The brand forms an increasing part of the intangible investments of the company. Related to the value of the company ($38 million) the brand accounts for 40 to 50 per cent according to the estimates.

In some cases, large groups invest in designations of origin to segment their range and differentiate products with good reputations that should ensure new markets. For example, the Lactalys group has invested in PDO French cheeses and the LVMH group has invested in PDO Champagne. The latter uses the Moët & Chandon brand that has strong growth potential and brand value estimated at around $4.5 thousand million in 2011 (Interbrand, 2011).

Economic stakeholders with investment capacity and power of anticipation in material and immaterial capital play both on the effect of size and on the effect of differentiation: domination by costs and by segmentation is part of the regime of competition in origin and quality that has developed since the hinge point in the 1990s. The major private and public economic stakeholders that are capable of steering global chains of value by economies of scale and differentiation are positioned on the world market.

Table 5.2 Classification of agrofood brand values

Company	Brand value BrandZ, 2011 Thousand million USD	Brand value Interbrand, 2011 Thousand million USD
Coca-Cola	73,752	71,861
MacDonald	66,005	35,593
Budweiser	15,952	12,252
Starbuck	11,901	
Pizza Hut	5,305	40,092
Moët & Chandon	4,570	4,383

Source: BrandZ, MillwardBrown and Interbrand, J.P Morgan Chase and Co, Citigroup and Morgan Stanley.

5.4 Conclusion: the largest common denominator?

The universe of brands remains the distinctive sign with the largest common denominator for all of the operators who are active in the world market. It is embedded by geographical indications handled by stakeholders whose numbers have increased continuously over the past 20 years. The legal (principles of territoriality and anteriority of laws) and economic (principles of reciprocity or competition) arguments are accompanied by political and cultural arguments (sovereignty and heritage protection) evaluated by measurement against the rules of international trade (non-discrimination, national treatment, and so on).

The differentials in arguments and in the legal, economic and political measures between countries in the New World and Europe aggravate tensions as the calendar for the implementation of the opening of economies is performed at various levels (multilateral and bilateral agreements, associations, and so on). The economic rent is at stake:

- The very large companies with brand equity and reputational goods exert pressure on governments. Even if transaction costs are high – court cases, political lobbying at WTO panels and so on – they struggle *ex ante* to set the rules awarding the right to institute proceedings and anteriority. Governance of the brand image and its portfolio, sometimes combined with designations of origin, strengthens the monopolistic power of the very large companies able to overcome free trade barriers, because they know how to manage the global knowledge economy.
- The governments involved in the defence of heritage value or origin and quality intervene to legitimize practices of the formalization of know-how. Countries with potentially marketable reputational goods claim rights to the emblematic value of names that cannot be dissociated from national territories or exceptional quality practices. Focused on export markets, they promote goods with reputations and operate at internal and external levels.

The search for opportunities to protect investments and gain export market shares mobilizes governments and the private sector. Pressure is focused on the ability and the legitimacy of drawing economic rent from a reputed name. The parallel between tradition and innovation makes the use of intellectual property rights legitimate as an essential factor for economic growth. Unsurprisingly, the strategies used are those of the market and competitiveness. Considered as tools that can protect innovations and enhance technology transfer or access to markets, intellectual property rights are strategic for companies – and governments – involved in international competition.

Far from withdrawing from the market, states intervene to set up incentive regulations for the private sector. Tradition and historical depth are used in relation to a set of attributes for the world market. It is not the '*terroirs*' as such that give value to the good, but the signs attached or related to them, as long as they comply with the rule of free trade and equivalent treatment at frontiers.

Reciprocal treatment at frontiers functions like an economic golden rule. Territorial privileges are considered as barriers to entry. Indeed, as the subject of a transaction on the world market, the good sold is considered to be free of regional links: it must move freely in a market governed according to the principles of national treatment and non-discrimination.

Progressive adjustments to become 'WTO-compatible' curve the horizon of institutional arrangements. The search to anticipate positions or to protect against the risks of counterfeits is a driving force. It is not a simple generalization of the rules governing intellectual property rights but the deployment of organized universes so that access to and methods of transfer of knowledge or know-how can be codified according to the rules of global markets. Focused on effectiveness and strategies for the defence of innovations or know-how, the international quality and origin regime is organized by sets of definitions, mechanisms or procedures whose stability in time depends on adjustments and repeated compromises by the parties.

Repetition is used by the infinite power of markets ever ready to find a new candidate for a new monopoly whose temporality depends on skill in coordinating different bodies of soft laws and marketing strategies. The procedures and modes of coordination between private and public lobbies eliminate discussions of the order induced by the extension of the intellectual property rights regime with regard to free trade. The problem of the balance between the free movement of knowledge and the right to limit access to it is a major point: territories, landscapes, specific foods and persons are attributes in global competition, whatever their size. Absorbed by the speed and power of capital, the daily experience of people is changed into proof of reputation and anteriority. The human question of public use, free inter- and intra-generational transfer of knowledge, is beyond the scope of this contribution. Do not agriculture and foodstuffs fulfill social, cultural, environmental and political functions that go beyond priority to an economic reputation?

Appendix 5.1 Names of European Union GI products likely to have an impact in world trade (wines and spirits not included)

	Meat products	Cheese	Oil	Other	Beer
Spain	Cecina De León Guijuelo Jamón de Huelva Jamón de Teruel Salchichón de Vic Sobrasada De Mallorca	Idiazába Mahón-Menorca Queso Manchego	Aceite del Baix-Ebre-Montsía Aceite del Bajo Aragón Antequera Baena Priego de Córdoba Sierra de Cádiz Sierra de Segura Sierra Mágina	Cítricos Valencianos Jijona Turrón de Alicante Azafrán de la Mancha	
Italy	Mortadella Bologna Pancetta Piacentina Prosciutto di Parma Prosciutto di San Daniele Prosciutto Toscano Zampone Modena	Asiago Fontina Gorgonzola Grana Padano Mozzarella di Bufala Campana Parmigiano Reggiano Pecorino Romano Provolone Valpadana Taleggio	Toscano	Balsamico Tradizionale di Modena	
France	Canard à foie gras du Sud-Ouest Jambon de Bayonne	Brie de Meaux Camembert de Normandie Comté Emmental de Savoie Reblochon Roquefort	Huile d'olive de Haute-Provence	Huile essentielle de lavande de Haute-Provence Huîtres Marennes Oléron Pruneaux d'Agen	

Germany	Nürnberger Bratwürste, Nürnberger Rostbratwürste	Allgäuer Bergkäse Allgäuer Emmentaler		Nürnberger Lebkuchen (*pastry*)	Bayerisches Bier Münchener Bier
Portugal		Queijo Sao Jorge Queijo Serra da Estrela	Azeite de Moura Azeites de Trás-os-Montes	Pêra Rocha do Oeste (fruit)	
Czech Republic				Žatecký chmel (*spices*)	České pivo Českobudějovické pivo Budějovický měšt'anský var Budějovické pivo
Greece		Feta	Siteia Lasithi Crete	Elia Kalamatas (*table olives*) Masticha chiou (*gums*)	
Austria	Tiroler Speck		Steirisches Kübiskernöl	Steirischer Kren (*fruits/ vegetables*)	
Denmark		Danablu			
Hungary	Szegedi téliszalámi/ Szegedi szalámi				

Source: Table compiled from an EU list (9.10.2009). Extract from the classification of GI products (EU510/200) according to export value.

Appendix 5.2 Comparative attributes of certifications, private brands and geographical indications

	Certification	Registered brand	Geographical indication
Type of right	Right certifying product quality, sometimes linked to origin	Right attesting human creation.	Right attesting a link between man and nature; proof of the link with terroir.
Duration of the right	Temporary, to be renewed	Life and death of the brand linked to the life of the company. An undefended brand becomes generic.	Imprescriptible: terroir and heritage are immemorial, without a limited duration.
Type of property (ownership and transferability)	– Individual or collective held by a registered person/persons (private law) – Not transferable.	– Individual by a legal entity (private law) – Renewable and saleable (sale and licences for use).	– Collective, even if registered by a single holder (joint right with no private holder) – Cannot be relocated, Inalienable (no licence, no sale).
Type of instrument	– Designation of a producer certifying the quality, origin characteristics, types of materials, etc. declared by the holders to the public authorities.	– Distinctive signs identifying a product according to the statements of the holder (no public intervention)	– Joint organisation handling the signs of tradition, constant uses and registration by the public authorities.
Type of obligation	Recognition of the quality of a product and coexistence with brands and GIs.	At the initiative of the body corporate, identifying the creator (court of justice in case of dispute)	Integration of multiple objectives related to communities: trans-generational obligation.
Function	Protection of the name and certification of quality.	Protection and remuneration of the body corporate.	– Protection of the public good in case of regional development or management, etc.

References

Allaire, G. (2009) 'Diversité des indications géographiques: positionnement dans le nouveau régime de commerce international', in Y. Tekelioglu, H. Ilbert and S. Tozanli (eds), *Les produits de terroir, les indications géographiques et le développement local durable des pays méditerranéens* (Montpellier: CIHEAM-IAM).

Appadurai, A. (1996) *Modernity at Large: Cultural Dimensions of Globalization* (Minneapolis: University of Minnesota Press).

Arhel, P. (2007) 'Travaux de l'OMC visant à étendre et à faciliter la protection des indications géographiques', *Revue mensuelle Jurisclasseur, Propriété industrielle (revue mensuelle Jurisclasseur)*, March, 7–12.

Aubertin, C., F. Pinton and V. Boisvert (eds) (2007) *Les marchés de la biodiversité* (Paris: IRD).

Audier, J. (1993) 'De la nature juridique de l'appellation d'origine', *Bulletin de l'OIV*, 66(743–4), 21–37.

Audier, J. (réd.) and Commission Européenne. Direction générale du Commerce (2000) *Indications géographiques* (Luxembourg: Office des publications officielles des Communautés européennes).

Axelrod, R. (1986) 'An Evolutionary Approach to Norms', *The American Political Science Review*, 80, 1096–111.

Barham, E. (ed.) (2010) *American Origin Products (AOPs): Protecting a Legacy* (Geneva: oriGIn).

Barton, J., D. Alexander, C. Correa, R. Mashelkar, G. Samuels and S. Thomas (eds) (2002) *Integrating Intellectual Property Rights and Development Policy: Report of the Commission on Intellectual Property Rights* (London: Commission on Intellectual Property Rights).

Barton, J.H., J. Goldstein, T.E. Josling and R.H. Steinberg (2006) *The Evolution of the Trade Regime: Politics, Law, and Economics of the GATT and the WTO* (Princeton, NJ: Princeton University Press).

Barzel, Y. (2002) *A Theory of the State: Economic Rights, Legal Rights, and the Scope of the State* (Cambridge: Cambridge University Press).

Beck, U. (2003) *La société du risque. Sur la voie d'une autre modernité* (Paris: Flammarion).

Bérard, L. and P. Marchenay (2007) *Les produits de terroir: entre cultures et règlements* (Paris: CNRS).

Berlottier, L. (2009) *L'agriculture de qualité et les signes distinctifs: les orientations de l'Union Européenne: le livre vert et la politique de voisinage, UE*). Séminaire international: la signalisation des terroirs. Pourquoi? Comment faire? Concepts, méthodes, pratiques et témoignages. 2 et 3 juillet 2009 au CIRAD (Paris), http://www.iamm.fr/ress_doc/multimedia/conferences/, date accessed November 2011.

Conseil Général du Développement Agricole (Rabat) and Conseil Général de l'Alimentation de l'Agriculture et des Territoires Ruraux (Paris) (2010) *Terroirs et origine: leçons d'une lecture croisée des expériences. Du Maroc à la France, pour une Méditerranée durable* (Rabat: Conseil Général du Développement Agricole).

Cormier-Salem, M.C., D. Juhé-Beaulaton, J. Boutrais and B. Roussel (eds) (2002) *Patrimonialiser la nature tropicale: dynamiques locales, enjeux internationaux* (Paris: IRD).

Delfosse, C. (ed.) (2011) *La mode du terroir et les produits alimentaires* (Paris: Les Indes savantes).

Dutfield, G. (2000) *Intellectual Property Rights, Trade and Biodiversity: Seeds and Plant Varieties* (London: IUCN, The World Conservation Union Earthscan Publications).

Ermenier, K. (2009) 'Bières: Budweiser intègre le portefeuille d'AB-InBev France', *Rayon Boissons. Actu Flash.* http://www.rayon-boissons.com/Actu-Flash/Bieres-Budweiser-integre-le-portefeuille-d-AB-InBev-France-7264, date accessed November 2011.

European Commission (2002) 'EC–Chile Association Agreement', *Official Journal L*, 352:30.12.2002.

European Commission (2011a) *EU–Singapore Free Trade Agreement Negotiations Progressing Well. Joint Statement by the EU and the Ministry of Trade and Industry of Singapore*, http://trade.ec.europa.eu/doclib/press/index.cfm?id=729, date accessed November 2011.

European Commission (2011b) *Quality Products: Four Chinese Agricultural Products Receive Protected Status in the EU*, http://ec.europa.eu/agriculture/newsroom/36_en.htm, date accessed November 2011.

European Commission (2011c) *Database on latest registered/published/applied designations*, http://ec.europa.eu/agriculture/quality/door/list.html?locale=en, date accessed November 2011.

European Commission DG Enterprise (2002) *The New IPR [Intellectual Property Rights] Regime under FP6 [Sixth Framework Programme (2002–2006)]* (Luxembourg: European IPR Helpdesk), http://images.to.camcom.it/f/ALPS_APRE_Convegni/IP/IPRunderFP6.pdf, date accessed November 2011.

Fanti, S. (2007) *GI as a Rural Development Tool in Europe: the Prosciuto di Parma Experience*, Third general assembly of OriGIn, Agadir (Morocco), 22–3 November.

Foucault, M. (1971) *L'ordre du discours* (Paris: Gallimard).

Geffroy, T. and D. Chabaud (2009) *Les marques de distributeurs au service du pouvoir d'achat: une nouvelle donne?*, 2ème journée ComIndus sur les relations entre industrie et grande distribution alimentaire, Jeudi 2 Avril 2009 – ISEM Montpellier.

GRAIN (Barcelona) (2002) 'Biodiversity, rights and livelihood', *Seedling*: July, 1–30.

Hannachi, M. (2008) *Construction de l'appellation d'origine et évolution des controverses internationales. Le cas de oriGIn* (Montpellier: CIHEAM-IAM).

Hughes, J. (2003) 'The Spirited Debate over Geographical Indications', *Law Review*, 20:10, 1–101.

Ilbert, H. (ed.) (2005) *Produits du terroir méditerranéen: conditions d'émergence, d'efficacité et mode de gouvernance (PTM: CEE et MG). Rapport final* (Montpellier: CIHEAM-IAM). FEMISE Research programme 2004–05.

Ilbert, H. (2009) 'Le marquage des terroirs par les indications géographiques: politiques internationales et stratégies nationales en Méditerranée', in H. Ilbert, S. Tozanli and Y. Tekelioglu (eds), *Les produits de terroir, les indications géographiques et le développement local durable des pays méditerranéens* (Montpellier: CIHEAM-IAMM).

Ilbert, H., K. Legouveln and M. Galvin (2000) 'La diversité des règles de protection de la biodiversité et de la propriété intellectuelle', *L'environnement dans les négociations commerciales multilatérales: un passage obligé* (Paris: SOLAGRAL).

Ilbert, H. and M. Petit (2009) 'Are Geographical Indications a Valid Property Right? Global Trends and Challenges', *Development Policy Review*, 27(5), 503–28.

Ilbert, H. and J.-L. Rastoin (2010) *Indications géographiques et marques territoriales agricoles et agroalimentaires dans l'espace euro-méditerranéen: orientations stratégiques pour un développement durable* (Paris: CIHEAM-IPEMed).

Interbrand (2011) *Best Global Brands 2010*, http://issuu.com/interbrand/docs/bgb_report_us_version?mode=a_p, date accessed November 2011.

Jacquet, O. (2008) 'Territoire politique socialiste et terroir viticole', *Cahiers d'histoire. Revue d'histoire critique*, 103, 24–36.

Josling, T. (2005) *What in a Name? The Economics, Law and Politics of Geographical Indications for Foods and Beverages* (Dublin: Institute for International Integration Studies).

Josling, T. (2006) 'The War on Terroir: Geographical Indications as a Transatlantic Trade Conflict', *Journal of Agricultural Economics*, 57(3), 337–63.

Krasner, S.D. (ed.) (1983) *International Regimes* (Ithaca, NY: Cornell University Press).

Laird, S.A. (ed.) (2002) *Biodiversity and Traditional Knowledge: Equitable Partnerships in Practice* (London: Earthscan).

Lence, S., S. Marette, D. Hayes and W. Foster (2007) 'Collective Marketing Arrangements for Geographical Differentiated Agricultural Products: Welfare Impacts and Policy Implications', *American Journal of Agricultural Economics*, 89(4), 947–63.

Louafi, S. and B. Roussel (eds) (2005) *Biodiversité et savoirs naturalistes locaux en France* (Paris: CIRAD-IDDRI-IFB-INRA).

Marette, S. (2003) 'Politique de concurrence et secteur agro-alimentaire dans l'Union Européenne', *INRA Sciences sociales*, 4/02, 1–4.

Mills, R. and N. Moorjani (2004) *United States Wins WTO Case Against EU Over Food Names*, Office of the US Trade Representative. http://www.freerepublic.com/focus/f-news/1306366/posts, date accessed November 2011.

Millward Brown Optimor (2010) *Top 100 Most Valuable Global Brands 2010 BrandZ* (New York: Millward Brown Optimor).

Morin, H. (2003) *Les accords bilatéraux et régionaux de propriété intellectuelle en Francophonie* (Montréal, Québec: Centre international Unisfera).

OECD (2000) *Appellations of Origin and Geographical Indications in OECD Member Countries: Economic and Legal Implications* (Paris: OCDE). Working party on agricultural policies and markets of the Committee for Agriculture, 15 December 2000, COM/AGR/APM/TD/WP (2000) 15 (final).

Olszak, N. (2001) *Droit des appellations d'origine et indications de provenance* (Paris: Editions Tec & Doc).

oriGIn (2005) *WTO Negotiations in Relation to Geographical Indications* (Genève: oriGIn).

oriGIn (2010a) 'Etude sur la "valeur de la production agricole sous AOP et IGP"', *Lettre d'oriGIn*, March, 1.

oriGIn (2010b) *American Origin Products (AOPs): Protecting a Legacy* (Genève: oriGIn).

oriGIn (2011a) 'Newsletter', October.

oriGIn (2011b) 'Newsletter', June.

oriGIn (2011c) *Organization for an International Geographical Indications Network [website]*, http://www.origin-gi.com/index.php, date accessed November 2011.

oriGIn (2011d) 'UE-Chine: projet sur la protection des IGs', *Lettre d'oriGIn*, March, 1.

Posey, D.A. and G. Dutfield (1997) *Le marché mondial de la propriété intellectuelle: droits des communautés traditionnelles et indigènes* (Ottawa: CRDI).
Rastoin, J.-L. and V. Vissac-Charles (1999) 'Le groupe stratégique des entreprises de terroir', *Revue internationale PME*, 12(1–2), 171–92.
Rayon Boissons (2009) 'Bières: Budweiser intègre le portefeuille d'AB-InBev France', *Rayon Boissons. Actu Flash.*
Rosa, H. (2010) *Accélération. Une critique sociale du temps* (Paris: La Découverte).
Ryan, M.P. (1998) *Knowledge Diplomacy: Global Competition and the Politics of Intellectual Property* (Washington, DC: Brookings Institution Press).
Saez, C. (2011) *With WTO Stalled, GI Industry Proponents Move to Create Their Own Register*: Intellectual Property Watch, http://www.ip-watch.org/, date accessed November 2011.
Sauvée, L. and E. Valceschini (2003) 'Agroalimentaire: la qualité au coeur des relations entre agriculteurs, industriels et distributeurs', in C. Déméter (ed.), *Déméter 2004: économie et stratégies agricoles* (Paris: A. Colin).
Schelling, T.C. (1960) *The Strategy of Conflict* (Cambridge, MA: Harvard University Press).
SOLAGRAL (1993) 'Biodiversité, le fruit convoité', *Courrier de la Planète*, 19, 1–46.
SOLAGRAL (1999) *Gestion des ressources naturelles: droits de propriété, institutions et marchés* (Montpellier: SOLAGRAL).
Sylvander, B. (2004) *Concerted Action DOLPHINS (Development of Origin Labelled Products: Humanity, Innovation and Sustainability): Final Report Synthesis and Recommendations* (Brussels: European Commission-Research Key action no. 5).
Tekelioglu, Y., H. Ilbert and S. Tozanli (eds) (2009) *Les produits de terroir, les indications géographiques et le développement local durable des pays méditerranéens* (Montpellier: CIHEAM-IAM).
USPTO (2008) *U.S. Patent Statistics, Calendar Years, 1963–2008* (Alexandria, VA: USPTO).
Valceschini, E. and S. Blanchemanche (2003) 'Valeur économique de la signalisation de la qualité et de l'origine', *Séminaire 'Les produits d'origine et de qualité: enjeux et stratégies'* (Montpellier: Agropolis International).
WIPO (2009) *WIPO Report Shows Growth in IP Rights Before Onset of Economic Crisis*, PR/2009/603. http://www.wipo.int/pressroom/en/articles/2009/article_0034.html, date accessed November 2011.
WTO (1994) 'Agreement on Trade-related Aspects of Intellectual Property Rights. Annex 1C', in WTO (ed.), *Marrakesh Agreement Establishing the World Trade Organization* (Geneva: WTO).
WTO (2003a) *Press Pack Briefing Notes: 5th Ministerial Conference, Cancun, Mexico, 10–14 September 2003* (Geneva: WTO).
WTO (2003b) *Council for Trade-related Aspects of Intellectual Property Rights – Special Session – Discussions on the Establishment of a Multilateral System of Notification and Registration of Geographical Indications for Wines and Spirits: Compilation of Issues and Points – Note by the Secretariat - Revision – TN/IP/W/7/ Rev.1* (Geneva: WTO).
WTO (2008) *The Results of the Uruguay Round of Multilateral Trade Negotiations: The Legal Texts* [CD ROM] (Geneva: WTO).

6

The Concept of *Terroir* as the Basis of Corporate Strategy in Agribusiness: The European Social, Economic and Institutional Model

Jean-Louis Rastoin

At the beginning of the current decade, more than half of the world's population live in a tertiary agro-industrial food system founded on long value chains in which a handful of very large retail companies practice quasi-integration between the consumers and the food supply mechanism as a whole (Rastoin and Ghersi, 2010). Food is therefore on the verge of becoming a trivialized function as a result of the globalization of products mass-produced by a small number of very large multinational agribusiness groups whose strategy is founded on standardization, economies of scale and the formatting of consumer behaviour[1] in a context of increasingly financialized governance. Nevertheless, in many countries, consumers are still attached to qualitative and social criteria in relation to their food. A survey conducted by BVA in France in 2006 indicated that 'food must above all be a pleasurable experience' (62 per cent of all answers). This concept, harking back to the most ancient civilizations (Mediterranean, Asian and pre-Columbian), is somewhat at odds with the utilitarian view of the 'new worlds' although when income increases, this point of view concerning the hierarchy of food attributes quickly becomes increasingly prevalent in all countries. The Eurobarometer of 2006 asserted that 'aiming to produce healthy food presenting no risk to the population' should be the priority for farmers (51 per cent) and for the Common Agricultural Policy (CAP) of the European Union (41 per cent). It cannot be denied that the food crises suffered in Europe in the second half of the 1990s have cast a certain shadow of doubt, if not anxiety, over society (Rastoin, 2009).

In this context marked by globalization and consumer anxiety, what strategies might agribusiness firms possibly adopt? While it has rapidly become a generalized phenomenon over the past half-century, the spread of the agro-industrial model would appear to have come to a standstill in high-income countries while doubts are surfacing with regard to the 'sustainability' of such a model. Furthermore, the food markets are adopting the structure of an oligopoly with fringes where the periphery retains a very dense and heterogeneous population of firms (Rastoin, 1994). This gives rise to several strategic alternatives for the production sector. After a theoretical presentation of these alternatives, we will analyze the prospects for the long-term development of the food system based on two alternative scenarios before presenting the conditions for developing a strategy founded on the concept of *terroir*.

6.1 Corporate strategies in the food system

At the beginning of the 1980s, Michael Porter was one of the first people to define the concept of the strategic group (Porter, 1980). He perceived it as a group of firms adopting a common strategic behaviour within a particular sector. In the case in hand, this sector is the agribusiness industry, including all types ranging from farms processing their raw materials to multinational agribusiness companies.

Identifying strategic groups as described by Porter calls on another concept defined by the author – that of 'competitive advantage' (Porter, 1985). Porter suggests that there are two main types of competitive advantage:

- Cost leadership
- Differentiation

Cost leadership means that the firm is capable of producing goods at a lower unit cost. From the ideas stage to the commercialization of a product there are numerous opportunities to reduce costs, and companies must endeavour to implement them systematically. In all cases, the use of economies of scale in the production process remains the safest means of reducing costs significantly in any industry.

Differentiation is the ability to provide buyers with a product they perceive as unique and superior to other products with regard to one or more of its attributes. This can be achieved either by means of marketing techniques (for example, segmentation of the clientele and the construction of a brand image), or through a strong product 'characterization', for example, by means of a quality level.

In both cases, the competitive advantage will take the form of increased productivity of the resources used, through either a reduction in the denominator (factor cost) or an increase in the numerator (price), thereby improving the firm's margins.

By considering that these advantages can be exercised on broad or narrow markets (competitive fields), Porter developed a strategic four-box matrix which has become a classic in the field of strategic analysis. Examining the food system concept using Porter's grid highlights five types of strategic position (Rastoin and Vissac-Charles, 1999):[2]

1. Costs minimized by mass production;
2. Costs reduced by subcontracting small volumes;
3. 'Peripheral' product differentiation (modelling of taste by ingredients and the construction of an image by means of packaging and communication) based on refined market segmentation (segmentation);
4. Differentiation through product innovation (distinction);
5. Differentiation through the territory/history pairing (singularity/typicality).

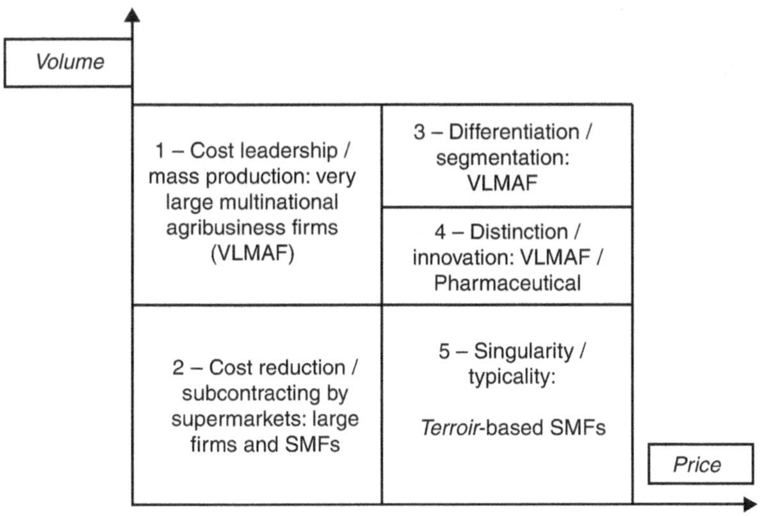

Figure 6.1 The strategies of competitive positioning in the agribusiness sector
Source: Adapted by Rastoin (1999) from Porter (1985).

Applying the Porterian concept of competitive advantage to the food system leads to four strategic groups being envisaged in response to the five positions presented above. Two strategic groups draw on the principle of cost leadership and segmentation while the other two call on the principle of 'specialized' differentiation:

- The strategic group of very large multinational agribusiness firms on mass markets (1);
- The strategic group of small and medium-sized subcontracting firms on standard markets (2);
- The strategic group of very large multinational agribusiness and pharmaceutical firms on mass markets (3) and (4);
- The strategic group of *terroir*-based firms (5).

The first strategic group is by far the largest as it occupies approximately 90 per cent of the food products market in high-income countries. It concerns 'basic' food products, that is, products of standard quality which comply with public health standards but for which the price remains the decisive variable conditioning consumer purchases. This phenomenon is amplified, if not caused, by the market power exercised by large-scale distributors (in France, three-quarters of all products are currently sold by supermarkets). Consequently, firms operating in this market are forced to minimize costs by means of mass production while segmenting their clientele in response to increasingly fierce competition. Achieving critical international size is a decisive factor of the strategy adopted by agribusiness firms which, in order to ensure their survival in a context of fierce competition, must be prepared to make considerable physical and intangible investments (primarily in the field of communication). This has led to the creation of an oligopoly of certain firms which, on average in 2005, recorded an annual turnover of $9 billion and net earnings of $700 million with a workforce of 33,000 employees in 15 countries. The top 15 of these firms accounts for 45 per cent of the turnover of the top 100 companies.

Subcontracting is the second means of reducing the financial burden of a company by eliminating marketing costs and a proportion of R&D costs which are instead covered by the contractor: this solution is adopted by companies which are prepared to accept a downstream partnership for the manufacture of products under the distributor's brand. In such a context, SMEs (small and medium enterprises) become competitive. The desire of distributors to become autonomous in relation to the industrial giants and the benefits of an image gained from a publicized cooperation with regional firms provides opportunities for a certain number of SMEs willing to accept (or actively looking to adopt) a position of subcontractor.

The third group concerns the rapidly growing 'nutriceuticals' market (nutritional pharmaceuticals intended for specific groups of consumers, for example, babies, pregnant women, seniors, sportspeople and consumers suffering from pathological disorders such as obesity, diabetes, HIV and so on). Initially developed by pharmaceutical firms, these products play an increasingly important role in the strategic fields of activity of food-producing groups. For example, following the transfer of its assets from the pasta and grocery sector, Danone is currently restructuring its activity to comprise three major divisions: health products (including Actimel), snack foods and drinks. In this area we could also cite the 'Weight Watchers' line of products from H. J. Heinz, 'Health's Choice' from Conagra and the clinical foods of the BioItalia and Euro-Aspartame subsidiaries of the Japanese firm Ajinomoto. Nutriceuticals have a very distinct image of 'health and safety', a field where consumer decisions are not guided by retail prices but by the expected efficiency and technical nature of the product.

The fourth group is guided by a strategy of 'qualitative/cultural' differentiation. It concerns **food products with a strong identity**. Alongside the consumption of standard 'daily' foods which continue to account for the majority of total consumption in quantitative terms, a market is also developing that is dedicated to food products that are differentiated by distinctive, identifiable characteristics: organoleptic criteria, the production process, the social history and place of origin as well as the 'occasion' of consumption (aesthetic or festive). In light of these elements, we can build a typology of food products distinguishing what we might call *terroir*-based products from *innovative* products and *basic* products.

A group of French researchers put forward the following definition of the term '*terroir*':

> A *terroir* is (1) a clearly defined geographical entity, (2) where a human community, (3) has developed a collective intellectual production know-how throughout history, (4) founded on a system of interaction between a physical and biological environment and a series of human factors, (5) in which the socio-technical orientations adopted, (6) reveal an originality, (7) confer typical characteristics, (8) and create a reputation for a product originating within this *terroir*. (Casabianca et al., 2005)

Terroir-based products are rooted firmly in a specific history, culture and geographical area. They have a strong 'intrinsic' value, both material (organoleptic qualities) and subjective/evocative or symbolic, to such an extent that the price is not the decisive variable conditioning purchase. Innovative products draw their specific quality from a technology and an added value which might be a service (ease of preparation) or a nutritional advantage (health food). For these, too, the price may be high, thus offering substantial margins which enable the pioneer to benefit from innovation revenue over a certain period of time. Basic products are characterized by mass production and distribution practices, highly competitive prices, extensive marketing segmentation and the systematic use of the brand awareness effect (Rastoin and Vissac-Charles, 1999).

6.2 Strategic perspectives

As we have just seen, the landscape of the agribusiness sector is quite diverse, with the cohabitation of different forms of companies and the existence of numerous types of food systems throughout the world. The globalization of the markets is nevertheless accelerating the remodelling of the situation and we are witnessing a dichotomization giving rise to two potential development scenarios: a trend scenario, involving the generalization of the agro-industrial model of mass production and consumption on a global scale, and a contrasting scenario founded on the notion of proximity. These two scenarios clearly correspond to the two strategic groups of companies mentioned above and represented by large-scale multinationals (scenario 1) and *terroir*-based firms (scenario 2).

6.2.1 Trend scenario: multinational firms as the dominant operators in the food system

The strategies of multinational companies are based on a production model founded on the fragmentation and distribution of activities throughout long value chains, economies of scale and the implementation of considerable investments, both in physical installations or intangibles (R&D and communication). Following the segment of mass-produced products which continue to represent the lion's share of turnover, analysis of the strategies of large firms in the agribusiness sector (in particular, European firms such as Nestlé, Danone and Unilever) has revealed a recent shift towards the inclusion of a second segment of goods consisting of innovative products (Rastoin, 2008). Multinationals, focusing on standardized and highly marketed mass-produced products since the 1970s, have now begun to base their product strategies on the health/fitness issue and thus develop prophylactic products (by integrating probiotics, *omega-3* and so on), a process we refer to as the 'medicalization of foodstuffs'.

Enjoying considerable marketing expertise, the major multinational agribusiness firms are eager to employ arguments which are appealing to the consumer. Thus, in the wake of the food crises of the mid-1990s, they seized upon the concept of *terroir*, thereby yielding to the pressure of the supermarkets which quickly developed their own retail brands rooted in this concept (for example, Reflets de France from the Carrefour group).

More recently, the themes of ethical products or fair trade have also been adopted by the marketing departments of the major supermarket chains. The intensity of the marketing practices and, more particularly, of advertising through packaging or the media, is exacerbated by the competitive environment and now poses social problems because the level of incentive can alter consumer choices when information becomes persuasion or even manipulation, with the potentially pathogenic effects already shown.

6.2.2 Alternative scenario: strategies founded on proximity

Despite the fact that the major players use the *terroir* argument,[3] the strategic map of the agribusiness sector nevertheless includes a second, highly active subgroup consisting of *terroir*-based firms. The strategies of these firms are grounded in two areas, of which one is specific resources, which are original in the true sense of the word as they relate to a geographic origin, a territory which provides the raw materials. The second is an entire range of goods and services required to manufacture the products through short value chains using specific techniques and forming part of a local social network and an entire history. The products manufactured within the framework of these strategies can therefore be described as 'authentic' and the strategies involve three types of asset:

- Material or tangible assets – natural resources, agro-climatic resources and the specific equipment required to manufacture the products as the production methods bear a greater resemblance to those used in the kitchen than in a factory;
- Immaterial or intangible assets – skills, know-how, tricks of the trade and original recipes;
- Temporal assets – a history generally involving several generations of professionals, often linked by family ties and firmly rooted in a small region.

This relation with farming land, technologies and time also represents a link to a natural (countryside) and architectural heritage, to local traditions (folklore) or to a social group – in short to a culture, all of which constitutes a territory. A localized food system (LFS, Fourcade et al., 2005), or cluster, is therefore a combination of a geographic area and one or more agribusiness value chains. From an economic standpoint, this type of production is based on proximity, whereas production in large-scale firms is founded on size. LFSs bring together hundreds of thousands of VSEs (very small enterprises)/SMEs worldwide and represent millions of jobs. They are often fragmented and have not always been able to organize and profit from their cohesion. They could play an important role in peri-urban areas and numerous examples can be observed: organic products and honey in Europe, bread in Romania, beer in Belgium, gastronomic festival in Hungary, meat and delicatessen products in Latin America and so on (Noronha Vaz et al., 2008).

By comparing the two models present in the food system, we can question the social relevance of the technological choice by large-scale firms to medicalize/artificialize foodstuffs. The quality of our diet may be derived from 'natural', varied and balanced food[4] which implies other choices concerning the production model (short value chains and factory formats). It is possible that consumers will increase their future information demands and will become aware of the dissonance between the messages broadcast by firms (recovery of the symbolic asset in the guise of the image) and the desired characteristics of the products. We might also expect more active lobbying from the VSEs/SMEs with a view to protecting their territorial revenue as well as regulatory action on the part of the public authorities. Under these conditions, the *terroir*-based products segment could become the domain of firms displaying a certain legitimacy in this sphere, thereby accelerating the shift towards an alternative model.

6.3 The factors of development of the strategic proximity model

The numerous crises which have affected the global food system since the end of the nineteenth century probably mark a break in the historical continuity that began with the industrial revolution. These crises have been health-related ('Mad Cow' disease, dioxin, salmonellosis, listeriosis, avian flu and, recently, the *Escherichia coli* bacterium), pathological (epidemics of obesity and food-related non-transmissible diseases including cardiovascular disease, cancer and diabetes affecting more than one billion individuals worldwide), economic and social (poverty and conflicts leading to the undernutrition of almost two billion people), and environmental (exhaustion of fossil fuels and chemical pollution). This worrying situation indicates that the industrial, intensive, concentrated and financialized model is unable to meet the challenges of sustainable food production. One alternative has emerged in the form of the proximity model, which would seem better suited to the criterion of sustainable development in spite of limitations resulting from the reluctance of the majority of consumers to pay for high-quality food products. It is therefore essential to support the expansion of the proximity food model by means of different institutional, economic and educational actions.

6.3.1 The institutional framework of *terroir*-based firms

The international regulatory GI (geographical indication) framework is currently defined by the ADPIC/TRIPS agreement signed in 1994 within the WTO (articles 22 to 24), although it does not demonstrate any restrictive nature concerning the protection of the GIs as it is situated in a paradigm guided by the market. Following a complaint filed by the United States and Australia in 2003 against EU regulation 2081/92, a panel of experts interpreted the section of the TRIPS agreement relating to GIs and offered a Pyrrhic victory by recognizing the validity and legitimacy of regulation 2081/92 and the validity of the control system while nevertheless indicating that it discriminated illegally against third-world producers because only the member states of the European Union could take advantage of it. Furthermore, while the European regulation correctly allows the coexistence of a GI and an existing brand, WTO members are free either to impose or not to impose limits on brand protection. The international legal context remains highly complex and continues to be the subject of 'disputes' within the WTO (Josling, 2006; Arhel, 2007).

The EU learned quickly from the decision of the WTO Dispute Settlement Body and published (EC) regulations no. 509 and 510/2006 in April 2006, thereby guaranteeing compliance with the panel's observations. These regulations specified two major provisions:

- Openness to the EU system of geographic designations (PDO-PGI-TSG) for products from non-member states;
- Elimination of the requirement that non-member states must apply comparable protection to that practiced by the EU on a basis of reciprocity and equivalence.

The TRIPS agreement imposes minimum protection for most intellectual property rights on WTO members, in particular geographical indications. This is indeed a minimum standard which is imposed; any member can therefore exceed this minimum. It is therefore possible to complement the existing protection of the geographical indicators by means of a regional label taking the form of a collective brand.

The concept of GIs is first and foremost European. It can be traced back to the creation of the National Institute of Origin and Quality (INAO) and the AOCs (designated origin) in France in 1919 and to the subsequent development of the labels of origin in a certain number of countries, primarily in the Mediterranean basin. In 1992, through regulations EC 2081/92 and EC 2082/92, the European Community created a system drawing heavily on the French concepts of *appellation d'origine* (PDO – protected designation of origin) and *indication géographique* (PGI – protected geographical indication). In August 2011, the EU had a total of 1,288 GIs, consisting of 1,049 registered, 71 published (awaiting registration) and 168 under consideration (cf. Appendix 6.1). Six GIs from non-member states are currently registered by the European Commission: five Chinese GIs and one Colombian (Colombian coffee), while another four have been published (two Chinese, one Indian and one Thai) and a further ten are under consideration. This demonstrates little interest shown by foreign countries, probably as a result of the power struggles existing at the WTO and the technique of bartering concessions between countries. In total, only thirty countries support the position of the EU, which is insufficient to impose the European system. However, the open attitude of China could represent an element conducive to the progress of the European dossier in the TRIPS discussions.

Within the EU, the Mediterranean countries are largely dominant with three-quarters of the GIs registered. Nevertheless, the number of demands filed by non-Mediterranean countries (30 per cent) shows that the mechanism also stimulates interest in northern Europe.

The main products benefitting from GIs in Europe are fruit and vegetables (27 per cent of the 712 registered designations in August 2011), cheese (20 per cent), meat-based products (13 per cent), fresh meat and offal (12 per cent) and oil and fat products (11 per cent, mainly olive oil). The number of GIs almost doubled between 2000 and 2011 with a strong increase in bread/pastry products (by a factor of 5.4) and fish, molluscs and shellfish (by a factor of 4.6). This increase bears witness to the interest shown in the proximity production model. Wine, a very old and culturally important commodity, is not subject to any agreement

Table 6.1 Agricultural and food products with geographic indications in the European Union as at 17 August 2011

Product category	**Number of GIs***		
	2011	**2000**	**Change 2000–2011**
Raw or processed fruit, vegetables and cereals	273	117	133%
Cheese	200	142	41%
Meat-based products (cooked, cured, smoked, etc.)	131	54	143%
Fresh meat (and offal)	124	82	51%
Oils and fats (butter, margarine, oil, etc.)	114	65	75%
Bread, pastry, confectionery and biscuit products	*54*	10	440%
Other products from appendix I of the treaty (spices, etc.)	37	8	363%
Other animal products (eggs, honey, dairy products excl. butter, etc.)	30	17	76%
Beers	27	14	93%
Fresh fish, molluscs, crustaceans and by-products	23	5	360%
Natural mineral water and spring water (interrupted)	23	31	−26%
Non-food products (hay, natural flavours, flowers)	5	2	150%
Pasta	5	0	–
Natural rubber and resins	2	1	100%
Mustard paste	1	0	–
Total	1,049	548	91%

* PDOs, PGIs and TSGs in 2011.
Source: European Commission, DOOR database, http://ec.europa.eu/agriculture/quality/door/list.html?recordStart=0&recordPerPage=10&recordEnd=10&filter:status=REGISTERED&sort.milestone=desc, *18 August 2011.*

concerning GIs. It is subject to a simple European Commission registration list (regulation EC 1493/99, article 54–4) which included 1860 designations in 2006, with 29 per cent in Slovenia, 25 per cent in France, 20 per cent in Italy and 6 per cent in Spain.

6.3.2 Advantages and constraints of the *terroir*-based strategic approach

The *terroir*-based approach represents a 'resource-based strategy' (Wernerfelt, 1984) which stipulates that, in a highly competitive market such as the agribusiness sector, one solution for companies unable to benefit from the size effect (cost reduction) is to differentiate their products according to specific, inimitable skills and original resources. These skills and resources can be called upon by firms firmly rooted in their territory of activity. It is primarily a matter of the specific quality of the product resulting from the particular agro-climatic and agro-ecological conditions (and thus from a clearly identified geographical area) and the production know-how resulting from a historical accumulation of experience (Sylvander et al., 2006). These considerations encapsulate the very definition of *terroir*-based products and the conditions for awarding a designation of origin under European regulations.

We can put forward three types of advantages linked to a strategy based on the concept of *terroir* and the GIs.

The first advantage is that firms producing *terroir*-based products cannot be delocalized and consequently maintain economic activity, and therefore jobs, in rural areas. In a study focusing on the agribusiness industry in France, we established that this industry has maintained a stable level of employees over a long period of time with only a 5 per cent decline over the past 30 years, whereas the manufacturing industry recorded a fall in employment of 30 per cent. This phenomenon can be explained by the fact that the disappearance of jobs in large companies (those with more than 500 employees) is offset by the creation of jobs in very small firms (those with fewer than ten employees). This development can be observed in most countries throughout the world (Rastoin, 2000).

The strategic approach founded on the concept of *terroir* presents a second advantage. It has been demonstrated empirically that the use of an official quality sign on a food product gives rise to above-average prices at the agricultural level (15 per cent for registered designations of origin) and higher incomes (equal to 14 per cent for the gross operating surplus) in the case of milk in France (Desbois and Nefussi, 2007). In the case of olive oil from Nyons, which carries a designated origin, the price is 51 per cent higher than a non-designated origin oil from the same region, and oil of a designated origin showed a growth rate of 9.5 per cent compared with 7.4 per cent for the oil of a non-designated over the period 1999–2002 (INAO, 2004).

Third, the market for *terroir*-based products, some of which are protected by an indication of origin, is becoming more structured and is beginning to represent significant volumes while enjoying much higher growth than the markets for standard mass-produced products, as can be seen in France. According to our estimates, GI products represented a market worth €17 billion in France in 2009, accounting for 10 per cent of food spending and demonstrating an annual growth of between 5 and 10 per cent over the previous ten years. These products concern slightly more than 100,000 farmers and approximately 6,000 agribusiness firms.

Table 6.2 Estimation of the European market of *terroir*-based food products (EU-27, 2009)

Type of product	Northern countries	Mediterranean countries	Total EU
Food and non-alcoholic drinks (billion €)	4.362	11.429	15.791
Food and non-alcoholic drinks (%)	1.0	2.6	1.8
Alcoholic drinks (billion €)	18.615	20.471	39.086
Alcoholic drinks (%)	12.9	23.1	16.8
Total food products and drinks (billion €)	22.977	31.900	54.877
Total food products and drinks (%)	4.1	6.2	5.1

Source: Our estimates based on Eurostat data 2011, http://appsso.eurostat.ec.europa.eu/nui/show.do?dataset=nama_co2_c&lang=fr, 17 August 2011.

At the European level, estimates are somewhat more difficult to obtain as there are no statistics concerning turnover resulting from GI products and not all of the products covered by our definition of *terroir* are protected by an official GI. Basing our estimates on the case of France, for which we have access to relatively precise figures, we have calculated that the European market (EU-27) for *terroir*-based products could have exceeded €50 billion for 2009 (Table 6.2).

The importance of *terroir*-based products varies from one country to the next. The market nevertheless extends beyond national borders. In reality, it is a dual market:

- Locally, in the different countries, it goes hand in hand with the consumption model which, in many countries and in particular in regions which were home to ancient civilizations such as the Mediterranean basin, attaches considerable importance to traditional products;
- Internationally, it is stimulated by the development of tourism, on the condition that this tourism promotes local produce (which is far from being the general situation). Products discovered during foreign holidays may indeed give rise to so-called 'exotic' export flows.

In certain countries, regulations exist allowing national authorities to grant geographical indications. However, little or no use is made of these provisions due both to a lack of interest from professionals (protected designations give rise to constraints for companies) and to an institutional framework which generally has a low level of resources and thus offers very few incentives.

Interest among farmers and small-scale industrialists in the agribusiness sector wishing to enhance their products is nevertheless on the increase, as shown by the following initiatives: wines, olive-based products and dates in Algeria and Tunisia; wines, argan tree and oasis products in Morocco; and sultanas and *Cezerye* loukoum from Mersin in Turkey (Ilbert, 2005). These initiatives remain well outside the strict framework applied in the Mediterranean countries of the EU, but nonetheless bear witness to considerations relating to the dominant model of modernization applied to agriculture. The public authorities in Europe and in certain countries enjoying long-standing food traditions (Mediterranean, Asian and Latin American countries) demonstrate an interest in the GI dynamic. The number of academic works has increased as researchers seek to expand the link between the institutional provisions such as the GIs and local development (see, for example, Hinrichs, 2000, on the entrenchment of local food systems; Rangnekar, 2004, on the socio-economic impact of GIs; and Marchesnay, 1998, and Usunier, 2006, on entrepreneurial approaches).

While numerous, the constraints imposed on *terroir*-based firms wishing to benefit from these advantages are not insurmountable. These constraints include:

- Low competitiveness in terms of prices due to the reduced scale of the volumes produced;
- Poor organization of the value chains, in terms of both production and distribution networks;
- Difficulty in adhering to national and international product standards;
- Low level of qualification of human resources in the value chains; and
- Lack of information and education of consumers.

These constraints can be removed by means of investment in research and development (R&D), be it with regard to the products, the technological or organizational procedures or training and information. Finally, the development of *terroir*-based products is largely subject to the reorientation of public agricultural and food policies.

6.4 Conclusion: legitimacy and relevance of the *terroir*-based strategic project

We can summarize the arguments in favour of a *terroir*-based approach by focusing on four main issues, the first of which is public health. Numerous clinical studies have established that diet can contribute to the prevention of food-related diseases which now represent more than half of all deaths worldwide. Paradoxically, the occurrence of these diseases is increasing rapidly in countries where the historical food consumption model has been favourable to good health, such as the Mediterranean countries at present. Perhaps the Asian countries will experience the same phenomenon in the future, due to people abandoning their traditional diet – a fact which can easily be explained by the expansion of the agro-industrial food supply model. The second favourable element is local development, which maintains economic activities and employment in rural areas against a backdrop of SMEs/VSEs. From a macroeconomic standpoint, the cliometric works conducted by Robert Fogel, who was awarded the Nobel prize for economics in 1993, clearly demonstrate the link between economic/population growth and physiology, and primarily nutrition (Fogel, 1994). Finally, considerations relating to identity (safeguarding an intangible heritage) offer not only cultural wealth and diversity but also a social link and economic repercussions through tourism, which can increase the value of typical cuisine.

An additional argument is supplied by globalization. Every country, and the entrepreneurs within each, is searching for commercial development opportunities. In the agribusiness sector, *terroir*-based products represent one of these opportunities, although they also risk being usurped by means of marketing techniques. Thus, wherever there is a Mediterranean-type agro-climatic environment, suitable perennial crops are developed. This was the case of vines several years ago in Australia with the '2025 vision', the aim of which was to make the country the world's leading wine exporter by this date. It is now the case with similar plans for olive growing in Australia, Chile and California. Those countries which traditionally produce these commodities therefore suffer the clear threat of aggressive competition from countries which already apply or are turning to the agro-industrial model, which is capable of hijacking market income by means of imitation and suggestion.

In order to retain or increase the market share of *terroir*-based products, it is therefore essential to implement a proactive programme with a view to ensuring that the benefits of this expanding market are felt locally. Nevertheless, each GI, which by definition has a small production volume, cannot ensure the efficient development of the associated product. It is therefore necessary to create group effects through collective action. For example, it is possible to create 'baskets of products' (Bérard et al., 2005) and 'umbrella brands' by bringing together several GIs at a regional level. The concept of congruence used in marketing demonstrates the interest in strengthening a corporate brand by means of an indication referring to the origin of the products (Aurier and Fort, 2007) on the condition that it incorporates modern product labelling tools, which involves a detailed knowledge of consumer perceptions of these signs (Codron et al., 2006).

Pooling resources may also concern transversal actions aimed at improving the quality of both products and managerial practices. Other points are important in consolidating the proximity model: institutional support (governmental and professional) for the organization of the value chains and markets (information system, legal framework, implementation of commercialization platforms) and producer training as well as the introduction of local governance with the participation of local authorities (Allaire, 2011). Furthermore, through the creation of multi-sector VSE/SME networks, a cluster-type territorial development process is also implemented (Torre and Traversac, 2011). The role of public policies accompanying this process is essential, as the dynamics of globalization tend to marginalize small-scale economic structures before causing them to disappear altogether. The public authorities also play an essential role – through the education system and institutional communication – in encouraging a change in the behaviour of consumers who are observed, in a society of mass consumption, to favour economic choices and time management practices which are often harmful both individually and collectively.

The contribution of *terroir*-based products in taking up the major challenges – the right to food and food security – through a development model founded on proximity and solidarity therefore appears to be potentially very large, both in the South and the North.

Appendix A6.1 Geographic indications in the European Union as at 17 August 2011*

Country	**Number of GIs**			
	Registered	**Published**	**Requested**	**Total**
Italy	273	19	23	273
France	187	8	34	229
Spain	150	9	29	188
Portugal	116	1	11	128
Greece	92	3	5	100
Germany	79	3	17	99
United Kingdom	38	4	12	54
Poland	29	5	3	37
Czech Republic	31		4	35
Slovenia	5	8	7	20
Austria	14			14
Slovakia	13	1		14
Belgium	13			13
Hungary	8	2	3	13
Finland	8		1	9
Netherlands	9			9
Denmark	3		4	7
Sweden	6		1	7
Lithuania	1	1	3	5
Ireland	4			4
Luxembourg	4			4
Cyprus	1	1	1	3
Bulgaria		2		2
Romania	1			1
Sub-total EU member states	**1,043**	67	**158**	**1,268**
of which Mediterranean countries	782	49	110	941
Share of Mediterranean countries	75%	73%	70%	74%
China	5	2	3	10
Thailand		1	2	3
India		1	1	2
Turkey			2	2
Andorra			1	1
Colombia	1			1
Vietnam			1	1
Sub-total other countries	**6**	**4**	**10**	**20**
Overall total	**1,049**	**71**	**168**	**1,288**

* PDO: protected designation of origin, PGI: protected geographical indication, TSG: traditional specialty guaranteed, not including wines and spirits.
Source: European Commission, DOOR database, http://ec.europa.eu/agriculture/quality/door/list.html?recordStart=0&recordPerPage=10&recordEnd=10&filter:status=REGISTERED&sort.milestone=desc, 18 August 2011.

Notes

1. This movement was named the 'fabrique du consentement' (manufacture of consent) by the philosopher Gilles Deleuze (Deleuze, 2003).
2. The four-box paradigm is structured here to comply with the empirical observations made on the food product markets.
3. Marketing has become a fearsomely effective tool. To cite Bernard Stiegler, it facilitates '... [the standardization] of consumers' behaviour by formatting and artificially manufacturing their desires. They [consumers in a post-industrial society] lose their know-how, their chance to exist. They are replaced by the standards decreed by the brands "rationally" produced by "marketing"' (Stiegler, 2007). Marketing specialists would qualify this point of view, reminding us that while the act of purchasing may be influenced, it nevertheless presupposes the simultaneous existence of an appropriate supply. Stiegler's interpretation, however, pushes us to consider the risks of excessive commoditization of what must be referred to as public good – food.
4. One of the paradoxes of the agro-industrial food system is that the level of health spending in a country such as France tends to converge with that of spending on food. In 2004, 13 per cent of the average household budget – including public transfers – was allocated to the former, demonstrating a high rate of growth, while 17 per cent was allocated to the latter, with a decreasing relative value, while the relationship between health and nutrition has long been established. In other words, a varied and balanced diet would appear to exercise a powerful prophylactic effect, thereby mechanically reducing health spending!

References

Allaire, G. (2011) *Petits acteurs et marchés locaux dans le contexte de la politique européenne de la qualité*, Note (Brussels: Directorate General for Internal Policies of the Union, European Parliament).

Arhel, P. (2007) 'Travaux de l'Organisation mondiale du commerce visant à étendre et à faciliter la protection des indications géographiques, Propriété industrielle', *Lexisnexis-Jurisclasseur monthly review* (Paris: Études), pp. 7–12.

Aurier, P. and F. Fort (2007) 'The Effect of Perceived Congruity Between Origin, Brand, and Product on the Purchase Intention of a Branded Product of Origin', *Advances in Consumer Research*. 34, 55–63.

Bérard, L., M. Hirczak, P. Marchenay, A. Mollard, and B. Pecqueur (2005) 'Le panier de biens: une construction patrimoniale et territoriale. l'exemple de la Bresse', *The International Symposium of 'Territoires et enjeux du développement régional'* (Lyon).

BVA (2006) Barometer of food perception, Ministry of Agriculture, Paris.

Casabianca, F., B. Sylvander, Y. Noël, C. Béranger, J.B. Coulon and F. Roncin (2005) 'Terroir et typicité: deux concepts clés des appellations d'origine controlée, Essai de définitions scientifiques et opérationnelles', The International Symposium 'Territoires et enjeux du dévelopement régional', Lyon, 9–11 March.

Codron, J.M., L. Sirieix and T. Reardon (2006) 'Social and Environmental Attributes of Food Products in an Emerging Mass Market: Challenges of

Signaling and Consumer Perception, with European Illustration', *Agriculture and Human Values*, Summer 23(2).

Deleuze, G. (2003) *Pourparlers* (Paris: éd. de Minuit).

Desbois, D. and J. Nefussi (2007) 'Signes de qualité: prix du lait et rentabilité des exploitations', *Agreste Cahiers*, no. 2, March (Paris).

European Commission (2006) Eurobarometer, http://ec.europa.eu/health/ph_publication/eurobarometers_en.htm.

Fogel, R. (1994) 'Economic Growth, Population Theory and Physiology: The Bearings of Long-Term Processes on the Making of Economic Policy', *The American Economic Review*, 84(3), 369–95.

Fourcade, C., J. Muchnik, and R. Treillon (2005) *Systèmes productifs localisés dans le domaine agro-alimentaire*, LPS GIS report to the MAAPAR and the DATAR, Innovation research unit (Montpellier).

Hinrichs, C. Clare (2000) 'Embeddedness and Local Food Systems: Notes on Two Types of Direct Agricultural Market', *Journal of Rural Studies*, 16, 295–303.

Ilbert, H. (coord.) (2005) *Produits du terroir méditerranéen: conditions d'émergence, d'efficacité et Modes de gouvernance*, Final report, FEMISE, Marseille (Montpellier: CIHEAM-IAM), pp. 39–64.

INAO (2004) AOC 'Olive et huile d'olive de Nyons' (Paris).

Josling, T. (2006) 'The War on Terroir: Geographical Indications as a Transatlantic Trade Conflict', *Journal of Agricultural Economics*, 57(3), 337–63.

Marchesnay, M. (1998) 'L'entrepreneuriat rural en quête de légitimité', in G. Miclet, L. Sirieix and S. Thoyer (eds), *Agriculture et alimentation en quête de nouvelles légitimités* (Paris: Economica), pp. 199–220.

(de) Noronha Vaz, M.T., P. Nijkamp, and J.L. Rastoin (2008) *Traditional Food Production Facing Sustainability: A European Challenge* (London: Ashgate).

Nossiter, J. (2007) *Le goût et le pouvoir* (Paris: Grasset).

Porter, M. (1980) *Competitive Strategy* (New York: The Free Press, Macmillan Publishing Co.). French translation: *Choix stratégiques et concurrence* (Paris: Economica, 1982), pp. 142–70.

Porter, M. (1985) *Competitive Advantage: Creating and Sustaining Superior Performance* (New York: The Free Press, Macmillan Publishing Co.). French translation: *L'avantage concurrentiel: comment devancer ses concurrents et maintenir son avance* (Paris: InterEditions, 1985).

Rangnekar, D. (2004) *The Socio-Economics of Geographical Indications: A Review of Empirical Evidence from Europe*, Issue Paper, 8 (Geneva: ICSTD, UNCTAD).

Rastoin, J.L. (1994) 'L'industrie alimentaire mondiale: vers un oligopole à franges', in *Politiques agricoles dans les PVD*, a collective work under the direction of M. Griffon, 3 volumes, special issue, *Economie Politique*, vol. 2 (Paris).

Rastoin, J.L. (2000) 'Une brève histoire économique de l'industrie alimentaire', *Économie Rurale* (Paris SFER), no. 255–256/2000, January–April (Paris), 61–85.

Rastoin, J.L. (2008) 'Les multinationales dans le système alimentaire', *Projet*, no. 306 (La Plaine: St Denis), 61–9.

Rastoin, J.L. (2009) 'Créer un label méditerranéen pour les produits agroalimentaires d'origine: quelques justifications théoriques et empiriques', in Y. Tekelioglu, H. Ilbert and S. Tozanli (eds), *Les produits de terroir, les indications géographiques et le développement local durable dans les pays méditerranéens*, OPTIONS méditerranéennes, Series A(89) (Paris: Ciheam), pp. 19–27.

Rastoin, J.L. and G. Ghersi (2010) *Le système alimentaire mondial, Concepts et méthodes, analyses et dynamiques* (Paris: Editions Quae). Preface by Olivier de Schutter, Special Rapporteur for the United Nations on the Right to Food.

Rastoin, J.L. and V. Vissac-Charles (1999) 'Le groupe stratégique des entreprises de terroir', *Revue Internationale des PME*, 12(1–2), 171–92.

Stiegler, B. (2007) 'Le désir asphyxié, ou comment l'industrie culturelle détruit l'individu, Manière de voir', *Le Monde diplomatique*, no. 96, December (Paris), 10–15.

Sylvander, B., G. Allaire, D. Barjolle and E. Thévenot-Mottet (2006) 'Qualité, origine et globalisation: Justifications générales et contextes nationaux, le cas des Indications géographiques', *Canadian Journal of Regional Science/Revue canadienne des sciences régionales*, 29(1), 43–54.

Torre, A. and J.B. Traversac (2011) *Territorial Governance* (Heidelberg and New York: Springer).

Usunier, J.-C. (2006) 'Relevance in Business Research: the Case of Country-of-origin Research in Marketing', *European Management Review*, 3 (Basingstoke: Palgrave Macmillan), pp. 60–73.

Wernerfelt, B. (1984) 'A Resource-Based View of the Firm', *Strategic Management Journal*, 5, 171–80.

Part II
Asian Challenges

7

From Products of Origin to Geographical Indications in Japan: Perspectives on the Construction of Quality for the Emblematic Productions of Kobe and Matsusaka Beef

Louis Augustin-Jean and Kae Sekine

In a context of tense agricultural negotiations at the WTO, Geographical Indications (GIs) are subject to intense bargaining. The way European and American standpoints can (or cannot) be conciliated affect the future of the products themselves, but also of the development potential of entire regions and the way they integrate into the world economy.

While GIs are recognized by the TRIPS (trade-related aspects of intellectual property rights) component of the Marrakech agreements (1994) of the GATT/WTO,[1] they are still the object of multiple interpretations. Generally speaking, the positions of governments have oscillated between the adoption of a system of (collective) trademarks and one of Protected Geographical Indication (PGI).

In recent years, stimulated by the TRIPS, the debate has reached new players, especially in Asia. The new interest of Asian countries in GIs is not an unexpected one, as they play an important role in the international agro-food business. Nevertheless, since GIs are relatively new in Asia, the respective positions of individual economies towards them are not always fully established. Many are still adapting their national regulations to the different international agreements they signed and have hesitated on the direction to follow. But that also explains why their attitude is so fundamental: the way in which GIs will be implemented is likely to modify the unstable balance between the tenets of the PGIs and those of the trademarks.[2]

Thus, Asia is becoming an arbiter. In developed countries such as Japan, consumers have a keen interest in the origins of the products they buy, which can be seen as an attachment to a (often reinvented) 'traditional way of life' and a suspicion about mass production and/or imported goods. GIs, therefore, not only reflect the interests of producers, but also target domestic (and overseas) consumers who have high purchasing power. In developing countries, the implementation of a GI mechanism may be seen as a tool to boost development in numerous regions, even though most of the potential consumers are overseas. In both cases, GIs should be sustainable and pose the questions of visibility and recognition.

Consequently, the evolving regulations concerning GIs in Asia have attracted the attention of professionals and scholars alike. For Beshaw (2008), the adoption of both the PGI and the trademark systems in China led to contradictions and ambiguities. Through the example of the Jinhua ham (a case analysed extensively in this volume), he tried to show, using a legal framework, that China should pursue the full adoption of a collective trademark system and get rid of the PGI one. By contrast, Wattanapruttipaisan (2009), who is in charge of the Intellectual Property Rights at the ASEAN secretariat, indicated that ASEAN as a whole could gain from European regulations and the current revision of the AOC system.

These debates are usually developed through a top-down approach with insufficient attention being paid to case studies and the relationships between actors. GIs in Asia, like elsewhere, depend not only on the legal framework, but also on the actions of producers, consumers, local authorities, and so on. This is not to deny the central position of the legal framework, but to emphasize that this framework (which is, by no means restricted to the legislation on GIs and is only a small part of the institutional context) and its implementation are shaped by actions at the local level.[3]

As Asian countries have only started to implement legislation over GIs, a clear picture of the links between GIs and local development is currently out of reach.[4] It is nevertheless possible to analyse how the interactions between agents influence the institutional context and vice versa – aspects that can be illuminated by an examination of the situation in Japan. As already stated, consumers have a keen interest in the origins of the products. The cultural practice of offering small presents (*o-miyage*) to colleagues or friends after one's travels has raised the level of interest in local products. More negatively, consumers have been affected by a crisis of confidence towards the mass production of agro-food goods following a series of incidents both in Japan (such as avian flu and an outbreak of foot-and-mouth disease among the cattle that produce the famous Miyazaki beef[5]) and also overseas (such as BSE in the United Kingdom and tainted powder milk from China). On the supply side, high-quality products have been developed for a long time, and products from certain regions, such as Kobe beef, have become emblematic worldwide. This promotion of local products, which involves a wide range of actors, is currently booming[6] and should affect the way Japan is implementing and modifying its GI system – not only nationally, but also locally.

More specifically, we hypothesize that while national institutions design a common setting, there is considerable leeway at the local level to alter this pattern. In practice, the cultural and social systems, as well as the interactions among the main stakeholders (including consumers), lead to differentiated 'models' of GIs locally. In turn, this may induce readjustments of this national institutional framework. We will test this hypothesis with a case study of the speciality beef from Japan. In order to do so, we performed an analysis of the way geographical indication systems have been built for the highly praised beef from Kobe and Matsusaka, which allowed us to highlight their similarities and differences.[7]

The reasons for this decision lay in the specificities of the top-grade beef market in Japan. This is a market characterized by two major elements: the first links a type of beef to a production area (as in the case of Kobe, Ômi, or Matsusaka); the second somewhat blurs this statement because most of the top-quality meat comes from the 'black hair Japanese beef' (*kuroge wagyu*) – the highest being the 'Tajima gyu', a strain that originated in the Tajima region of Hyogo Prefecture. The consequence of these two elements was that it resulted in competition between the two territories based on the capacity of each production area to develop strong links between the local culture/tradition and a specific method of production.

Thus, since it is commonly admitted that the highest grade of *kuroge wagyu* is the Tajima gyu strain, then what is the difference between beef from Matsusaka and beef from Kobe? And what is the relationship between the different elements we indicated earlier (the territories, the method of production, and the product) and how are geographical indications involved in this differentiation process?

This chapter aims to answer these questions. It is divided into three sections: the first one presents theoretical elements related to quality products and territorial development. The second section is devoted to the description of the geographical indication framework of Japan, as well as the debates related to this framework that are currently surfacing.

The final section analyses the relationship between the development of speciality beef in Kobe and Matsusaka. It shows that despite the same institutional pattern at the national level, the relationship among actors as well as the weight of the traditions that has resulted in the design of two different products and systems of competition.

7.1 Quality and territorial development: some theoretical perspectives

7.1.1 GI systems and territories: the role of actors in the construction of quality and territorial development

Whether the adoption of a Geographical Indication framework is based on trademark or PGI has different implications for territorial development. In particular, there are differences in the relationships that farmers maintain with other agents. Before elaborating on this statement, it is useful to introduce the notion of a 'GI system':

> ...the set of actors who are effectively engaged in creating value and improving the strategic marketing position of the GI product by spontaneous individual or organized collective action and those who are engaged in the activation and reproduction of those local resources (natural resources, knowledge, social capital) which make the GI product specific (SINER-GI Project, quoted by Barjolle et al., 2009, p. 1, note 1).[8]

Analytically, there are similarities between GI systems on one hand and, on the other hand, Localized Productive Systems (LPS) and 'Agrofood Localised Systems' (Moiti-Maïzy et al., 2002). Like LPS, GI systems stimulate spillovers and disseminate information. GIs offer a platform for actors (local authorities, trade unions, tourist associations, producers, distributors, and so on) to discuss and promote the name collectively – with PGIs more prone to stimulate this kind of synergy than collective trademarks. Thus, as individual producers tend to have lower visibility than the GI, competition between producers is replaced in part by competition between territories. When individual producers want to increase their visibility, they tend to exert a control over the definition and implementation of standards and/or establish a dominant position (ideally a monopoly). If they cannot impose their rules of the game on others, they may threaten to exit the GI, which may be damaging to its management and/or reputation. This situation can be seen either in the case of a PGI or a collective trademark.[9]

In this respect, there are not always major differences between agro-food products and other goods, as is demonstrated by the Swiss example:

> A simple geographical name merely noting the source of origin in order to comply with the customs regulations (...) is not necessarily a GI that can be protected. Watches and chocolate from Switzerland are notable exceptions. They serve to illustrate that in order for an indication to function as a GI, it must communicate that *the product from the noted region also has a particular reputation, thereby creating a link between some characteristic of the product and the particular region where it was produced.* (Giovannucci et al., 2009, p. 6; our emphasis)

From this definition of a GI (system), at least two insights can be inferred. First, the territorial dimension includes not only the geographical space, but also the links between people as well as institutions and objects. The product and its quality are no longer defined by their technical characteristics, but are a structure that encompasses 'intangible assets' such as local culture, specific know-how, geographical elements of the region, and so on.[10] When this notion of construction is taken into account, it is not surprising that possible changes to the rules of the game affect the future of the GI.

Second, since the publication of the work of Granovetter (1985), the notion of network has gained ground in the social sciences. Despite criticisms (see, for example, Powell, 1990), such a notion is well-suited to grasping not only market structures, but also other forms of relationships. Consequently, the definition of quality depends on a wide range of social actors that participate in its construction. 'Quality' can change depending on which social and economic actors are included in the network. Thus, a major problem is to delimit precisely the network: what (kind of) agents should be included in it? Where does it stop? These questions are at the centre of the creation of new GIs:[11]

> Defining the exact boundaries of a GI can be politically and socially controversial. Some who currently participate as producers or processors may be excluded. 'Free riders' may demand to be included. Producers within the same boundaries but who follow somewhat different methods may find themselves excluded. In fact, some will always be excluded (...) (Giovannucci et al., 2009, p. 22)

Therefore, the construction of a GI is in part a political process. It depends not only on national legislation (which results from social compromises), but also on existing social forces at the local level. The pattern of exclusion would be different if the GI is *sui generis*, as in Europe, or if it follows the collective trademark system or certification mark, as in the United States. Section 7.1.2 shows the differences between the American and the European systems of geographical indications and their consequences.

7.1.2 Trademarks and product promotion versus PDOs/PGIs, development and quality promotion

The American and European systems are dominant sources of inspiration for others. Nevertheless, inspiration is not copy, as the Japanese example shows (see section 7.2): while each framework can be classified as a 'trademark' or '*sui generis*', in practice, it often evolves into a unique blend. In order to understand how the Japanese system and its local implementation departs or looks like one of these two models, it is important to introduce them briefly:

> [In the United States,] Collective marks belong only to public or private groups, such as trade associations and are used by the members of a cooperative, association or other collective group to distinguish their offerings from those of non-members. Use of a collective mark requires membership in the group owning the mark. (Giovannucci et al., 2009, p. 67)

Thus, only members are allowed to use the mark (others being excluded), which can be sold and bought like any other trademark. The system of the collective trademark is not as developed as the certification mark, but it has gained in popularity.

The certification mark is closer to the European system. In the certification mark, producers cannot be excluded from using the mark, provided that they have fulfilled all the obligations attached to it, including a 'code of practice'. The owner of the mark chooses what he believes are the most important characteristics of the products, which he can change at any time. 'A certification mark differs from *sui generis* GI controls in that: a) it is not required to meet any pre-defined public or private standard; b) it need not necessarily be confined to a specified geographic area; and c) the owner defines his or her own rules of participation that may or may not include quality parameters', for example (Giovannucci et al., 2009, p. 55). Thus, the role of GIs in the United States is to enhance marketing and product promotion rather than local development and quality promotion, which is the case in the European Union.

The stricter approach of the EU can be seen from the two existing forms of GI registration: (1) the Protected Designation of Origin (PDO); and (2) the Protected Geographical Indication (PGI). The differences between the two lie in the fact that in the case of a PDO, 'the product *must be produced AND processed in the geographical area*. This implies that the product exhibits qualities or characteristics that are essentially due to that geographical area', while for a PGI, the product *must be produced OR processed in the geographical area,* meaning that the product exhibits a specific quality, reputation, or other characteristics attributable to that area. For a PGI, the registration allows for greater flexibility based more on reputation and less on the qualities of a geographic region (Giovannucci et al., 2009, p. 60). Any producer in the area can use the GI, provided that he or she meets the certification criteria. There is no possibility of exclusion, while private trademarks can also be added to the GI. The PDO or PGI can be considered tools for local development, and all stakeholders participate in the negotiation process, leading to the underwriting of the 'code of practice' and the official recognition and registration of the GI. The GI is perceived as a public good that may belong to a group in the region, but is usually managed by the state; it cannot be sold or transferred.

The diverging systems of ownership of GIs have had different consequences for local development. As the proponents of the collective trademark have emphasized, private ownership may generate positive results because the collective interests of the owners are to develop their brand names and increase their market share. This approach does not lead to a real developmental project because other producers, consumers, distributors, and so on are de facto excluded from the creation of the GI. In other words, private ownership may benefit shareholders, but generally not the other members of the community. For PDOs and PGIs, this is exactly the opposite, because they are negotiated by all stakeholders and may be nurtured into a real development project for the community. But the case of the certification mark is unclear and should be analyzed case by case.

The next sections will show, within the given institutional framework of Japan, that the way agents organize themselves locally bends this framework towards one of the systems presented earlier. The sections also indicate that this interaction between agents not only determines two strategies of development, but also a different definition of the product and its quality. The next section is devoted to the presentation of the national institutional framework, while the last deals with our case studies.

7.2 The protection of Geographical Indications in Japan

Local actors are bounded by an institutional framework that is defined by formal and informal rules and regulations (North, 1990). The design of these rules and regulations follows a complicated process, since at all levels, from the international to the local, they are affected by the involvement of individual actors. The legal structure occupies a central position due to its framing effect and coercive and constraining nature. As the institutional framework for GIs was implemented only recently in Japan, it continues to evolve, and some of its main features are still under discussion. This section presents some of the most striking characteristics of the regulations pertaining to Japanese GIs.

7.2.1 A negative protection system for Geographical Indications in Japan

Japan has signed most international agreements related to GIs: the Paris Convention of 1883, the Madrid Agreement for the Repression of False or Deceptive Indications of Source on Goods of 1891 and, most importantly, the TRIPS of 1994 (Aoki, 2006). Japan did not sign the Lisbon convention, which is not really significant, as only 26 countries have currently done so.[12]

In accordance with its participation in the major international agreements on GIs, Japan implemented a series of domestic laws. Yuki Obinata, from the Japan Patent Office (JPO), described the existing framework as a 'negative protection system':

> Japan adopts the negative protection system (i.e., the prohibition of registrations and uses of GI by people who do not have an exclusive right to use it) instead of the affirmative protection (i.e., the registration and the protection of GI by people like producers who have right to use it) in place in European countries. (Obinata, 2009, p. 64)

To support her argumentation, Obinata showed how some articles of TRIPS were incorporated into domestic legislation. For example, Article 22(2) of the TRIPS Agreement (restriction of use) was put into practice by the Unfair Competition Prevention Act (Act No. 47 of 19 May 1993). Similarly, Articles 22(3) and 23(2) (which both concern the restriction of registration as a trademark) were already implemented through the Trademark Act (Act No. 127 of 13 April 1959). Finally, Article 23(1) (restriction of usage) was applied through the Act on Securing of Liquor

Tax and on Liquor Business Associations (Act No. 50 of 2 June 2006) (Obinata, 2009, p. 66).[13]

Similarly, Japan passed significant laws to prevent the registration and possession of GIs with the aim of not misleading people about the origin or quality of goods. The protections provided by these laws are not mutually exclusive (Obinata, 2009, pp. 64–5). On the same token, the Act against Unjustifiable Premium and Misleading Representations (Act No. 134 of 15 May 1962) 'prohibits any representation by which any matter relating to transactions of goods or services is likely to be misunderstood by general consumers and which is designated by the Fair Trade Commission as such, finding it likely to induce customers unjustly and to impede fair competition' (ibid., 66). The Act for Standardization and Proper Labeling of Agricultural and Forestry Products (Act No. 31 of 30 April 2009) 'forces producers to show the signs of the place of origin on food and beverage packaging. If vendors make false indications on the places of origin of the food and beverages they sell, they can be punished by imprisonment with labor or with a fine' (ibid., pp. 65–6). The Custom Act (Act No. 61 of 2 April 1954) 'stipulates the prohibition to import the foreign goods which show directly or indirectly signs in a manner that are likely to mislead the public as to the place of origin' (ibid., p. 65).

Thus, the 'negative protection system' described by Obinata is based on the protection of consumers against deceptive producers. The next section presents this system and its limitations, as well as exhibiting its major differences with the American equivalent.

7.2.2 GI protection within the trademark system

The 'negative protection system' indicates that Japan has not taken a very dynamic path with regards to its GI legislation. Despite having signed most international agreements on GIs, Japan was slow to develop its system. It was only in 2006 that a trademark legislation for the protection of GIs was implemented, but the system still needs some improvement.

Before 2006, there was 'no registration system for recording GIs' (Aoki, 2006, p. 7).

> The Japan Patent Office refused the registration of geographical designations as trademarks, referring to Article 3 (1) (iii) of the Trademark Law, which specifically denied registration eligibility to 'marks indicating in a common way the origin of the goods'. A registration of such trademarks was regarded as inappropriate, since nobody should

> receive a monopoly right over geographical names. The only way to obtain a trademark with a geographical name was to demonstrate the name had become famous enough to have a distinctive meaning of its own, apart from the purely geographical description of origin (Article 3 (2) Trademark Law). Only very few trademark applications were able to climb that hurdle. (Ries and Weede, 1999, p. 1)

At the same time, there were 'frequent media reports about foreign "counterfeit" products mislabeled as famous Japanese agricultural products, which led to increasing demand from producers of local specialty' (ibid.) agro-food products, as well as consumers for a new law. The fact that a number of Japanese geographical names were granted trademarks in China also made Japanese policy makers and local governments feel threatened. They thus resolved to protect GIs in Japan – in addition to the duty Japan had to abide by the international agreements it signed.[14]

The implementation of the current system is the result of a complex power relationship between the governmental bodies concerned with the management of GIs, namely the Ministry of Agriculture, Fisheries and Forestry (MAFF) and the Ministry of Economy, Trade and Industry of Japan (METI). In 2003, MAFF planned to establish its own *sui generis* system, based on European legislation (Aoki, 2006, p. 7; interview at MAFF, 15 March 2010). Nevertheless METI, while aware of the discussions at MAFF, took quick action and 'established the Regionally Based Collective Trademark System in order to easily protect GIs under the Trademark Law' (Aoki, 2006, p. 7). The law came into effect in April 2006.

On the first day of implementation, '258 regionally-based collective trademarks' were filed, including one for Kobe beef (ibid.).[15] Since then, more than 970 regionally-based collective trademarks have been applied for and 450 of them have been registered (JPO, 2011). Not only agricultural products, but handicrafts (for example, *Mino* pottery) and services (like *Arima* hot spring) have been recognized as GIs (which matches the international system), while the Japanese registration is also open to the registration of foreign products; in 2010, two foreign GIs were recorded.

The 2006 legislation provided business cooperative associations and similar legal entities with a tool to protect GIs:

> The key points of the new law are that: (1) the mark can be applied for by a Collective Association, which is recognized by law. Such marks must be applied to goods which come from that area or have

> a close connection with it. (2) The mark should consist of both the place and product name; e.g. Kobe beef. (3) Since it consists of a geographical name, it will have to show acquired distinctiveness. (4) There are strict limitations on the transfer or assignment of such marks. (5) Provision is made for a 'fair use' right for prior users from the area to continue using the mark. (6) If the requirements for registration are violated, the marks registration may be opposed or if it has been granted, then invalidated. (Gangjee, 2006, p. 12)

While under the Trademark Law, the trademark with a geographical term was required as the 'secondary meaning', and the new legislation only required it to 'be well-known through use in Japan' (Ries and Weede, 1999, p. 2). It is sufficient for the registration of a regionally-based collective trademark that this trademark is 'readily recognized in two or more prefectures or another definable area of considerable size. As a result, the registration of regional trademark names has become much easier' (ibid.).

Nevertheless, there are still problems in Japan with the international protection of GIs as collective marks. Gangjee pointed out that 'there is a critical danger with using the trademark system' as 'the system operates along the lines of "First in Time, First in Right"'. This means that, in the 'case of a conflict between two marks which are similar or the same, the one which has prior rights will triumph'. If the principle of 'first in time' is followed, for instance, the use of the 'valuable brand of Kobe Beef', which was 'applied for as a trademark in various depictions in the US, in Australia and in Canada by non-Kobe producers', would be prohibited for authentic Kobe producers. However, according to a recent WTO Panel Ruling on GIs (WTO, 2005), the trademark system permits the coexistence of similar or identical trademarks as 'a fair use exception under Article 17 of TRIPS despite the rights to exclusive use which trademark owners are guaranteed under Article 16' (Gangjee, 2006, pp. 14–15). In any case, under the trademark system, the burden for producers who need to bring proof against the misuse of the name by other producers may be quite heavy, especially the small and middle-sized ones.

In conclusion, the Japanese trademark system is more flexible than its American counterpart. While the property belongs to one or more association(s), the registration of regionally based trademarks offers possibilities for local development – but also for the promotion of brands like in the United States. Nonetheless, the complicated framework may well explain why, despite the implementation of a trademark system, Japan still claims a neutral position in the current WTO debate between the supporters of the European *sui generis* system for GIs and those of the (collective) trademark system (MAFF, 2010). Finally, the existing law offers the prospect of a brand promotion and/or local development, depending on the decision-making process at the local level, the relationship among the actors, and so on. The last part of this chapter shows how the application of the 2006 law has led to differentiated paths in Kobe and Matsusaka.

7.3 Kobe beef and Matsusaka beef: two qualities, two strategies

Every Japanese consumer knows about Kobe beef and Matsusaka beef, which are produced, respectively, in Hyogo and Mie Prefectures. But what s/he may not know is what those products and their differences really are: consumers are not always aware of the construction of quality for these top-grade beefs. This construction has a lot to do with the existence of traditions, as well as a unique and complicated pattern of relationships among the main stakeholders (see section 7.1).

As we have seen, Japan adopted a trademark system that borrows from the American one, but with at least two major differences. First, in Japan, the debate between the tenets of the trademark system (supported by the JPO under METI) and those of the PDO/PGI at MAFF, is an ongoing process. Second, local initiatives give considerable leeway to the implementation of an original system of certification for each product. In practice, while Japan has legislated on GIs (as requested by the WTO), there remain considerable possibilities to 'manipulate' the system.

The purpose of this section is not to analyse conflicting situations, but to show how agents at the local level interact to produce different patterns of GIs and development. The first part of this section defines the Kobe and Matsusaka beef and analyses the consequences of the differences. The second gives some statistical consequences of these definitions, while the last one provides elements of analysis with regards to local development.

7.3.1 The definition of Kobe beef and Matsusaka beef

If Kobe and Matsusaka beef are both high-grade *kuroge wagyu*[16] and are valued similarly by Japanese consumers, there are still major differences between them (see Table 7.1). Kobe beef is exclusively produced from a special strain, the 'Tajima-gyu', which is registered with some special pedigrees. The cattle for it has to be raised in Hyogo by registered

Table 7.1 Definitions of Kobe and Matsusaka beef

	Kobe beef	Matsusaka beef
Breed	Tajima strain in Black-hair Wagyu strain	Black-hair Wagyu breed
Sex	Heifer and ox	Heifer
Age	28–60 months	No criterion excepting 'Speciality' which needs 900 days of fattening
Area	All of Kobe Prefecture	Limited zone in Mie Prefecture
Duration of		
Production Period in the Area	From birth to slaughter	Duration of fattening period in the area must be the longest and the last
Meat Grading	Yield Rate: Class A or B BMS Rate: from No. 6 to No. 12	No criterion about meat grading

Source: Documents and interviews from Kobe Beef Distribution Promotion Council and Matsusaka Beef Liaison Council.

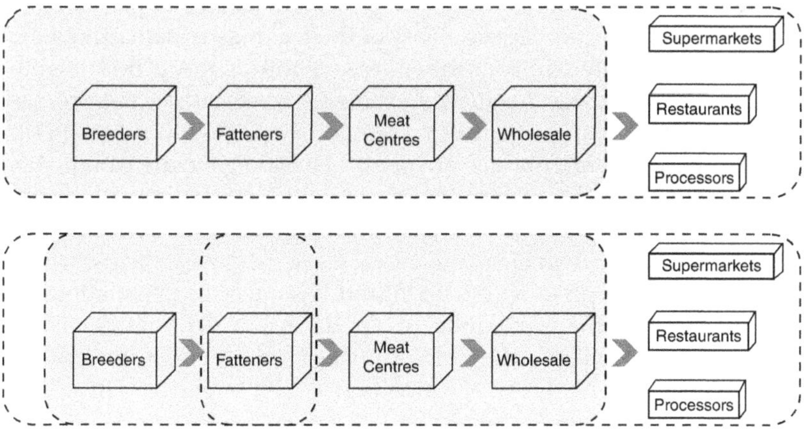

Figure 7.1 Stages of production in zoning area of Kobe beef and Matsusaka beef
Source: Documents and interviews from Kobe Beef Distribution Promotion Council and Matsusaka Beef Liaison Council.

farmers (cf. below) and slaughtered in designated slaughterhouses within the prefecture. The cattle must also be a heifer or steer.

Articles 20 and 21 of the Kobe Beef Marketing and Distribution Promotion Association (*Kobe Niku Ryutsu Suishin Kyogikai*) provide extra details:

> Art. 20. Hyogo Prefecture produce 'Tajima-gyu' refers to cows and bullocks between the ages of 28 and 60 months, bred solely from 'Motoushi' or purebred Tajima seedstock cattle obtained by cross-breeding only generations of cattle in Hyogo Prefecture by registered members (producers) of this Council[17] until they are processed at a slaughterhouse in Hyogo Prefecture and shipped to market, and that have been certified as having a yield score of A or B (…).[18]

Article 21 adds details concerning the weight of the carcass (230kg to 470kg for a heifer; 260kg to 470 for a steer), the score of Beef Marbling Standard (BMS) (a score from 4 or 5 qualifies), and the yield grade (Grade A or B – like for the Tajima beef) (see Table 7.1).[19]

The criteria indicated in Articles 20 and 21 are of a different nature. Article 20 includes information regarding the area of production and the exclusive usage of the Tajima strain. In other words, the definition includes an element of tradition, a geographical area, and the specificity of the product – all elements that are necessary for the construction of a GI, especially in the PDO/PGI system. In short, the definition implies a strong link between the product (the meat) and its area of production.

Article 20 also shows the specificity of the Japanese trademark system. It is somewhat different from the American one (as it was described in section 7.1), since the membership remains open subject only to the payment of fees. It still remains a trademark system, as, unlike the PDO/PGI European system, not just anyone in Hyogo Prefecture can qualify as a Kobe beef producer. Membership of the Association is necessary. A difference with the European system is that the definition is established by the Association (which is linked to the local government), which can change it anytime. If this definition is subject to negotiations, it does not lead to the elaboration of a code of practice that details all the production processes. In particular, the definition does not include elements concerning the feed, which is generally imported. This major aspect is also found in Matsusaka.

On the other hand, Article 21 only provides technical and measurable criteria, as defined by the Japanese Meat Quality Grading Association (*Nihon Shokuniku Kakuzuke Kyokai*): the repartition and percentage of fat or the yield, for example, are all objective indicators that are used to define the grade of the meat, regardless of its geographical and strain origin: Article 21 defines the kind of Tajima beef that technically qualifies as Kobe beef.

As it appears, the definition of Kobe beef is strict and precise, despite its lack of a code of practice, and is based on at least five types of parameters: (1) geography (Hyogo Prefecture); (2) tradition (know-how, history – the embeddedness of these two types being possibly assimilated into the notion of *terroir*[20]); (3) race (Tajima strain); (4) technical (percentage of fat and so on); and (5) association membership (trademark).

The definition of Matsusaka beef is less strict than that for Kobe beef. The only stricter parameter relates to the zoning, which only covers part of Mie Prefecture (while the production area for Kobe beef covers all of Hyogo Prefecture). Nevertheless, as both have a precise geographical delimitation, what matters more is the production processes that relate to two definitions of quality.

First, although the definition of Matsusaka beef states that the cattle must be a heifer, it does not impose the utilization of a specific strain like 'Tajima'. Still, the breed must be *kuroge wagyu* (Table 7.1). Second, unlike Kobe beef, there is no obligation for cow/calf to be born and slaughtered within the zone; the standard only specifies that the longest period of growing/fattening should occur within the geographical area (Figure 7.1). This means that the cow/calf can be imported from anywhere in Japan as long as it is of the *kuroge wagyu* breed. Similarly, the slaughtering can occur in designated slaughterhouses within Mie Prefecture or in Tokyo. This factor has important implications with regards to beef consumption, as well as to brand promotion (see section 7.3.3).

The existence of disagreements among the actors of the value chain explains this 'minimal' definition. If, during our fieldwork, it was difficult to unveil the various positions of these actors, the construction of the Matsusaka beef definition shows how their diverging positions lead to a limited agreement, of which some major producers, like Wadakin, did not approve. First, unlike in Kobe, the quality of Matsusaka beef has experienced some deregulation. As we have seen, in order to be labelled Kobe beef, the meat has to be graded 'Class A or B' with a yield score of between No. 6 and No. 12 for the marbling – the grades for which were established by the Japanese Meat Quality Grading Association (Table 7.1). But there is no minimum grade for Matsusaka beef, even though marbling and fat are major quality considerations for Japanese consumers.

Another important element in the determination of quality is the age of the cattle. By general understanding, the cattle must be raised over a certain period of time to reach its best and mature taste. The age of Kobe beef has been fixed at between 28 and 60 months before slaughter. In Matsusaka, heated discussions have led to the cancellation of the age criteria. With the cancellation of the meat grading and age determination standards, there have been great worries about the credibility of the product, as well as greater difficulties in controlling its quality. On the other hand, the new, looser standards have provided room for increasing production with some consequences for the direction of development. More details will be provided on this topic in the next two sections.

Finally, while the Matsusaka beef has such weak standards, it must be noted that a compromise was found for the production of the 'speciality Matsusaka beef' (*Tokusan Matsusaka Gyu*). Its definition is closer to the one for Kobe beef and the tradition in Matsusaka, including a fattening period of 900 days (see Table 7.1) and the use of heifers of the Tajima strain. This compromise shows the existence of a pattern within at least two conflicting groups. The first one is willing to design a product based on tradition and strict criteria in order to protect the brand and the quality. The second disagrees with such strict parameters, so it has pushed for the elaboration of the weaker definition to increase production.

These differences in definitions and production systems, as well as the conflicting situation in Matsusaka, might be due to different institutional settings (Table 7.2). While the Kobe and Matsusaka beef trademarks are both managed by two organizations (respectively, the Kobe Beef Marketing and Distribution Promotion Association and the Matsusaka Beef Liaison Council), the ownership structure of these organizations is different. The Kobe Association has a single owner,

Table 7.2 Property rights of Kobe beef and Matsusaka beef

	Kobe Beef	**Matsusaka Beef**
Registered names	Kobe Beef, Kobe Cattle, Kobe Meat	Matsusaka Beef, Matsusaka Meat
Proprietors of trademarks	Hyogo Meat Industry Cooperative Association	6 Agricultural Cooperatives, 3 Meat Industry Cooperatives, 2 Livestock Broker Cooperatives
Managers of trademarks	Kobe Beef Distribution Promotion Council	Matsusaka Beef Liaison Council

Source: Documents and interviews from Kobe Beef Distribution Promotion Council and Matsusaka Beef Liaison Council.

but there are 11 for the Matsusaka Council, which is not helpful for reaching a consensus. More research on the relationships between these owners needs to be conducted, and at this stage, we can only suggest the following hypothesis: the different institutional structure influences the decision-making related to the definitions of each kind of beef and on the brands' management, with different implications on development.

Finally, these definitions demonstrate that even within the Japanese trademark framework, two different systems have been designed locally. Both meet, to different degrees, the WTO legislation. While, despite its lack of a code of practice, the Kobe beef is relatively close to a PDO (the product must be produced and processed within a geographical area), the Matsusaka beef looks more like a PGI (the product must be produced or processed within a geographical area), as 'it exhibits specific quality, reputation or other characteristics attributable to that area' (see section 7.1). The consequences for these differences, starting with the volume of production, are important.

7.3.2 The production volume of Kobe beef and Matsusaka beef

Matsusaka beef's deregulated definition has allowed fatteners to raise more cattle than those for Kobe beef. While 300 fatteners in Kobe raised 1,500 heads of cattle to slaughter 600 to 700 heads a year, 130 fatteners of Matsusaka beef raised 9,350 heads of cattle to slaughter 4,600 heads a year (interview, March 2009). The production of meat remains small for both, but much higher in Matsusaka. While Japanese consumers eat about 1.2 million tons of beef every year,[21] the annual production of Kobe beef only reaches 700 tons, and that for Matsusaka beef totals about 3,000 tons.

However, this rapid expansion of Matsusaka beef production has made small-sized fatteners, especially the older ones, concerned about a loss of quality. As one of them told us in May 2009, 'recently, there have been more and more Matsusaka beef fatteners who have raised lots of cattle and produced low quality grade meat. If they continue to sell meat of such poor quality, the "Matsusaka Beef" brand will quickly lose ground in comparison to the other regions producing Wagyu beef.'

The newly-adopted production system for Matsusaka beef does not always guarantee quality. At the moment, however, it has not caused major problems for at least three reasons. First, the high price of Matsusaka beef in urban markets (in Tokyo, it can fetch up to 50,000 yen per kg for the most expensive parts) may sufficiently guarantee quality for customers (a traditional function of prices). Second, even though research on the topic has been limited, what little information exists indicates that many consumers cannot make a clear distinction between the quality of the Matsusaka and Kobe beef (which they often perceived as similar). Finally, in order to compensate for the less strict definition, a strict tracking system has been implemented by Matsusaka Prefecture that is independent from the one created by MAFF. Nevertheless, according to the people who manage traceability at the slaughterhouse of Mie Prefecture, the ability to track Matsusaka beef has not fully eliminated fraudulent or substandard producers or distributors, although it has greatly reduced their numbers (interview, 13 July 2009).[22]

7.3.3 In search of local development

The definitions of Kobe and Matsusaka beef, while following the trademark system implemented by the JPO, has induced different strategies for the management of GIs. The first strategy, which is for Kobe beef, could be termed 'protective', while the other strategy looks more 'expansive'. They might not have been established consciously by the actors in the value chain, but they determine different dynamics.

As we have seen, in Kobe, there is a strong 'embeddedness' between the material quality (defined by technical criteria), tradition (methods of production and the genealogy of the Tajima strain), history, and so on. The Kobe Beef Marketing and Distribution Promotion Association aims to protect this 'embeddedness', despite its direct effect is to limit production. While Kobe beef is renowned both within Japan and beyond, its limited production means consumption is only for the happy few, often in the Kansai area. Officials from the Association told us that they never export, so the so-called 'Kobe beef' on sale in China or the United States is not genuine. The following analysis drawn by John Longworth in 1983 is still pretty much valid.

> The emerging 'HQ' [high quality] market includes all the Wagyu beef production which does not achieve 'super beef' [i.e. Kobe beef] status and the best of the best of the domestic dairy steer beef. (...) [T]here is a great temptation to describe 'HQ beef' as 'Kobe beef'. The distinction between 'HQ beef' and 'Kobe beef' is becoming increasingly blurred as the supply of genuine 'super beef' declines relative to the size of the market for this specialty. (Longworth, 1983, p. 20)

Similar observations led the Association to protect its brand name as early as 1983. Since then, the tendency has been towards a clearer separation of the two markets, but ambiguity remains for two reasons. First, if consumers know 'Kobe beef', they do not necessarily know about the brands and its symbols (the chrysanthemum, for example). Second, the production of genuine Kobe beef is too low (a parameter already isolated by Longworth).

Thus, respect for the traditions and the promotion of the brand have had two opposite effects. On one hand, they have allowed for an increased reputation and territorial development. The general agreement among local actors has generated a strong territorial dynamic, leading to a recognition of the know-how or quality, nationally and internationally. With the brand name well-established at the JPO, Hyogo Prefecture can enter into domestic competition in the higher end beef market. This synergy between the actors of the value chain is stimulated by the Association. It acts as a platform that aims to create and promote the GI. This platform regroups most actors of the value chains and reinforces existing networks.

On the other hand, the difficulty of increasing production seems damaging to potential development, since territorial competition in this market segment has become fiercer than ever (in addition to Kobe and Matsusaka, one can also include Ômi, Miyazaki, Hida, and so on). This limited production can be attributed in part to the strict definition of Kobe beef, which also explains why the number of animals per fattener remains small. Another difficulty is in maintaining a certain margin of profits. Despite high prices, farmers (especially smaller ones) are in a difficult situation due to the increasing prices for feed, which is mostly imported, and calves. This has been especially the case since 2008, when agricultural prices jumped worldwide.[23]

In order to match this increased competition, actors of a certain size tend to develop individual strategies in Kobe. First, they produce and distribute other kinds of high-grade beef under their own brands. The idea is that since profits from the production and sales of Kobe beef are small, it is more rewarding to deal with other beef categories, but without withdrawing from the Kobe beef market. For consumers, since these producers/distributors can deal with top-grade Kobe beef, they cannot sell poor-quality products (interview with a producer/distributor, 15 March 2009). Second, they also aim to control more segments of the value chain from production (they have their own farms) to distribution (they are also butchers and own restaurants). Thus, the solution for coping with the difficult market situation is to increase one's control over the value chain and also to introduce a degree of diversification. This strategy can only be put into practice by large producers and could threaten the existing form of unity in the management of the brand and local dynamics, as promoted by the Association and its members, in the future. Beyond the territorial competition with other top-grade beef-producing areas, there is also a new tendency from large producers to gain extra control over the value chain and distribution of the limited production, which reintroduces competition among producers (see section 7.1).

In Matsusaka, the dynamics are different, as only a minimal consensus can be reached. The supply of cattle is diversified beyond the Tajima strain, while the slaughter of Matsusaka beef in Tokyo increases its market there. The diversification has allowed a larger volume of production, which is beneficial to producers in the short term. There is also a positive commitment by the Council and other actors to promote the 'Matsusaka' brand.

At the same time, there is a fear of the possible loss of quality. This is of great importance for producers, especially the smaller and older ones, which are concerned with the respect of traditions (an important factor for the existence of the GI). The more 'expansive' attitude in Matsusaka could be a threat to the reputation of the Matsusaka beef in the future, if consumers start doubting the quality of the meat. This may be even more likely, as Wadakin did not join the Council. Technically, this producer (and distributor) is not allowed to sell Matsusaka beef, but its reputation is sufficient to attract consumers. Thus, if the Council, in Matsusaka, conducts a policy of expansion, this policy is threatened by the dual behaviour of producers, as well as the possible lack of confidence of consumers in the future. Resorting to a trademark system offers certain guarantees, but not all of them, because the definition can be changed at any time without the knowledge of (potential) consumers. Unlike in Europe, Japanese legislation does not require a code of practice that is supervised outside the local system (for example, an agency under governmental control). The same may apply to Kobe beef, but the general consensus for the protection of the product, the tradition, the brand, and the attitude from local consumers have thus far prevented such an outcome.

7.4 Conclusion

There are differences in the ways the GIs of Kobe and Matsusaka beef were developed under the same institutional framework. In Kobe, the focus is on local development with strong implications for local actors. This strategy shows its own limitations with few possibilities to expand the production (strong control of the strain, a small number of fatteners, few animals per fattener, and so on). In Matsusaka, the emphasis has been on brand promotion, but at the possible expense of compromising quality and a limited consensus among the actors. Interestingly, while Japan has implemented a trademark system for GIs, the dynamic in Kobe seems closer to a European PDO/PGI, while Matsusaka may more closely resemble the American system.

More importantly, these differences signify that Matsusaka beef and Kobe beef are two different products, a point of which most consumers are unaware. Unfortunately, the implementation of a trademark system in Japan cannot fully lift the ambiguities related to the quality of these products. As indicated in the introduction, while Japanese consumers are concerned about the origins of traditional products (including GIs), the existing system needs to be upgraded. It seems especially important to reinforce the domestic system during the current negotiations process at the international level. This is more urgent even as disagreements between Japan and the United States occur, which resemble those between the United States and Europe, as the following example demonstrates. In 2007, MAFF sent a draft to the US Government via the USDA Bureau of the American Embassy in Tokyo concerning Wagyu beef.

> The Government of the United States of America appreciates the opportunity provided by the Ministry of Agriculture, Forestry, and Fisheries to comment on its draft 'Labeling Guidelines for Distinctive Meats such as Wagyu. (...)
>
> With respect to beef, the United States has a number of concerns regarding the purpose of the draft guideline and its impact on future trade (...).
>
> One function of the draft guideline is to prevent imported beef from being labeled as 'Wagyu'. In particular, Section VI, 1 (1) ((2)) requires cattle bearing the Wagyu label must be born and raised in Japan. We believe that beef that meets the requirements under the draft guideline and that is raised outside of Japan can also be termed Wagyu. (...)
>
> In summary, the characteristics of Wagyu beef, such as meat quality, texture, and flavor, which give Wagyu its product value, are derived from specific animal genetics. Wagyu genetics are not constrained by geography nor are otherwise limited to Japan. (...) Any measure that limits the labeling of Wagyu beef to animals raised in Japan would provide strong disincentive for the future foreign production of Wagyu and negatively impact trade. (USDA, 2007)

In short, the United States does not recognize the validity of a GI for Wagyu beef because it wishes to protect the American Wagyu

Association and its possible sales in Japan. The Americans consider 'Wagyu' a generic label.

Japan's answer is also clear and close to what the European attitude would have been if a similar situation have occurred. A document available from MAFF states that '[Wagyu beef] is increasing in popularity all over the world. Unfortunately, this has resulted in the appearance of many non-authentic Wagyu beef *impostors*. (...) Only authentic Wagyu bears the 'Universal Wagyu Mark'. (...) [Wagyu beef] must be cattle born and bred in Japan (...)' (MAFF, 2011; our emphasis).

The position of Japan is strongly stated with the use of a word like 'impostor'. Nevertheless, in the absence of a code of practice, this position seems difficult to support. The existing trademark system and the negative protection system (Obinata, 2009) have led to divergence and confusion over the nature of the products, even for top-grade Kobe and Matsusaka beef. As we have seen, the networks between the main actors define an LPS that is different in the two cases so that the result is the existence of two divergent dynamics of local development. Again, given that the unclear domestic situation implies a necessary revision of existing laws regulating GIs, it also weakens Japan's position in the international negotiation process. In any case, this close examination of Kobe and Matsusaka beef demonstrates all the potential Japan has to strengthen these regulations and support existing local initiatives.

Notes

1. For an updated discussion of this point, see Ilbert and Petit (2009).
2. On this debate, see the general introduction of this volume.
3. For more discussions on these points, see Giovannucci et al. (2009).
4. It is nearly impossible to determine which legal system is more conducive to local development. More generally, some studies have concluded that GIs are beneficial to local development, but they are partial and not unambiguous (Barjolle et al., 2009).
5. Many newspapers articles refer to the foot-and-mouth disease of beef cattle in Miyasaki Prefecture. See, for example, *Asahi Shimbun* (2008).
6. For an analysis of the products of 'regionally-based collective trademarks' from a marketing perspective, see Saitoh (2007) and Saitoh et al. (2008).
7. This study was conducted in March and July 2009, and in March 2010. The 2010 fieldwork was organized by a team from the Graduate School of Agriculture, Kyoto University, under the leadership of Professor Yoko Niiyama. More generally, we want to thank Professor Niiyama for her generous help and advice during the course of this research.

8. SINER-GI (Strengthening International Research on Geographical Indication) is a project of the European Union and supported by the European Commission under the Sixth Framework Programme.
9. The 'camembert war' in France, is illustrative of this attitude. Camembert is traditionally produced from raw milk, which increases the risks of contamination for mass production. Consequently, large producers, such as Lactalis, tried to change the code of practice of the AOC 'Camembert de Normandie' in order to use pasteurized milk. They were unsuccessful, meaning that over 80 percent of the camembert production no longer qualifies as 'true' camembert (Sciolino, 2007; Chrisafis, 2008). Similarly, one of the main producers/retailers of Matsusaka beef, Wadakin, refused to adopt the collective trademark. Another example of marketing strategy is presented below in relation to Kobe beef. We would like to thank Dr Boutonnet for bringing the example of camembert to our attention.
10. On the notion of quality, see Allaire (2009) and his article in this volume, along with Nicolas and Valceschini (1995) and the pioneering work of Eymard-Duvernay (1994). On the notion of the 'social life of things' and the commodification of 'intangible assets', cf. Appadurai (1988).
11. Again, the examples of Lactalis and Wadakin perfectly illustrate this statement (see note 9).
12. The Lisbon Convention consists of an International Protection System of GIs, but the limited number of countries that have adopted its provisions makes the agreement relatively ineffective (Giovannucci et al., 2009).
13. See Baumert in this volume on the protection of GIs on Japanese Sake (rice wine). Baumert also described the efforts undertaken at the prefectural government level to strengthen the protection of GIs.
14. For instance, the Aomori prefecture is well known as a producer of apples, which are exported to Hong Kong, Taiwan, and China. Yet, the geographical name was used for the application of trademarks to five different products (meat and dairy, fruits and vegetables, processed food, drinks, and clothing) in China in May 2003. Formal protests have been issued against the Chinese authorities through diplomatic channels from apple producers in Aomori (see the website of Aomori prefecture, http://www.pref.aomori.lg.jp/kenminno-koe/h18nourinsuisan-e-019.html, date accessed 10 December 2010).
15. The story is more complicated than that. In 1983, due to pressure from consumers, the Association for the Promotion of Kobe beef was established in order to protect the 'Kobe beef' brand. The brand name was created that year, even though it was not protected by the JPO. In 2001, the logo (a stylized chrysanthemum) and the 'tridimensional monument' (a statue of a cow's head) were approved by the Patent Office. At that time, it was not possible to register the GI, but it was possible to register its symbols, which provided a form of protection (interviews with the Association, 18 March 2009). This shows how pressure from consumers and local authorities pushed for the establishment of a GI system, a subject detailed in section 7.3.3.
16. According to MAFF, Wagyu (Japanese beef) is defined by four specific varieties of beef from cattle such as Japanese Black and Japanese Brown, along with their breeding. In addition, a Wagyu cattle must be born and bred in Japan. For more details, see the website of MAFF (2011). The consequences of this definition are explained in the conclusion of this article.

17. The Association has just been renamed; it was previously a Council.
18. See the website of the Association, http://www.kobe-niku.jp/english/contents/pu/pu_b.html, date accessed 1 August 2011.
19. As MAFF explained (2011), 'Beef is graded based on the yield grade and meat quality. The yield grade refers to the ratio of meat to total weight of the carcass and is classified into three grades from A to C with A being a grade of higher yield. Meat quality is classified into four elements and graded from 5 to 1 based on "marbling", "colour and firmness of the meat", and the "colour and quality of the fat". The lowest of the four individual elements is the final grade of the meat.'
20. On the notion of *terroir*, see Baumert and Chan in this volume.
21. In 2000, the consumption of beef in Japan was 1.56 million tons (imports totalling 1.05 million tons) – decreasing to 1.19 million tons in 2010 (imports totaling 0.678 tons). See Obara et al. (2010), who quoted sources from MAFF.
22. On the traceability system of beef in Japan and its evolution, cf. Niiyama et al. (2004).
23. On the price of feed for beef producers in Japan, see Obara et al. (2010).

References

Allaire, G. (2009) 'Economics of Conventions and the New Economic Sociology and our Understanding of Food Quality and New Food Markets and Trade Institutions. What Are Markets That Pure Economics Does Not Know?', 27th International Conference of Agricultural Economists, Beijing, China, August.

Asahi Shimbum (2008) 'Outbreak Hits Famed Miyazaki Beef Cattle', 18 May.

Aoki, H. (2006) 'Protection of Geographical Indications (GIs) under the New Japanese Trademark Law', Document provided by MAFF, May, pp. 6–11.

Appadurai, A. (ed.) (1988) *The Social Life of Things. Commodities in Cultural Perspectives* (Cambridge: Cambridge University Press).

Barjolle, D., M. Paus and A. Perret (2009) 'Impacts of Geographical Indications, Review of Methods and Empirical Evidences', International Association of Agricultural Economists Conference, Beijing, China, 16–22 August.

Beshaw, B.M. (2008) 'Geographical Indications in China: Why Protect GIs with Both Trademark Law and AOC-type Legislation?', *Pacific Rim Law and Policy Journal*, 17(1), 73–102.

Chrisafis, A. (2008) 'Camembert Wars Get Dirty in Fight for France's Soul', *The Guardian*, 18 April.

Eymard-Duvernay, F. (1994) 'Coordination des échanges par l'entreprise et qualité des biens' in A. Orléan (ed.), *Analyse économique des conventions* (Paris: Presses Universitaires de France).

Gangjee, D. (2006) 'Protecting Geographical Indications as Collective Trademarks: The Prospects and Pitfalls', IIP Bulletin, p. 149, http://www.lse.ac.uk/collections/law/staff%20publications%20full%20text/gangjee/Gangjee_IIP%20Report%202006.pdf, date accessed 15 November 2010.

Granovetter, M. (1985) 'Economic Action and Social Structure: the Problem of Embeddedness', *American Journal of Sociology*, 91(November), 481–510.

Giovannucci, D. et al. (2009) *Guide to Geographical Indications. Linking Products to their Origin* (Geneva: International Trade Centre).

Ilbert, H. and M. Petit (2009) 'Are Geographical Indications a Valid Property Right? Global Trends and Challenges', *Development Policy Review*, 27(5), 503–28.

Japan Patent Office (2010), 'Report on Regionally Based Collective Trademark Legislation', http://www.jpo.go.jp/cgi/link.cgi?url=/torikumi/t_torikumi/t_dantai_syouhyou.htm, date accessed 29 August 2011.

Japan Patent Office (JPO) (2011) 'Homepage on Regionally Based Collective Trademark Legislation', p. 1, http://www.jpo.go.jp/cgi/link.cgi?url=/torikumi/t_torikumi/t_dantai_syouhyou.htm, date accessed 29 August 2011.

Longworth, J.W. (1983) *Beef in Japan: Politics, Production, Marketing and Trade* (St Lucia, London and New York: University of Queensland Press).

Ministry of Agriculture, Fishery and Forestry (MAFF) (2010) 'Situation Around Geographical Indication in Japan', March, pp. 1–11 (in Japanese with translation in English).

Ministry of Agriculture, Fishery and Forestry (2011) 'Authentic Wagyu Bears the "Authentic Wagyu Mark"', http://www.maff.go.jp/j/export/e_info/syoku_niku/pdf/4_en_beef.pdf, date accessed 15 May 2011.

Moiti-Maïzy, P. et al. (2002) *Systèmes Agroalimentaires localisés: terroirs, savoir-faire, innovations* (Paris: INRA).

Nicolas, F. and E. Valceschini (eds) (1995) *Agro-alimentaire: une économie de la qualité* (Paris: INRA/Economica).

Niiyama, Y. et al. (2004) *Practical Theory for Food Safety System (Syokuhin Anzen no Jissen Riron)* (Kyoto: Showado) (in Japanese).

North, D.C. (1990) *Institutions, Institutional Change and Economic Performance* (Cambridge: Cambridge University Press).

Obara, K. et al. (2010) *Japan's Beef Market*, USDA. LDP-M-194-01 Report, August.

Obinata, Y. (2009) *Geographical Indication Systems in European Countries* (Oxford: Oxford Intellectual Property Research Centre).

Powell, W. (1990) 'Neither Market nor Hierarchy: Network Forms of Organization', *Research in Organizational Behavior*, 12, 295–336.

Ries, M. and R. Weede (2009) 'Registration of Regional Collective Trademarks in Japan: Requirements and Statistics', pp. 1–3, www.country-index.com/articles/article_10.pdf, date accessed 10 December 2010.

Saitoh, O. (2007) *Food Industry Clusters and Local Brands (Syokuryou Sangyou Clusters to Chiiki Brands)* (Tokyo: Noubunkyou) (in Japanese).

Saitoh, O. et al. (2008) *Strategies and Managements of Local Brands (Chiiki Brands no Senryaku to Kanri)* (Tokyo: Noubunkyou) (in Japanese).

Sciolino, E. (2007) 'If Rules Change, Will Camembert Stay the Same?', *The New York Times*, 20 June.

USDA (2007) 'US Comments on Draft Wagyu Labelling Guidelines', http://www.usdajapan.org/en/newsroom/2007/jpnews070213.html, date accessed 15 May 2011.

Wattanapruttipaisan, T. (2009) 'Trademarks and Geographical Indications: Policy Issues and Options in Trade Negotiations and Implementation', *Asian Development Review*, 26(1), 166–205.

World Trade Organization (WTO) (2005) 'Report of the WTO Panel: European Communities – Protection of Trademarks and Geographical Indications', WT/DS174/R, 15 March.

8

The Development of Geographical Standards for *Sake* in Japan[1]

Nicolas Baumert

As a cultural product, *sake* is as important in Japan as wine in Europe. Despite differences in scale, nature, and ingredients, these two beverages have experienced similar challenges in quality development. They have been the drink of elites and have contributed to the fortune of makers and merchants (Dion, 1959; Yunoki, 1998). They have also been regarded as popular beverages and 'cheap calories' (Nourrisson, 1990; Aoki, 2006); furthermore, both are now contested in their own territories by the globalization movement (Baumert, 2006). Consequently, their legislations are subject to examination. For example, the *terroir* model is now put into question even in France by the rise of new producing countries and the penetration of wine-based classification (Garcia-Papet, 2004). In Japan, the appreciation of quality, traditionally based on production standards, is now being questioned by the emergence of geographical classifications.

Nowadays, similar to the situation of wine in Europe, *sake* is at a turning point in its history. In Japan, the consumption of *sake* has decreased, and the consumers are seeking something more than an ordinary alcoholic drink. For about a decade, *sake* has enjoyed greater popularity and consumption in foreign countries. This overseas expansion has led to new sales opportunities and changes in traditional perceptions of its quality standards. Quality becomes a keyword, often associated with representations of authenticity and origin, but lacks a concrete definition. As in the case with any alimentary production, the quality of *sake* can be based on 'objective' criteria, norms, or processes of judgement implying producers, consumers, and intermediates. The origin contributes to this process and could change the actual construction of quality.[2]

This study aims to demonstrate that in an old country like Japan, the territorial dimension of quality is emerging to be an important factor again for *sake* consumers, which inclines them to adopt geographically specific labels under the influence of Southern Europe's representations of *terroir*. For *sake*, as for many beverages coming from a long tradition, a producing territory could be seen as an appropriate space, constructed by a human community during time that produces know-how and quality. In this respect, the scale is voluntary and imprecise and can change in terms of ingredients, the nature of the beverage, the historical period, or legislation (Hinnewinkel, 2002; Baumert, 2011).

To fully comprehend the challenge in creating geographical origin standards for *sake*, we first consider the actual production and investigate where the regional territories of *sake* are located. Then, we examine the characteristics of each of them before considering the limits and challenges of creating a geographic indication system for this particular beverage.

8.1 Which production territories are suitable for rice-wine?

Understanding which territories are most suited for *sake* production obliges us to first take a brief look at its production methods. Contrary to popular belief, *sake* is not a strong distilled beverage; instead, it is a 'rice wine', produced by the fermentation of rice in water. Its alcohol degrees usually range between 12 and 17. Outside the Far-East regions, fermented drinks based on brewed cereals are often regarded as beers, but the producing methods and final results of rice-wines are different. What distinguishes *sake* from other brewing methods is a process known as 'multiple parallel fermentation'. To produce *sake*, brewers use a mould called *kôji*[3] (which transforms the rice starch into simple sugars) and yeast (which transforms the sugar into alcohol) instead of using malt in beer.[4] Although rice-wines have been produced in Japan since the introduction of rice around the fourth century BC, *sake* production using the 'multiple parallel fermentation' has been known since the mid-sixteenth century, and its components have not changed much since this time (Kamatani, 1995).

By following legislation, *sake* quality can be defined in two ways (Table 8.1). Considering the brewing process, which represents a technical quality, the use of pure rice (which means 'without any additives') is the most important. The other criterion is the degree of rice polishing (polishing removes proteins and undesired minerals on grain shells). This legislation is controlled by Japan's Ministry of Taxation.[5] It started in 1969 with the creation of the *honjôzô* class to solve the

Table 8.1 *Sake's* quality categories

	Criteria	
	1. Ingredients	**2. Rice polishing***
High-class *sake*	***Junmaishu*** (Only rice, water, *kôji* and yeast)	***Daiginjô***** (less than 50%) ***Ginjô***** (between 50 and 60%)
Ordinary *sake*	***Futsûshu*** (additional ingredients are allowed in the mash, in particular distilled alcohol up to 25% of the rice volume)	***Honjôzô***** (between 60 and 75%) ***Futsûshu*** (more than 75%)

*Percentage indicates the volume of grain left.
**Only one ad of distilled alcohol is allowed for these categories, until 10 per cent of the rice volume.
Source: Baumert (2009), p. 335.

problem of adding too many additional ingredients in the mash (for example, distilled alcohol or sugar). The *junmai* criteria were established in the 1980s.

Official legislation does not refer directly to origins of production, except for the bottling location. Considering the region, to identify a measurable link between origin and taste, best-quality water and rice are cited by brewers to explain that both regions famous for growing rice and snowy mountainous regions are the best locations for *sake* breweries because the water, which is low in mineral content, is ideal for *sake*. The regional know-how, relating to a long tradition of brewing, is also a selling point mainly used by well-known and long established brands.

However, it is difficult to establish a link between *sake* production and a specific location. It is true that the process of producing *sake* is difficult and its mastery has been an area of distinction before the introduction of modern science and the full comprehension of the biochemical process of brewing at the end of the nineteenth century (Yoshida, 1997; Yunoki, 1998). However, to address the question on territories, its ingredients (rice, *kôji*, and yeast) are no longer difficult to find or transport, even over long distances. This is the major difference from wine making. Thus, it is possible for *sake* brewers to use different varieties of rice; furthermore, the producing regions of *sake* and particular kinds of rice used in its making are not always the same. In fact, the only ingredient for *sake* that could make a difference is water, but this difference only occurs on a local scale. As it is true that *sake* breweries are located near the best water sources, in a mountainous and volcanic country like Japan, good water can be found everywhere. It is thus very difficult to justify *terroir* by objective criteria, and *sake* can theoretically be produced in every region of the country. Actual territories are then results of a complex history (Baumert, 2011).

A look at the geography of *sake* production presents us with an idea of the actual territories of *sake*. Currently in Japan, approximately nine million hectolitres of *sake* are produced. 99 per cent is consumed in the country and only one per cent is exported (NTA, 2006). According to the 2005 map of *sake* production (Figure 8.1), elaborated with regional statistics, *sake* is mostly produced in two regions of Japan. In 2005, the first region is Kansai with principally Hyôgo (30 per cent of the production) and Kyôto (15 per cent of the production) prefectures. The second region is the north-west of Japan, around Niigata prefecture along the Sea of Japan (*Nihonkai*).

This distribution trend, showing two major producing regions (one in central Japan and the other in the north-west), is relatively recent (about 20 years). If we look at the distribution of *sake* production in

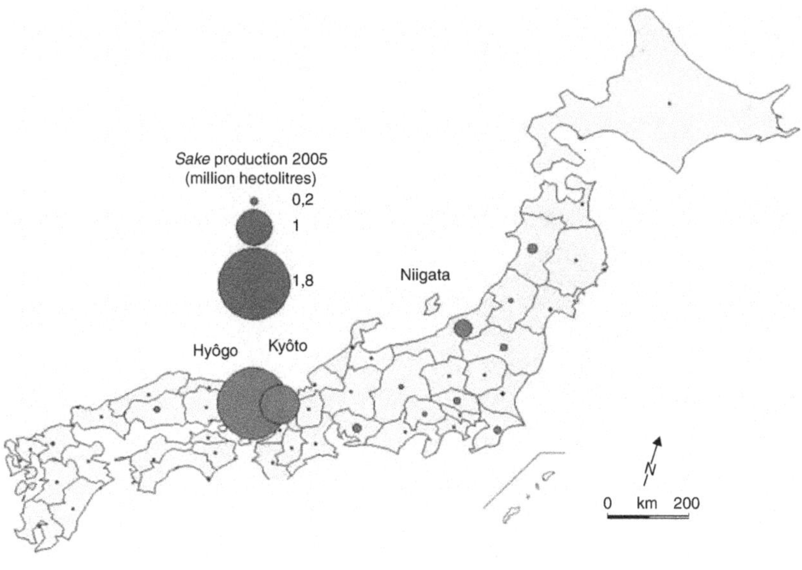

Figure 8.1 *Sake*'s departmental production in 2005
Source: National Tax Agency Report; Cartography: Nicolas Baumert (2009).

1985, for example (Figure 8.2), this one was a little bit different. At this time, the Kansai region was producing the major part of *sake*, while the rest of the country's production was, in most of the prefectures, larger than it is at present but similar in scale. In 1985, high-quality classes of *sake*, nationally distributed, were produced by the big firms of Kyôto and Hyôgo. Firms in the countryside produced ordinary *sake* limited to regional distribution for the most part.

Between 1985 and 2005, the quantity of *sake* produced decreased (eleven million hectolitres in 1985; six million hectolitres in 2005), but we should consider that the overall quality of the production increased in every region. We will see in the second part of this paper that the high-quality classes of *sake* are now produced in the north-west.

Most noteworthy are certainly changes in distribution. The decrease in global production in the whole country has changed the geography of *sake*. Since the north-west around Niigata is the only region where production has not decreased (or has decreased less than in the rest of the country), it appears as a new territory. Instead of being concentrated only in the Kansai region, as had been the case since the Meiji period (1868–1912), the actual geography now shows two major poles, presenting two cultures of *sake* and a strong rivalry between them.

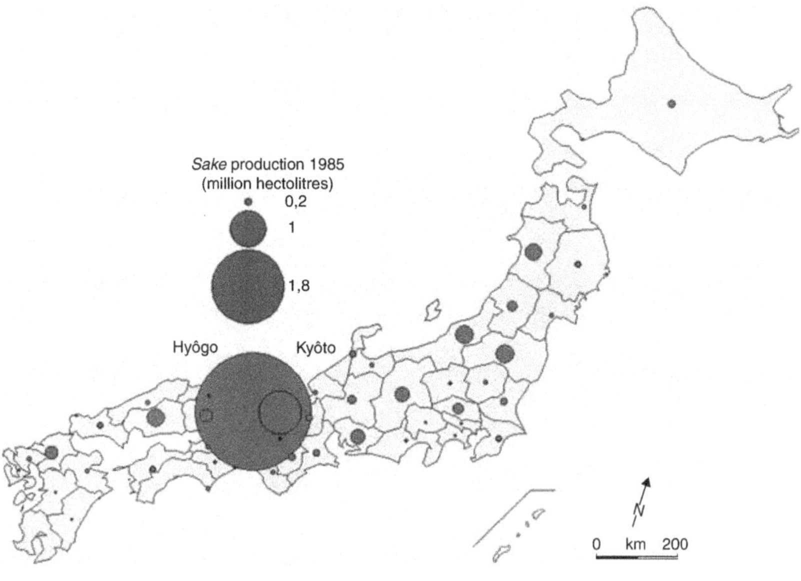

Figure 8.2 *Sake*'s departmental production in 1985
Source: National Tax Agency Report; Cartography: Nicolas Baumert (2009).

This analysis of producing regions leads to two questions concerning: (1) the importance of Hyôgo and Kyôto in Japan's *sake* geography; and (2) the reasons for the emergence of these new territories around Niigata for the past 20–30 years. A look at their history can explain this evolution.

8.2 Two main producing regions and their characteristics

8.2.1 The Kinai culture of *sake*

Kinai is the ancient appellation of what is now the most important part of the Kansai region around Kyôto, Kôbe, and Osaka. The importance of this region for the production of *sake* is related to the importance of the old capital, Kyôto, during the Antique and Middle Ages. At the early times of Japanese history, *sake* was considered as the drink of Gods. There are records of uses of rice-wines in rituals and as a medicine (Ashton, 1993). In the Antique period, court brewers were producing several forms of *sake* for the emperor, different levels of the nobility, and different kinds of ritual ceremony.

Sake has been commercially produced since the Middle Ages and sold locally, and, as with most cultural products that have become commodities at these times, it was made mostly for the elite and for special events, while the rest of the population drank it occasionally. Before the mid-sixteenth century and the spread of new techniques concerning the 'multiple parallel fermentation' production methods developed by the Buddhist temples of Nara, *sake* breweries were always located close to the consumption areas to make preservation easier. Polishing rice grains before cooking them gives *sake* a higher degree of alcohol, and pasteurization helps preservation. Another important point is in explaining the situation of breweries in the Kinai region in the Antique and the Middle Ages; Kyôto, the capital, was the only big city in the country and the residence of the elites, so the most important part of *sake* production was found in Kyôto countryside.

During the Edo period (1603–1867), the political capital was moved to Edo (the actual Tôkyô). The city of Edo developed rapidly (one million inhabitants in the beginning of the eighteenth century), and, because of system obliging the feudal lords to come to the shôgunate's capital for one year in every two and leave their family there as hostage while they returned to administer their lands, the city was populated mostly by well-educated male inhabitants[6] who demanded quality food and drinks, most of which were produced in the Kinai region. The Edo period marked the beginning of a larger social consumption in urban Japan as well as the appearance of large factories and merchants' corporations. Despite the move of a large number of consumers in the North, the Kinai region has continued to dominate the high-quality *sake* production, and a rich commerce has developed between Kinai and Edo. Kinai's comparative advantage can be explained by the superior quality of *sake* it produces by mastering production techniques (Yoshida, 1997).

After the Meiji restoration (1868) and the opening of Japan to modern and western sciences, new brewing techniques and a new legislation appeared. The *sake* industry underwent modernization. In 1904, the government created a *sake*-brewing research institute as well as improved hygiene and quality standards (Morris-Suzuki, 1995). These developments benefitted the biggest firms, most of which located, for the historical reasons already provided, in the Kinai, while the development of modern transportation permitted them to sell throughout the country. The legislation passed in 1881 on taxation, which favoured large breweries over smaller producers is another reason for the dominance of the Kinai region. Between 1880 and 1912, more than 60 per cent of the brewers disappeared (Hurt, 2000). After the Second World War, the industrial transformation of breweries and the fast-growing demand during the high-growth period reinforced the quantitative superiority of Kansai firms (but often at the expense of quality), which explains the importance of this region (Kondo, 1996).

Currently, 12 of the 15 most important brewers of Japan, together producing about 50 per cent of annual production, are located in Kansai. Most of them are old breweries from the Edo period and are located principally in the urban environment of the Kyôto-Kôbe-Osaka conurbation. Local big makers also trade, buying *sake* from smaller breweries in their region or all over the country, and commercialize it under their own brand label.

8.2.2 *Sake* culture in the north-west

Many *sake* breweries in the North-West were created in the Edo period and their production was sold locally. However, the emergence of this region as a territory of *sake* was a success story that began in Niigata in the 1980s. This change was made possible and can be explained by an evolving perception of *sake* quality since the mid-1970s.

Before the mid-1970s, consumers recognized national brands as providers of quality *sake*, which was available everywhere in Japan, while the local *sake* called *jizake* was mostly available only in the regions where they were produced. The national brands were then most respected, and perceptions of their quality were closely associated with the firms' names, which were used to guarantee standard production. However, following the big push for modernization following the Second World War and the outbreak of many scandals concerning the use of alcohol and sugar in the *sake* mash or the subcontracting system of buying *sake* from other regions to blend it with the *sake* produced locally, consumers changed their perception of quality and started showing preference for *jizake*, marketed as a traditional and preserved product (Kondo, 1996; Frank, 2009[7]).

A few producers of Niigata felt this change before the other regions did, and at the beginning of the 1980s, at a time when most brewers in Japan were still attempting to increase production volume, Niigata brewers focused on quality and produced higher-level *sake* with more polished rice and dry taste. This change occurred at a turning point of the *sake* consumption in Japan because at this period, *sake* stopped being a product of mass consumption, and consumers in Japan, like others in most developed countries, began to drink less but better. The *jizake* of Niigata gained popularity in Tôkyô where its dry taste matched well with the local cuisine before establishing its reputation all over Japan. As noted before, while analysing the evolution for 30 years, despite a decrease in global production, the Niigata prefecture has maintained its share volume of production. This is truly exceptional because in most cases, the transition from producing for mass consumption to producing for quality is generally characterized by volume decrease. If we consider the actual production of a superior class of *sake*, Niigata is the first producing region, before the Hyôgo and Kyôto prefectures (Figure 8.5).

Following Niigata, the *jizake* success was duplicated in other prefectures, such as Nagano, Ishikawa, Akita, or Yamagata. The old *sake* breweries of these regions, which had missed the turn of modernization and mass consumption after the war, are now assimilated into romantic marketing representations as the guardians of ancestral techniques and places of taste, quality, and authenticity (Sumihara, 2004). The North-West discourse about quality refers generally to two advantages, both related to physical factors (its climate and rice quality). It is true that this part of Japan along the Sea of Japan is famous for its superior rice quality and has the largest snow precipitation, which provides good and pure water for *sake* production. During the last decades, brewers and farmers have developed several regional varieties of special *sake* rice, which contribute now to regionally distinct types of *sake*. Presently, Niigata is, for example, the second largest producer of *sake* rice (Figure 8.3).

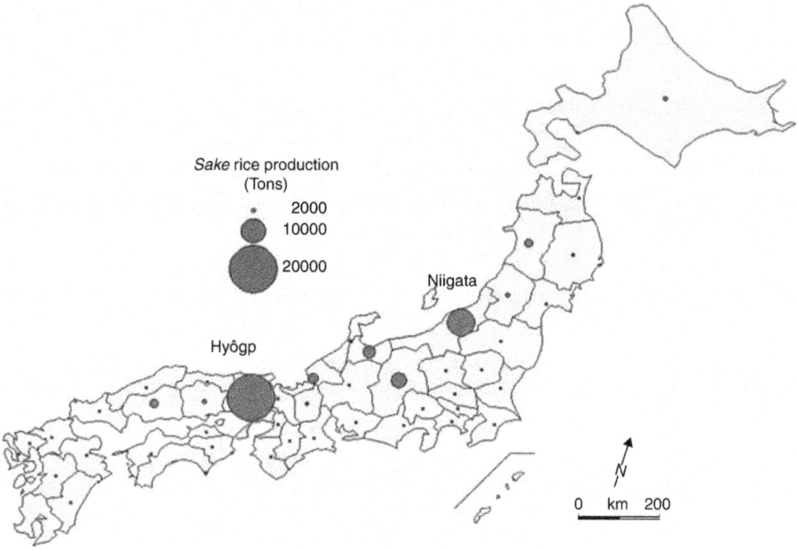

Figure 8.3 Departmental *sake*-rice production in 2005
Source: National Tax Agency Report; *Cartography*: Nicolas Baumert (2009).

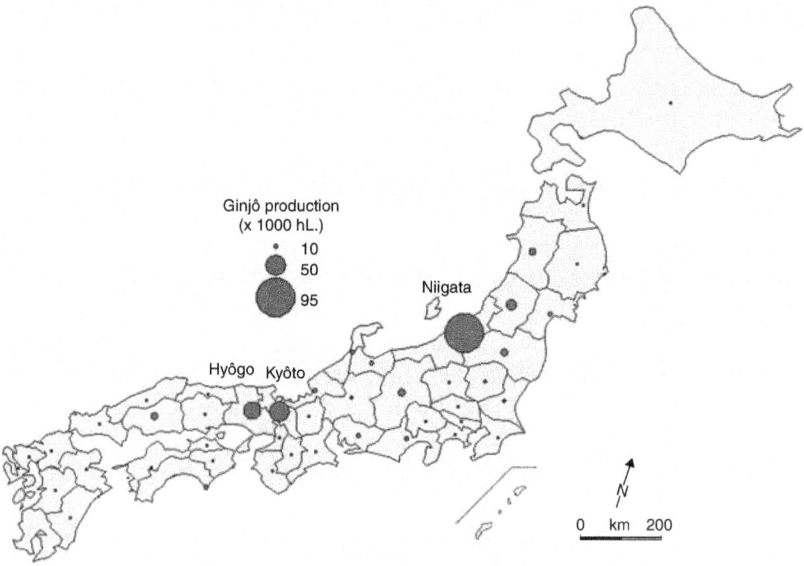

Figure 8.4 Departmental production of superior *sake* in 2005
Source: National Tax Agency Report; *Cartography*: Nicolas Baumert (2009).

The new territories of *sake* in the North-West of Japan have a culture of rice-wine distinct from that in the Kansai region, and are now a rival territory for the ancient region of Central Japan. The breweries of the North-West are smaller and mostly artisanal. Most of them are located in a rural environment where physical factors play a major part in the discourse of quality.

8.2.3 Two different cultures and two conceptions of quality

The two main producing regions present two cultures of rice-wine: one is rural and mostly comprised small makers; the other is urban and is mostly represented by big firms. Discourses about quality differ. For the ancient Kinai region, brand recognition associated with production standards is sufficient; for the new north-western regions, quality is associated with the origin of the *sake* ingredients and the region's name.

Behind these two conceptions of quality appears the historical evolution in *sake* brewing that has occurred since the modernization period. Before Meiji, mastering the fermentation technique was the main problem, which was also associated with transportation facilities. With modernization and the emergence of industrial brewing, the overall quality improved and became certified by technical standards subject to revision. The technical quality based on the brewing process was sufficient in a context of increasing consumption but showed its limits when *sake* consumption began to fall. In the 1980s, with the acceptance of regional names as a reference for quality, two forms of competition took root in the Japanese market of *sake*, one traditional, between brands, and the other between regions and firms.

These forms of competition were related to changes in consumers, on the one hand, who now attached more importance to the origin of *sake* production and the emergence of regions other than the ancient Kinai, on the other hand. All this necessitated a new definition of quality for *sake*, in terms of not only production standards but also geographical origins.

8.3 Limits and challenges of the Geographic Indication system

The actual labelling rules are strict concerning *sake* ingredients and propose a good traceability too, but do not attribute importance to the origin. For example, *sake* can be brewed in Niigata with Hyôgo rice or using a blend of *sake* from other regions. In both cases, the *sake* produced will be called 'Niigata regional sake' if bottled in Niigata, which is absolutely legal but makes no sense, since consumers look for a real regional product.

Legislation concerning *sake* is also problematic because it is very complicated. Since the 1960s, national labelling rules by the Ministry of Taxation and the producers' associations have been inconsistent, and legislation has always been caught between the following two ways. The first way of legislation considers that good *sake* is obtained with heavily polished rice grains, while the second way considers that good *sake* is only obtained with pure fermented rice without including distilled alcohol in the mash. These two schools of thought in legislation, which combine more than ten categories, are very difficult to understand for non-specialists and even for Japanese consumers. They are the result of endless debate concerning the real nature of *sake*, and these debates are still ongoing, probably because of the political influence of big brewers who prefer the possibility of adding additional ingredients in the mash for their ordinary products.

Since the recent success of regional *sake* and the importance accorded by consumers to regional names, some regions are now attempting to protect their success and to protect themselves from the use of their name by defining rules associated with geographic contents. Their advocates include associations of producers and local governments and are creating their own origin labels. Since 2006, one Appellation of Origin, piloted by the Ministry of Taxation, has also occurred.[8]

The first region to have developed a geographically specific label is Niigata in 1997. Its label was called 'Niigata-O-C', with a clear reference to the French's 'Appellation d'Origine Contrôlée'. To be admitted into this label delivered by the Niigata brewers' association, the rice must be grown in Niigata and polished at, at least, 60 per cent. The use of local water and traditional techniques constituted parts of tasting tests. Approximately 50 per cent of the 92 breweries of Niigata participate in this label, which made it the most important in Japan. After Niigata, the Nagano prefecture has developed a product control system in 2002 where rice must be locally produced in the prefecture, and be polished at least 70 per cent. The final product is submitted to tasting tests. In 2004, the Saga and Hokkaido's prefectures came out with similar labels.

The Ishikawa Appellation of Origin called 'Hakusan Kikusake' is the only one who is managed by the Ministry of Taxation. It is, in fact, a trademark that does not involve the entire Ishikawa prefecture but a more specific territory that corresponds to the Hakusan Mountain from where the *sake* water comes. This collective trademark is used by five breweries and applied only to high-class *sake*. However, the appellation allows the use of rice produced outside the Ishikawa prefecture.

As evident from exploring the actual attempts of geographic indication systems, the factors concerning the link between quality and origin are quite different from one to the next. For some of them, rice is the most important part of the challenge, for others, it is only water. The maker's regional tradition seems to be another point, controlled by tasting tests. By considering the appellation scale, except for Hakusan, the reference is mainly the limit of the prefectures.

Despite the notable influence of Southern European legislations about wine on all of these attempts, it is certain that *sake* is, for the identification of producing territories, more complicated, and this explains the difficulty in adapting the French notion of *terroir*. The reason is simply that the nature of *sake*'s raw material is not the same as that for wine: rice can be easily stored and transported and mixing rice from different origins has worked for *sake* for a long time. For wine, on the other hand, grapes must be pressed quickly and close to their harvest areas because their fermentation occurs rapidly. The identification of *sake*'s *terroir* is then very difficult because this reality includes many human factors and cannot be reduced to the physical origin of *sake* ingredients.

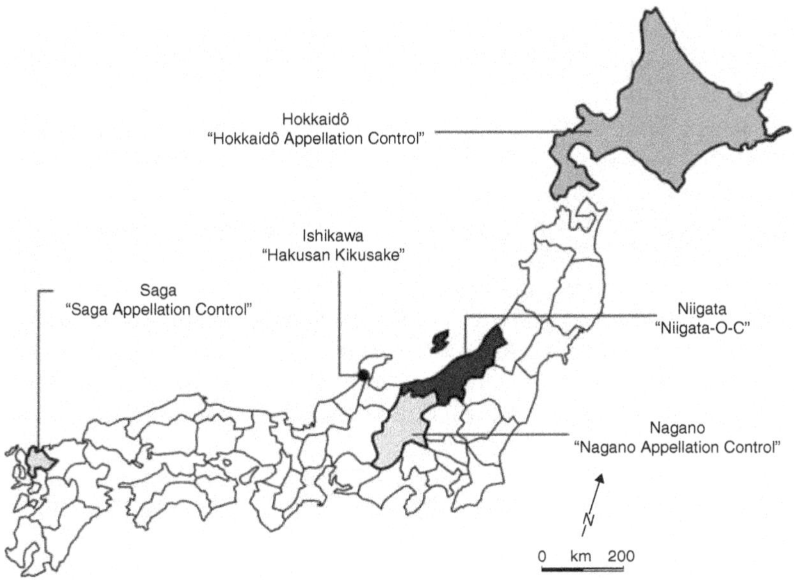

Figure 8.5 Geographical labels and appellations of origin for *sake* in Japan in 2008
Source: Baumert (2009).

In this light, the different geographical labels can be considered since the new territories of the north-west stand a good chance of reversing the standards of quality by developing geographical indications mostly based on physical features. At the opposite end, the ancient territories of Central Japan have not yet developed geographical labels. Their local producing places like Nada or Fushimi are well known and some geographical standards could be created. A choice exists between the two different cultures of *sake* or between the North-West and the Kansai. For the famous firms in the Kansai region, it is unnecessary to promote a region's or locality's name. This will be unproductive at the end because it will dissolve their famous names in a geographical entity, permitting other smaller makers of their region to use their notoriety.

However, actual consumer practices seem to turn in another way and are increasingly concerned with product origins. This is a global trend in Japan that does not occur only for *sake*. For nearly each region of Japan, except Kyûshû and Okinawa, *sake* is a part of culture identity and cuisine. Nowadays, with the *chisanchichô* movement, for example, there is a return to local food consumption, and the quality of regional *sake* for rural regions is very important for territorial marketing and tourism (Oyama, 2006; Sumihara, 2004; Baumert and Fukuda, 2008). As was the case for wine in 1930s France for the creation of the AOC system (Laferté, 2006),[9] changes in the representations of quality and the discourse of the actors involved could change the hierarchy of the regions in the future.

The geographical consequences of the development of *sake* origins can then be analysed as a system connecting the brewers, farmers, and producers of rice in each region. On the national scale, the multiplication of these forms of local development will induce a new form of competition among geographical entities (for example, Niigata, Fushimi, and Nada). Despite Hakusan's label experience in Ishikawa, the problem for *sake* is at present is the lack of a set of easily recognizable national geographical standards that guarantees the intrinsic quality of products. *Sake* of origins is not uniformly managed, the appellations scales are very different, and local initiatives have considerable leverage in deciding how to promote and protect their own products.

Dissent within Japan over the elaboration of quality standards also becomes a problem at the international level. As *sake* is becoming more popular and as it is competing in many international wine challenges, there are now imitations of Japanese *sake* using well-known names that are produced in Taiwan, Southeast Asia, and Korea. These products are also sold on the Japanese market and in other countries. That was the reason for creating the Hakusan's appellation in 2006 as a test to extend the protection to other regions. But for the moment, this initiative is not going further, while in North America and in Europe, although Japanese *sake* is becoming better known by consumers, it is not enough to really make them understand the differences in quality and the importance of origin. Therefore, the development of international sales is not only an opportunity to counter the decrease in national consumption but also an opportunity to redefine the nature and quality of *sake*.

8.4 Conclusion

The recent evolution of *sake* production in different territories shows the emergence of a new entity in North-West Japan around the Niigata Prefecture along the Sea of Japan, which contrasted with an ongoing process since the end of the nineteenth century, which is characterized by the concentration of industrial firms in the Kansai region. Those new territories are rural, their breweries are small, and the discourse about quality is mostly based on geographical elements such as the quality of water or rice instead of production standards. In the future, their importance will probably increase because of their importance in the high-class *sake*'s geography and in response to consumers who increasingly associate quality with geographical origin.

This importance of origin for Japanese consumers appears to be a part of their food identity. By analysing the evolution of the representations of food quality over a long period of time, the link with origin is ancient. In the Antique period, the production place of rice-wines was often written in poems. During the Edo period, the Kinai origin was also a guarantee of quality. In fact, it appears that modernization has induced an exception in these representations which slowly returned when the industrial *sake* showed its limits. Currently, there are three forms of competition for *sake* in Japan: (1) traditional competition among famous brands; (2) competition between brands and territories; and (3) competition among territories.

However, the lack of national management of local initiatives could be problematic in promoting *sake* in international markets. For a long time, Japanese legislation has been viewed as being disconnected from the rest of the world, but the globalization movement has led to changes. For example, the addition of alcohol in the mash at the end of the fermentation process puts, in many countries, *sake* in the category of liquor rather than wine (Jetro, 2003, 2004). In a world where local territories are now in competition with one another, Japanese legislation must adapt to international standards to protect its specific rice-wine, and propose easily recognizable 'made in Japan' products. The development of geographical standards is a part of this challenge.

Notes

1. I am grateful to the Academic Writing Unit of Nagoya University (Mei-Writing) for their invaluable assistance in the preparation of this work.
2. On this point, see general introduction of this volume.
3. The *kôji* mould is made with *Aspergillus oryzae* and rice. *Aspergillus oryzae* (*kôji-kin* in Japanese) is one of the filamentous fungi most widely used in fermentation industries in Japan. It is exploited in the production of *sake*, *miso* (soybean paste), *shoyu* (soy sauce) and other products.
4. Because cereals does not contain the amylase necessary for converting starch to sugar, it must undergo a process in which starch is converted to sugar by *kôji*, and sugar is converted to alcohol by yeast. In *sake* production these two processes take place at the same time rather than in separate steps in beer production, so *sake* is said to be made by 'multiple parallel fermentation'.
5. The importance of the Ministry of Taxation in the management of *sake* is related to the importance of the drink for the public finance at the beginning of the twentieth century. At this period *sake* was representing about 20 per cent of each year's ordinary tax income.
6. According to Yazaki (1968), in the city of Edo, men outnumbered women during all the Edo period. The sex ratio can mainly be explained by the large number of warriors and priests in the city. However, even exclusive of warriors and priests, the city was mainly populated by men. For example, in 1721, the ratio exclusive of warriors and priests was 181/100, it became smaller during the nineteenth century but never less than one to one (ibid., p. 141).
7. Frank (2009) offers a good comparative historical view about the evolution of European, North American and Japanese consumers during the twentieth century.
8. Details about the GI's tries conducted by the NTA, one for *sake* and four for *shôchû* (traditional distilled alcohol of Kyûshû and Okinawa) are available on NTA website: http://www.nta.go.jp/shiraberu/senmonjoho/sake/shiori-gaikyo/shiori/2010/pdf/09.pdf (see pp. 53–4), date accessed 23 September 2011.
9. Laferté (2006) has analyzed the shift from the domination of the wine market by the traders of Beaune to the vineyard owners around Dijon in 1930s France.

References

Aoki, T. (2006) 'Le mouvement anti-alcoolique au Japon de 1880 à 1920', *Ebisu*, 35, 73–95.

Ashton, W.G. (1993) *Nihongi: Chronicles of Japan from the Earliest Times to A.D. 697* (Tôkyô: Charles E. Tuttle Compagny).

Baumert, N. (2006) 'Vin et saké dans la mondialisation', *Ebisu*, 35, 97–109.
Baumert, N. and I. Fukuda (2008) 'Paysages, imaginaires et produits de qualité pour les consommateurs japonais', in V. Moriniaux (ed.), *Nourrir les Hommes* (Nantes: Editions du Temps), pp. 69–80.
Baumert, N. (2009) *Le saké: Géographie historique et culturelle d'une exception japonaise*, PhD dissertation, University of Paris 4 Sorbonne.
Baumert, N. (2011) *Le saké, une exception japonaise* (Rennes: Presses Universitaires de Rennes, collection 'Tables des hommes').
Dion, R. (1959) *Histoire de la vigne et du vin en France des origines au XIXe siècle* (Paris: Flammarion).
Frank, P. (2009) 'Inconspicuous Consumption: Sake, Beer and the Birth of the Consumer in Japan', *Journal of Asian Studies*, 68(1), 135–64.
Garcia-Papet, M.F. (2004) 'Le marché de l'excellence: le classement des grands crus à l'épreuve de la mondialisation', *Genèses*, 56, 72–96.
Hanai, S. (2003) 'Structural Characteristics and Modernization of Alcoholic Beverages Production in Japan and China', in *Japanese Civilization in the Modern World no. 18: Alcoholic Beverages* (Osaka: National Museum of Ethnology), pp. 17–33.
Hurt, P. (2000) 'L'assemblée des brasseurs de saké', *Cipango*, 9, 93–132.
Hinnewinkel, J.C. (2002) *Les Territoires de la vigne et du vin* (Bordeaux: Ferret).
Ishige, N. (2001) *The History and Culture of Japanese Food* (London: Kegan Paul).
Jetro (2003) *Heisei 14 nendo kaigai maketingu jittai chosa hôkoku sho (Foreign Marketing for Sake and Research Report for 2003)* (Tôkyô: Nihon bôeki shinkô kikô).
Jetro (2004) *Nihonshu o yushutsusuru sai no beikoku ryutsu kiseitô no chôsa (Exporting Sake to the United States, Research's Report and Legislation's Problems)* (Tôkyô: Nihon bôeki shinkô kikô).
Jetro (2006) *Beikoku ni okeru nihonshu to shôchû no yushutsu no kanôsei to shijyô dôkô (Exporting Sake and Shôchû to the United States)* (Tôkyô: Nihon bôeki shinkô kikô).
Kamatani, C. (1995) 'Sake brewing and its records in Edo Japan', *Historia Scientiarum*, 5(2), 117–25.
Kondo, H. (1996) *The Book of Sake* (Tôkyô and London: Kodansha International).
Laferté, G. (2006) *La Bourgogne et ses vins* (Paris: Belin).
Larson, J. (2007) *Relevance of Geographical Indications and Designations of Origin for the Sustainable Use of Genetic Resources* (Rome: GFU).
Morris-Suzuki, T. (1995) 'The Great Translation: Traditional and Modern Science in Japan Industrialization', *Historia Scientiarum*, 5(2), 103–16.
National Tax Agency (NTA) (1947–2010) *National Tax Agency Annual Statistics Report* (Tôkyô: Kokuzeichô).
Nourrisson, D. (1990) *Le buveur du XIXe siècle* (Paris: A. Michel).
Oyama, T. (2006) 'Le consommateur japonais face aux produits biologiques', *Ebisu*, 35, 9–29.
Sumihara, N. (2004) 'Tradition as a Solution to the Crisis of Japanese Sake Industry', *Agora*, 2, 27–37.
Yamaguchi, S. (2009) *Nihon no sakagura (Sake Breweries)* (Fukuoka: Kyûshû daigaku shuppankai).

Yazaki, T. (1968) *Social Change and the City in Japan* (New York, San Francisco and Tôkyô: Japan publication inc.)
Yoshida, H. (1997) *Edo no sake (Sake of the Edo Period)* (Tôkyô: Asahi Shinbunsha).
Yunoki, M. (1998) *Shuzô keizaishi no kenkyû (Economical History of Sake Breweries)* (Tôkyô: Yuhikaku).

9

An Export Niche in the Philippines: The Commodification of a Speciality Rice in Ifugao Province

Suyako Sekimoto and Louis Augustin-Jean

The official recognition of a Geographical Indication (GI) is not always the magic wand that guarantees market access. In many instances, GIs only provide local recognition and minor economic benefits. Yet examples in which the implementation of a GI has helped farmers to access national or international markets proliferate. In some cases, especially in the developing world, the implementation of GIs may signify not only increased market access, but, more importantly, a base for the creation of that market (see Chapter 4 of this volume).

This chapter describes the way in which Tinawon rice, a speciality rice from Ifugao province, found its way into international markets, while a few years ago it was only cultivated for local consumption. In order to analyse this process, the authors scrutinized social changes (in the form of the new consciousness of farmers in the economic, cultural, and social values of their product), as well as the links of the territory and its main actors with the overseas world. More precisely, this 'glocalization' has integrated rural places into the world economy and has huge implications for local populations by effecting changes in traditional power relationships (Augustin-Jean, 2010; Fligstein, 2001). In other words, while Tinawon rice is still not a legal GI, the chapter shows the process by which some of its characteristics (not only its material attributes, but also its history and culture, along with the know-how of its people – the major components of a GI), acquire market values and are at the basis of the creation of the market. Consequently, the study of Tinawon rice provides a good opportunity to analyse two related factors: (1) the historical experience of the implementation of the market (Polanyi, 1944); and (2) the commodification process of an agricultural product, which permitted the creation of a market for it (Appadurai, 1988).

Both factors implied the 'requalification' of Tinawon rice – that is, the redefinition of its 'quality' at every level of the value chain, which we will detail in section 9.3.

Until recently, Ifugao was an isolated province in the north of Luzon Island, characterized by a romantic landscape of rice terraces. The main link of its people with the outside economy was through migration. Since the 1960s, many young people have left Ifugao in search of better opportunities in the lowlands. This drift from the land has had a negative impact on the preservation of the environment. The situation changed in 2005 when an American company, Eighth Wonder, became attracted by the specificity of Tinawon rice. While this rice had no economic value for the local people (even though it had important cultural values) at the time, Eighth Wonder gave it a new function as an export commodity – with implications for social organization, local development, and sustainability.

The case study of Ifugao highlights the role of a foreign venture in the integration of a community into the world economy. The arrival of Eighth Wonder in Ifugao led to a series of events in which some members of the community became aware of the potential of GIs. Thus, despite its specificity, Ifugao, along with the positive and negative aspects of the commodification of Tinawon rice, can serve as an example for localities in developing economies to boost markets for their own unique products.

With these considerations in mind, the first part of this chapter focuses on agriculture and describes the commodification process of Tinawon rice. The second part analyses the evolution of the production method and the commodity chain since the start of Eighth Wonder's involvement, while the final part discusses the construction of the quality of Tinawon rice, and also its theoretical and practical consequences. The analysis is primarily based on fieldwork conducted in Ifugao province in 2007 and 2008.[1]

9.1 Tinawon rice and its modification

9.1.1 Ifugao province and rice farming

Ifugao is located in Luzon's Cordillera Administrative Region (CAR). Like the other provinces in the CAR, its population had to overcome geographical handicaps in its farming and has therefore developed stunning elevated rice paddies. Irrigation associations and land systems have been the main determinants of Ifugao's social organization, leading to an equal distribution of water and welfare. In connection with this complex system, a wide range of rituals related to rice farming reaffirms the symbolic solidarity among the community members and serves as a manifestation of the identity of the Ifugaos. In 1995, the rice terraces[2] in the CAR were inscribed in the UNESCO World Heritage list under the category of 'living cultural landscape'.

Historically, the Ifugao people have engaged in rice farming in fields that were passed from generation to generation, especially in the higher areas where the terraces are located. To meet family needs, camote (sweet potato) and yam were also cultivated, as well as hunting or gathering in the forests. Traditionally, because of Ifugao's geographically isolated location, most of its products circulated in a barter system within the province (Kainuma, 2003, p. 118). Since 1960, however, the pace of its integration into a cash-based economy accelerated and more people started to leave their terraces.

During the mid-1960s, the widely known 'Green Revolution' brought to Ifugao a package of agricultural practices, including the adoption of high-yielding varieties of rice, the use of fertilizer, and an expansion of irrigated areas. Nevertheless, in 1973, the Ifugao rice terraces were given recognition by the government as a national landmark for their high cultural value and as one of the country's irreplaceable treasures. Since then, the diversified efforts to ensure the continued existence of the rice terraces have undergone various governance mechanisms, with input coming not only from the government, but also from international organizations and NGOs, which were involved in revitalizing agriculture, especially rice farming. These programmes, however, could not stop the Ifugaos from leaving for the lowlands in search for contract labour in farms located in Nueva Vizcaya and Cagayan or for jobs in mining companies. As a result, the deterioration of the rice paddies became serious.[3] As we will see, the actions of Eighth Wonder might have changed this pattern positively and/or negatively, but before we elaborate on this assertion, it is necessary to provide a background on Tinawon rice.

9.1.2 A brief history of Tinawon rice

9.1.2.1 The characteristics of Tinawon rice

As 'Tinawon' literally means 'once a year' in the Ifugao language, the rice variety called Tinawon rice can be harvested only once a year due to its long growing season. According to Druguet (2009, p. 1), the 'meticulous techniques to select rice, which is harvested panicle per panicle according to multiple criteria of quality (size, shape, colour, aroma), significantly vary from one community to the other and are at the root of the great diversity of species within the generic category of Tinawon.' During her fieldwork, Druguet was able to identify about 30 varieties of Tinawon rice (ibid.). This suggests both a strong specificity of the rice and a great genetic diversity among its different species. Its aromatic characteristic forms a second specificity. Rice experts widely agree that Tinawon rice is the most aromatic variety of rice in Ifugao. Whenever interviewees and locals were asked to identify Tinawon rice, they would always cite its aroma before referring to its other characteristics. Third, according to its farmers, Tinawon rice tends to boast bigger and bolder grains than other rice varieties. This was confirmed by an examination done by Brown, who showed that 100 grains of traditional Ifugao rice weigh 3.5g compared to 2.5g for ordinary Modern Rice Variety (MRV) (Brown, 1987, quoted from Osman, 1990; see also Cappleman, 2006). In addition, its bigger and bolder grain seems to easily give consumers of Ifugaos rice a greater feeling of fulfilment after repeated chewing. Thus, what some Ifugaos often say becomes quite understandable: 'When I eat Tinawon rice, one plate of rice is enough, but if it is California rice or Miracle rice (MRV is often referred by those words in Banaue), I would need to eat more than three plates.'[4] Finally, Tinawon rice has only three to seven panicles, while others have between seven and 12 panicles. Along with its longer growing season, this means that Tinawon rice has fewer yields than most rice.[5] Thus, despite its qualities, rice farmers find it difficult to grow Tinawon rice after they have adopted MRV.

With its distinctive characteristics, Tinawon rice was consumed within Ifugao communities and only on a few occasions was it served as a delicacy to outsiders. Even following the integration of Ifugao into the Philippines' cash-based economy, Tinawon rice was never regarded as a commercial product to be sold to consumers outside Ifugao. In other words, its farmers never assigned a monetary value to their product, but rather took it as a staple with an important cultural dimension. These comments are reinforced by the long history and the specific culture of Tinawon rice.

9.1.2.2 Tinawon rice and its culture

A series of rites[6] involving Tinawon rice show its integration into Ifugao's cultural and religious life. In performing the rice ceremonies, the 'Mumbaki' needs the help of the god of rice to bless, care for, and protect the seeds from natural disturbances such as rodents, calamities, and so on. Nevertheless, the practice of performing rituals is currently diminishing; in the words of a farmer, 'we know what kind of rituals should be conducted at each cultivation phase but we cannot always afford to perform them. Only those who have many rice paddies can afford to do all of them. Few farmers practice those cultural rituals, and the younger generations have even lost the knowledge about them.'[7]

But, as its farmers say, the long history of Tinawon rice has made the Ifugaos feel that it is something different and special, even though the rituals are being gradually beginning to be forgotten. In any case, this loss of identity has been combined with the commodification of Tinawon rice. The next section elaborates on this point.

9.1.3 The new economic importance of Tinawon rice

As shown in the previous section, Tinawon rice is at the centre of Ifugao culture but has never been regarded as a tool for income generation until the launch of the Cordillera Heirloom Rice Project (CHRP), which values Tinawon rice as a speciality food product (SFP).

The official commencement of CHRP was July 2005, when the Revitalize Indigenous Cordilleran Entrepreneurs Inc. (RICE) was established through the registration with the Republic of the Philippines Security and Exchange Commission.[8] RICE, a non-governmental organization, aims to assist interested farmers to either establish or strengthen their own cooperative organizations. It supports sustainable agriculture within their communities in cooperation with government bodies and other NGOs. As a non-profit organization, RICE relies on grants and donations for its operations and has only five local board members and coordinators. As a market arm of RICE for international markets, Eighth Wonder Inc. was established in the US state of Montana. RICE and Eighth Wonder first selected a traditional rice variety from the Cordillera region to be delivered to consumers in speciality food markets in the USA and Canada and gourmet restaurants in the USA.

Initially, CHRP started in five municipalities in Ifugao Province and two from Kalinga in 2005. With support from various actors such as UNESCO, PhiliRice (the Philippine Rice Research Institute), the National Food Authority, and local government units, the project quickly reached 18 municipalities from three provinces: Ifugao, Mountain and Kalinga. As of 2008, a total of 1,358 farmers had become involved in the project.

In Ifugao, CHRP started in Banaue, Kiangan, Hingyon, Hungduan and Mayoyao municipalities and later added two new municipalities (Aguinald and Adipulo) in 2007 plus a third one (Tinoc) in 2009. Although the precise number of farmers participating is not available, the number of participants from Ifugao Province was 219 in 2005, 396 in 2006, and 418 in 2007.

Unlike the ordinary commercial rice that is generally consumed within the country, Tinawon rice is delivered to consumers through specific supply chains (see below). Since the beginning of the project, the per kilo farm-gate price of Tinawon rice has been set at 50 pesos (or one US dollar) by RICE and Eighth Wonder. According to the director of RICE, this rate has been fixed based on various measurements related to the project's costs (such as shipping, packaging, tracking, and so on), as well as to a marketing rate that specifically refers to fair trade prices in the USA.[9]

In the fields, farmers have diverging opinions about this price. One interviewee stressed, 'if I sell one kilo of Tinawon, I can buy two kilos of commercial rice. I can make a plan for the future'.[10] This fixed price seems to give her regular income and a feeling of security, since the payment is guaranteed as long as farmers can produce as requested. On the other hand, most interviewees claimed that 'the rate is too low, especially since everything is getting more expensive'.[11] They also added that 'they [that is, RICE and Eight Wonder Inc.] promised they would increase the price if we could produce more. But they did not.' One officer of the agricultural department in Banaue pointed out that the price setting may become a more serious problem because many farmers are concerned about it.

Participating farmers have benefited from CHRP in various ways. One of them is the opening up of the international market for their product. From self-consumption, Tinawon rice has become a commodity sold internationally and farmers understand its new economic importance. The involvement of RICE and Eighth Wonder has led to the commodification of a local product in the sense indicated by Appadurai (1988). It is interesting to note that the new market for Tinawon rice was first international, not domestic or local (Polanyi, 1944).[12] Differently stated, the establishment of RICE and Eighth Wonder in Ifugao has given monetary value to some cultural (symbolic) and material elements of Tinawon rice, a prerequisite to its commodification. Consequently, the creation of an international market for Tinawon rice have created quality – the specific quality of Tinawon, compared to other fair trade rice, being roughly evaluated as the difference between the price of Tinawon rice minus the price of the fair trade rice (also minus residuals like the difference in packaging, transportation, and so on). There are therefore two problems that remain: (1) the need to understand if local actors value Tinawon rice as much as RICE and Eighth Wonder; and (2) if they think the share they can get from the commodification of Tinawon rice is 'fair'. These questions lead us to describe the production process and the value chain, as well as the social construction of quality of Tinawon rice – the topic of the two remaining sections.

9.2 The evolution of Tinawon rice production

The new economic importance of Tinawon rice for Ifugao has led to changes in the province, as well as consequences for the sustainability of its economic growth.

9.2.1 Changes in social organizations

Under CHRP, existing associations and newly organized groups have had to work together. In Banaue Municipality, as of 2008, most participating farmers came from two newly-created local farmers' associations: the Tukububan Farmers' Association (TFA) and the Bocos Poitan Kinakin Ibayong Farmers' Association (BPKIFA – see Figure 9.1), both of which were already in existence before the launch of the project. The TFA was founded in 2002 to improve and maintain good relations within the community, to preserve good cultural practices that were elaborated on by their forebears, and to help the national government develop the country by maintaining good unity and peaceful living in the years ahead. The TFA was organized by farmers from two barangays.[13] The BPKIFA was created in 2000 by farmers from four barangays and was officially registered in 2003. Actually, if these two farmers' associations already existed in Banaue even before the launch of the project, they did not have a close relationship with each other: they defined their

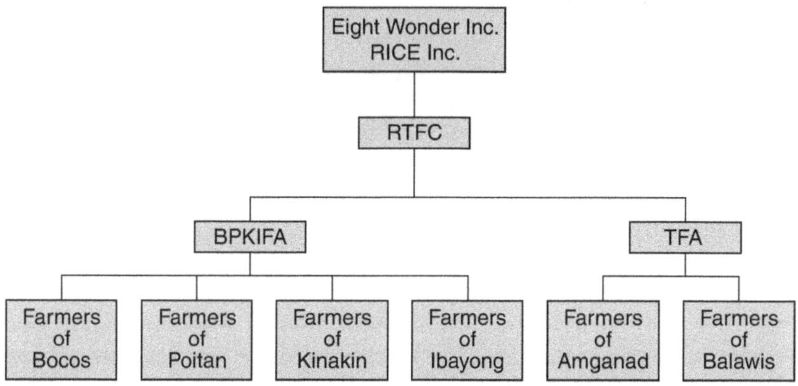

Figure 9.1 Organizations of CHRP members in Banaue, Ifugao

respective goals and programmes within each barangay to cope with the difficulties they faced.

In addition to these existing associations, a farmers' cooperative, the Rice Terraces Farmers' Cooperative (RTFC), was set up for the project in April 2006. Farmers' representatives, who were elected from the barangays or the municipal level units, convened a province-wide meeting in order to form the new cooperative. Government units at both the provincial and municipal levels, especially the Department of Agriculture, showed an interest in the project.

What it is important to understand is that despite their divergences, the TFA and BPKIFA have played an effective role in performing quality control checks by training farmers in organic farming and regularly monitoring their members' rice fields to check for compliance with a no-chemical products rule.[14] Representatives from the TFA and BPKIFA regularly gather at the RICE office and have opportunities to share problems or information regarding the project. This has resulted in closer links between the two associations within the municipality.

The interesting point is that the establishment of a market for Tinawon rice has been accompanied by the development or reinforcement of institutions linking the foreign company, the NGO, the local government, and the farmers. These institutions are necessary, not only for linking farmers to distant markets (the supply chains will be examined in the next section), but for ensuring the definition of and respect for quality (to be determined in the last section) that are necessary for this market to exist. Interestingly enough, the requirements for quality are only marginally set by farmers (contrary to the construction of many European GIs). More often, they are set by demand, which is located in places beyond the reach of the producers. The creation of a market for Tinawon rice, like any kind of market, cannot exist *ex nihilo* by the simple virtue of supply and demand, and without suitable institutions (Fligstein, 2001; Garcia-Parpet, 2007).

Nonetheless, these institutions and the commodification of the rice have created a new consciousness for local actors in relation to the quality and value of their product. At the same time, government action seems necessary, in the short to medium term. It cannot ignore the complex process of building up the quality of Tinawon rice, which lies beyond its reach because of the new awareness of the producers and international influence. As we indicated, the producers are not in control of the build-up of the quality of their product, which also depends on Eighth Wonder and overseas consumers. This path has hit a few bumps. The study of the supply chains illustrates this point.

9.2.2 Diversifying supply chains of Tinawon rice

Generally, commercial rice takes a long path before it reaches Filipino consumers, as shown in Figure 9.2. It changes hands from farmers to trade-millers, agent-assemblers, capitalist-users or the National Food Authority (NFA), and then it passes to large traders-distributors, wholesalers, and retailers before finally reaching consumers. It is often said that middlemen and traders benefit more than producers or consumers, even though rice markets are controlled by the governmental agency, the NFA, which ensures the profitability of rice farming and its availability at affordable prices (Philippines Peasant Institute, 1994). Since joining the WTO and commuting the Agreement on Agriculture, the Philippines has shifted from a position of marginal exporter in rice production to a growing importer. This reflects the increasing gap between production and consumption, as well as a rising dependency on the international rice market to meet food requirements. The Philippines' rice imports[15] increased from 1,000 tons in 1970 to 1.9 million tons in 2005, or approximately 12.6 per cent of domestic production. Despite high tariff rates, the prices of imported rice were substantially lower than those of locally produced rice (at least before 2008). As a result, it became even harder for farmers, especially small-scale ones with less land and/or investments, to sell their rice in favourable conditions, under which they can earn enough to support their families (Intal, Jr. and Garcia, 2005).[16]

Before the implementation of CHRP, most of the Tinawon rice was circulated within the communities, while its supply chain was quite simple (see Figure 9.3). Except for family consumption, Tinawon rice was distributed to individuals as compensation for their labour in

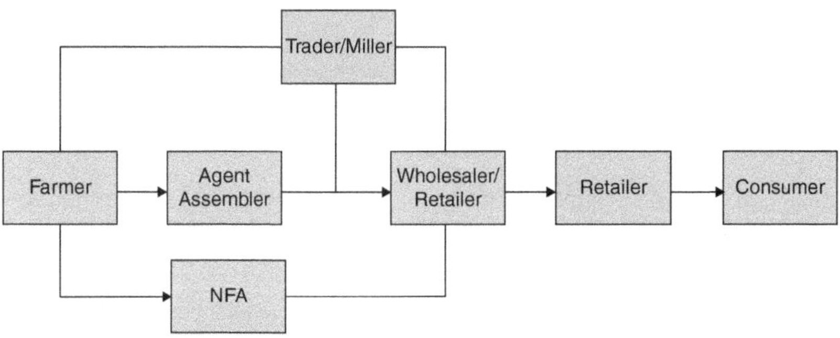

Figure 9.2 Supply chain of commercial rice in the Philippines

the rice paddies. Usually, five bundles[17] of Tinawon rice were allotted for each labour-day in place of cash.

According to Supply Chain B in Figure 9.3, since the start of CHRP in 2005, Tinawon rice has been distributed to other countries, especially the USA and Canada. It has sold for relatively high prices in the United States (US$12.5 per kg in 2009)[18] when compared to those for domestic rice ($1.7) or imported rice from India ($2.8). Despite this price discrepancy, increasing amounts of Tinawon rice have been exported to these two countries: 720kg in 2005, 3,119kg in 2006, and 7,950kg in 2007 were shipped, although the percentage of exports to total Tinawon production remains small (see Table 9.1). In 2009, the export volume increased again to reach 20 tons (up from seven tons the previous year).[19]

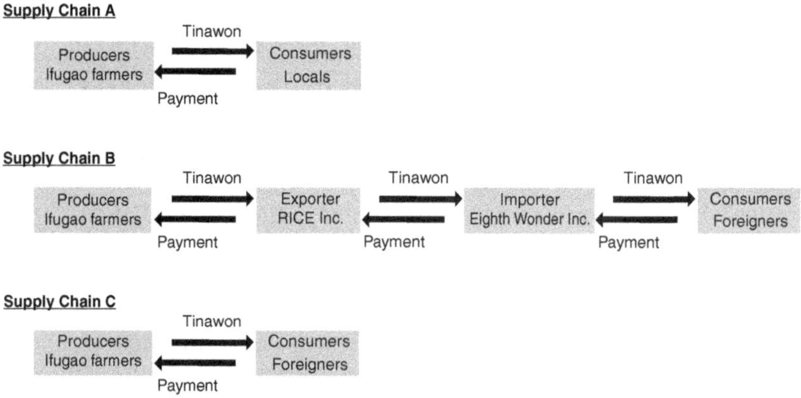

Figure 9.3 Supply chains for Tinawon rice

Table 9.1 Export of commercial Tinawon rice and rice production in Ifugao

Year	Total rice production	Exported Tinawon rice	
	(Metric ton)	(kg)	(%)
2005	49,921	720	0.004
2006	54,653	3,119	0.005
2007	61,047	7,950	0.013

Source: RICE annual reports 2005, 2006, 2007, and BAS.

Finally, the supply chain C, which is currently under development, establishes a direct link between the participating farmers to their consumers ('direct selling'). The farmers are involved in the whole process, from production to marketing. Significantly, they set the retail price for the product, usually from 100 pesos to 150 pesos,[20] and are more aware of Tinawon rice as a commercial product. Some of them seem very motivated to expand their lines of business. For example, unmarketable grains such as broken or chalky grains can be processed into rice snacks or cakes instead of being consumed as daily staple.[21] Supply chain C also shows that members are also interested in linking this project to tourism or agro-tourism where visitors can experience rice planting, harvesting, hand-pounding, and so on. A significant difference between the supply chains B and C is that in supply chain C, farmers can directly see consumers' reactions towards Tinawon rice, which can generate new social relationships between locals and visitors. The office of the RTFC, where Tinawon rice is sold, is decorated with agricultural tools such as knives for harvesting, pounders, and shifting devices that farmers use in their fields. The RTFC has also developed original packages decorated with Ifugao heirloom weaving, which can be bought only by those who visit the office. The closer links between Tinawon and its geographical origin of production may allow consumers to form informed opinions on the desirability of the product on the basis of their own knowledge, experiences, or perceived imageries.[22] In short, a new definition of quality is developed through the interaction between the traditional knowledge and know-how of farmers and the one of their consumers who are often urban dwellers and base their judgements on the information they receive from different sources (Boltanski and Thévenot, 2006; Karpik, 2010). This aspect is elaborated on in the last section of this chapter.

9.3 The construction of quality

In the previous sections, we detailed the commodification of Tinawon rice, together with the creation of its international and domestic markets. This commodification of a good originally not produced for sale implied a quality build-up that involves agents located in different geographical and cultural spheres and generally with no physical or direct contact with each other: consumers in the United States, local actors within the rice-producing community, and, increasingly, urban dwellers in the Philippines. RICE and Eighth Wonder act as middlemen whose main advantage is being able to link these different spheres for a profit (which is an innovation, in the sense of Schumpeter, 1934).

This section explains the elements that enter into the creation of quality and which give value to the rice. But before we develop this point further, a short approach on quality is necessary.[23] According to Dubuisson-Quellier and Neuville (2003) and Karpik (2010), quality is not an objective factor that is fixed. On the contrary, perception of it involves a judgemental standpoint from people, especially when they make the decision to buy (or not buy) a product or service. The judgemental process suggests that everyone can theoretically have a different opinion on the quality of any given good, since this judgement is based on their personal experiences, expectations, levels of knowledge, and so on. But if everybody has a different opinion on quality, it is difficult for exchanges to occur and markets to exist. This position is more fundamental than those of Akerlof (1970) or Arnot and Stiglitz (1988) because it is not limited to an asymmetry of information, but is concerned by the way people make their own judgemental decisions. For example, tradition may be a qualitative factor for European consumers, but not so much for Americans. As a consequence, there is an ontological uncertainty over quality, which can be partly lifted by the existence of focal points or, in the words of Karpik (2010), 'judgement devices'. These devices help consumers, depending on their level of expertise, to make 'reasonable choices' that are similar to the choices of other consumers who rely on similar devices.[24] This is especially the case in the market of 'singularities', which can be defined as goods or services that are multidimensional,[25] incommensurable,[26] and of uncertain quality[27] – a definition that perfectly suits Tinawon rice.

Nevertheless, our purpose is slightly different from that of Karpik, as it intends to check how the actions of RICE and Eighth Wonder make way for the construction of a market by establishing a difficult match between the different judgemental standpoints of American consumers and Ifugao farmers. Under this configuration, ontological uncertainty remains, but RICE and Eighth Wonder are able to use existing 'judgemental devices' (for example, fair trade) or to incorporate other elements into existing devices. For example, their actions will lead to the establishment of a GI that does not yet exist (see below). In doing so, the middlemen are changing the existing perception related to the product, which creates a 'dynamic of quality': the quality of the product is progressively transformed until it reaches a situation of equilibrium that can be sanctioned by an 'ultimate device' such as a code of practice. In the following section, we will examine the actions of RICE/Eighth Wonder in the construction of quality and their consequences for local farmers and urban consumers in the Philippines. Unfortunately, due to fieldwork constraints, it was not possible to analyse the judgemental decisions of American consumers. In other words, the analysis is limited by the lack of understanding of the judgemental process leading to purchase decisions.

9.3.1 At the root of the commodification: Eighth Wonder and RICE

The marketing strategy of Eighth Wonder links the preservation of the terraces to the rice (Druguet, 2009, p. 1). This starts with a brand name, as the terraces are locally said to be the eighth wonder of the world.

> In the words of the company, 'the rugged mountain terrain of Luzon' (...) holds what is known as the 'Eighth Wonder of the World'. Over the centuries, indigenous farmers carved into the steep mountainsides an engineering masterpiece of integrated rice terraces.
>
> These terraces stand in quiet cultures that have received around rice, ecology and relationship with environment. (...)
>
> In 1995, UNESCO designated five of the most spectacular terrace areas as World Heritage sites (...)[28]

By this means, the company aims to sell a 'symbolic quality' that is attached to a 'romantic' landscape of a cultural significance and officially recognized by an independent institution (an international organization). But the 'romantic landscape' may not be enough for the development of an international market. This is why Eighth Wonder also linked the product to other criteria such as history and tradition, which are important elements that enter into the composition of a geographical indication. In addition, the company added an important point to try to make consumers responsible for their own purchases: when people buy Tinawon rice, they not only buy a nutritious and organic variety of rice, as we will see below, but they also participate in the protection of these terraces (which were relisted as endangered world heritage by UNESCO in 2001). In a way, consumers are associated symbolically and materially with the construction of the quality of the rice they buy. They can also go one step beyond that by adopting their own terraces, as indicated in the project's website.

In short, the company surfs between several components that do not change the taste or nutritional qualities of the rice (this is why we use the term, 'symbolic quality', in this article), but creates value for the American consumer: a good and protected environment, history, and tradition that are supposed to support good cultural practices (see below), fair trade (also emphasized in the company's website), social responsibility, and so on.

Of course, a well-identified 'material quality' is also necessary for stimulating one's judgemental decision to buy a product. We saw how RICE and Eighth Wonder have carefully selected varieties of Tinawon rice, based on specific characteristics, including its aroma and uniqueness, but it also had to be organic. The company also claims to respect fair trade rules. If it is impossible to precisely measure the monetary value of each of these characteristics, the symbolic quality captures an important share of the product: while RICE and Eighth Wonder buy the rice at US$1 per kg from the farmers, they sell it at US$12.5 per kg in specialized markets in the USA and Canada. This is not without problems, as will be shown in section 9.3.3. Another important element is that the extra value generated in such a way (as well as the market itself) was not created by the producers, but by the middlemen that are in direct contact with both potential consumers and the producers (similar to the coffee trade, as studied by Daviron and Ponte, 2005).

9.3.2 Filipino urban consumers

This market, developed from agro-tourism, is relatively new and less mature. For this reason, we will devote less time to it. Like American consumers, urban Filipinos are interested in the material qualities of rice (organic, nutritional, and so on). They are also interested in the history, traditions, and beauty of the landscape where the rice is grown. But two dimensions differentiate this case from the previous one. First, the traditions that Filipinos seek are often reconstructed from their own experiences or by the experiences of their ancestors; this is actually a well-known phenomenon that was the subject of deep analysis by Selina Chan (2010) in the context of Taiwan. The second difference lies in the fact that these consumers tend to have direct contact with the producers; not only can they share in some 'countryside experiences' with the practice of cultivating rice, they can also directly exchange views with the producers. In this way, urban dwellers can transmit their beliefs to farmers, who can then modify their views of the world. Of course, their views can also be modified by the actions of Eighth Wonder and RICE, but in this case, the direct contact with their compatriots implies the confrontation of judgements. Here, the way that the beliefs of urban dwellers are constructed (with different devices like newspapers, television, advertising, and so on) matters less than the way that these exchanges give new ideas to farmers about the economic value of their product.

9.3.3 The farmers

The arrival of Eighth Wonder in Ifugao has led to the commodification of Tinawon rice and changed the perception locals have of their product. The creation and extension of the market have imposed changes that were not fully predicted by the company and are the basis of existing problems (a well-known phenomenon of bounded rationality; Simon, 1997). The farmers did not remain passive after the implementation of the project and they quickly understood that the monetary value of their rice comes from two elements: (1) those to which they had already assigned an important place (such as culture and tradition), but not a monetary value; and (2) purely exogenous elements that were 'imported' by Eighth Wonder and urban dwellers. From this dual approach, they started to question the 'fairness' of the price paid to them by Eighth Wonder, even though the company claims to follow fair trade practices. In addition, the strict approach of RICE in order to match international standards (material quality) has led to resentment from some farmers. The last section explores these points.

The most directly observable factors relate to the determination of a quality that matches international standards. Regarding the production phase, the concept of organic farming is widely shared among participating farmers. 'Organic farming' refers to methods in which there is strict compliance with the use of no chemical pesticides or inorganic fertilizer. Fortunately, this did not lead the farmers to completely change their farming methods, which seem, at first glance, sufficient to satisfy international requirements. Mr Menen, the vice chairman of TFA, stressed that, 'We are proud of our farming. We will be happy to have our rice paddies checked whether it is really organic or not.' Hence, there was already a foundation for Ifugao rice farming to enter international markets without big changes.

Nevertheless, the necessary quality controls set up by RICE have had important consequences for the farmers. Contrary to the previous positive reactions from some members, many others have had difficulties meeting the criteria fixed by Eighth Wonder and RICE. One farmer described his experience as such: 'I tried the Tinawon rice project last year but I had only two third of the usual production.'[29] According to a municipal agriculturist,[30] the differences in terms of farming methods among local farmers are not so big, but the availability of acceptable cultivars are different in the higher and lower areas. Rice farmers in the lower zones tend to produce MRV or improved Tinawon varieties compared to farmers located in the higher areas. Therefore, it is more challenging for farmers in the lower areas to partake in a project that accepts only specific cultivars of Tinawon rice because their rice practices are already close to the necessary requirements. In addition, since every community has its own variety of rice, Eighth Wonder's policy has modified the unstable balance between these communities. Similarly, the decision to have only one cooperative has exacerbated the rivalry and jealousy among participating municipalities and barangays (Druguet, 2009, p. 3).

Another problem stems from the fact that the farmers did not expect, since their traditional practices were basically suitable, that any of their rice would be rejected by RICE. The processing created a situation in which some rice was rejected, despite the manual labour and time the farmer expended to grow it. As a result, some farmers became discouraged and stopped producing Tinawon rice for a while to see if the project would continue to succeed. Others left the project and shifted to other rice varieties, claiming that the requirements for Tinawon rice were beyond their capabilities.

In response to these reactions, RICE decided, in 2007, to purchase a milling machine to deal with the painful manual cleaning necessary after the harvest, but preliminary results showed that the new equipment did not resolve the problem entirely. In fact, from the farmers' point of view, the machine hardly alleviated their workload, which still involved a careful cleaning of the rice before processing. RICE refused to acknowledge this fact. On the contrary, it decided to decrease the price of the rice by 20 percent (from 50 to 40 pesos) to compensate for the extra cost of processing (Druguet, 2009, p. 4).

In any case, RICE's rigorous requirements have prompted farmers to understand that material, controllable quality is fundamental if they want to reach their markets effectively. In Banaue, motivated members of the farmers' associations introduced a two-step quality inspection system before the quality inspection by RICE. The first step is conducted at the individual level. Each member is requested to be aware of the kind of grain to be planted and how it should be produced. Second, members carry their products to the association during meetings held at the barangay halls. Then, the rice is examined by local quality inspectors who are nominated as representatives and have undertaken quality control training by RICE. Finally, the rice from each municipality is gathered at the office of RTFC and only products that are accepted through RICE's strict examinations are ready for export.

A final issue concerns the way farmers value their rice. As we have seen in section 9.1, they are proud of their rice culture, the specificity of Tinawon rice, their production methods, and so on. The involvement of Eighth Wonder, be it good or bad, has increased this feeling since they see how much (in every sense of the term) American consumers value their tradition, their work, and the uniqueness of their product. The question, then, is how much this rice, which the farmers believe to be given by the gods, along with its history and tradition can be valued. In some ways, Eighth Wonder answered the question by fixing a buying and a selling price. However, if the traditions belong to the local farmers, they can only get a small share of the pie. Following Druguet (2009, p. 5), it can be stated that while the farmers are now aware of the value of their product, the small share they can get from selling it increases the possibility of opportunistic behaviour. This includes the use of the brand and the American commercial networks to sell the lower-quality rice locally. More positively, it also includes the farmers' search for new networks in Europe that would be under their control (that is, more segments of the value chain – Kaplinsky, 2000).

In other words, the price of Tinawon rice reflects its quality, which is expressed by many material and symbolic criteria. This price also shows the commodification of this product, which gave value to elements of culture and tradition, but also imposed strict quality controls and specific methods of production, which are close to a 'code of practice', but were established by the enterprise (and thus changeable anytime). Then, the question remains: who is entitled to reap the largest share of the profits – Eighth Wonder, which literally created the price value and acts as a middleman, or the farmers? Different parties have different ideas on that question, but the way it will be answered and the compromise that may result may have a huge influence on the future of the project.

9.4 Conclusion

Unexceptionally, the so-called 'Green Revolution' brought Ifugao society repeated agricultural programmes focusing on increasing yield potential and an improved resistance to insects, pests, weeds, draught, cold temperatures, flooding, and so on. Unlike in the lowland areas in the Philippines, those agricultural practices based on the principle of mass production have not been well-adapted by the Ifugaos and did not stop migration out of the province.[31] They also cannot prevent the rice terraces from deteriorating and it is clear that these terraces cannot be preserved as a World Heritage site or for the enjoyment of tourists only.

Under these circumstances, CHRP was launched in 2005. For this project to become sustainable, at least three challenges had to be faced.

First, in the six years since the beginning of the project, it has not reached the point at which the farmers received a fairer share of the profits. They are prevented not only from controlling a greater share of the value chain, but also from accessing information concerning the way their product is perceived at different levels of the commodity chain. It is important for key actors in the chain to better coordinate their activities in order to improve their information flow so that farmers can enjoy a more accurate perception of the trade in their product instead of relying only on partial information provided by RICE and Eighth Wonder.

The second issue is related to the farm-gate price received by the farmers. The rate of 40–50 pesos is higher than the prices for other commercial rice varieties, while the farmers are protected from price fluctuations. However, almost 80 per cent of rice growers are unable to meet household consumption requirements and have to purchase most of their daily staples. The prices of other necessities (including inputs for rice cultivation) have also increased recently. Thus, some adjustments have to be made. If not, the relationship between the farmers and RICE/Eighth Wonder will deteriorate in the future. This is partly because both parties have different perspectives. While RICE makes its arguments based on the technical aspects of the international market, the farmers ask for price adjustments based on the socio-economic conditions they face. More importantly, the farmers now know the value of their rice and don't want to be short-changed on the profits it generates. Unsurprisingly, Eighth Wonder does not provide full information concerning the marginal profits per kilogramme of Tinawon rice, which raises suspicions among the farmers.

The last issue is related to GIs. Through the process of commodification, the link between the product (Tinawon rice) and the geographic origin (Ifugao) has been strengthened. As we have seen, the commodification was based on a specific product of a given material value; this product also bears a history, a tradition, a culture, and know-how. With the arrival of RICE and Eighth Wonder, some of these cultural practices were assembled ('codified' in a way) into what looks like a 'code of practice', but which is under the exclusive control of Eighth Wonder. In other words, if Tinawon rice has all of the characteristics of a geographical indication, beside official recognition, the establishment of a GI needs to associate with the farmers.

This seems like an urgent task, and many local actors are aware of it. In fact, while gaining public recognition Ifugao started to serve as an 'informal' brand name. Not only Tinawon rice but also the province's name, Ifugao, has been targeted by actors who seek business opportunities. The problem is also about the definition of Tinawon rice and its zone of production. The chairman of RTFC showed his concern as follows: 'If someone takes Tinawon rice to somewhere else and grow it, can it still be called Tinawon?' Its quality as a speciality food product was constructed not only from its material quality attributes, but also from various attributes strongly rooted in the geographic origin of production. Tinawon rice has value because it is produced by the Ifugaos in a specific way. Therefore, it can no longer be called Tinawon rice when it is produced in so many other places. In this sense, the protection of GIs may be a way of preventing Ifugao rice farmers from experiencing the undesirable outcomes that have befallen producers of Basmati rice. But given the strategy of Eighth Wonder, which aims to include the beautiful landscape and nature recognized by the UNESCO World Heritage label as an intrinsic part of the quality of Tinawon rice, how would consumers react if the rice were to be produced in another region?

Notes

1. The fieldwork information in this chapter draws on work by Sekimoto (2009).
2. A rice terrace can be defined as a rice field where a series of artificial steps are cut into the hillside, with the soil being retained by stone walls or earth banks. Water is allowed to move by gravity from the upper to the lower terraces (*Dictionary of Geography*, 2003, p. 67). In Northern Luzon, four types of rice terrace can be distinguished: 1) the Lanpunto-Bonton type, 2) the South Kalinga type, 3) the Ifugao type, and 4) the Tinguian type (Keesing, 1962). Anthropological and related studies have determined the origin of those terraces to have been at the time when the first occupants of Ifugao arrived. For lack of arable land, those people were forced to eke out a living from the mountains by terracing rice paddies on the slopes (Dulawan, 2001).
3. *Philippine Star*, 'Possible delisting of Ifugao terraces as world heritage site an empty threat', 13 September 2007.
4. Interview with Ana Habbilings, a leading farmer in Amganad, Banaue, 24 July 2008.
5. Interview with Jimmy Cabigat, the Director of the Department of Agriculture of Banaue, 25 July 2008.
6. The rituals spread during the whole period of rice cultivation. They involve a series of sacrifices of chickens and pigs that supposedly help to have plentiful yields. The sacrifice is performed by the Mumbaki, a priest who live in seclusion and is not allowed to work during the harvest season. Similarly, in that period, he can only eat the rice and chicken gathered for him (based on the interview with Mr Camhit, August 2007).
7. Interview with Malayya Tayaban, a farmer in Amganad, Banaue, 3 August 2008.

8. The SEC was established on 26 October 1936 by virtue of Commonwealth Act No. 83 or the Securities Act. Its major functions include a registration of securities, an analysis of every registered security, an evaluation of the financial condition and operations of applicants for security issue, a screening of applications for a broker's or dealer's license, and the supervision of stock and bond brokers, as well as the stock exchanges. (SEC: http://www.sec.gov.ph/, date accessed 28 January 2008).
9. Interview with the director of RICE, Vicky Garcia, 6 August 2008.
10. Interview with Sally Donque, 4 August 2008.
11. The public transports, on which most of the Ifugao rely, have increased their fares. The jeepney fee from Banaue to Lagawe increased by more than 1.5 times in 2008 compared to 2007. Other prices for food, agricultural inputs, and so on have also increased dramatically in 2008 (see Augustin-Jean, 2008, among many others).
12. For a deeper analysis of food markets as special markets and the seminal contribution of Polanyi in this analysis, see Steiner in this volume.
13. A barangay is the smallest administrative unit in the Philippines.
14. Organic agriculture is based on minimizing external inputs, avoiding the use of synthetic fertilizers and pesticides, and following the guidelines of the FAO/WHO Codex Alimentarius. Organic rice refers to rice grown without inorganic fertilizers and pesticides, but it is a misnomer, as the plants still absorb inorganic nutrients from the soil (Chaudhary et al., 2001; quoted from Juliano, 2003).
15. Thailand and Vietnam have been the country's main trading partners since the 1990s, accounting for at least 60 per cent of the total imports by volume. In recent years, India, Pakistan, and the USA have also been rice exporters to the Philippines. In 2008, during the food price crisis, the Philippines imported 2.34 million tons of rice, which pushed up prices. Since then, the government has announced plans to make the country self-sufficient in rice production by 2013 (*Philippines Star*, 23 May 2011).
16. The percentage of retail prices allocated to farmers fluctuated from the early 1970s to the late 1980s, but declined afterwards. The farm-gate price to retail price ratio was 0.51 from 1973 to 1975, 0.49 from 1989 to 2001, and 0.43 during 2001 to 2003 (Intal, Jr. and Garcia, 2005, p. 9).
17. Normally one bundle of rice is equivalent to one kilogramme.
18. From the website of Eighth Wonder, http://eightwonderheirloorice.foodoro.com/products/tinawon-white-rice-1-lb, date accessed 21 July 2011.
19. See 'Ifugao Tinawon Rice Export Market Opens', *Agribusiness Week*, 8 January 2009, http://agribusinessweek.com/ifugao-tinawon-rice-export-market-opens/, date accessed 21 July 2011.
20. From their marketing experiences in Manila and Baguio during Summer 2008, they started to develop their knowledge of marketing.
21. During the interviews, the farmers showed a deep interest in the rice-processing industry.
22. The study of agro-tourism in Ifugao is not the topic of this article, and thus, will not be elaborated on further. For one study on this topic in an Asian context, see Chan (2010) on Taiwan.
23. For a more theoretical and detailed analysis of quality in economics and sociology, see the chapters by Allaire and Steiner in this volume.

24. These devices are multiform and can be classified into several categories. We will not detail them further in this chapter, but we can give a few examples, such as restaurant's guides, standards and labels, word-to-mouth, and so on.
25. The price of the good cannot be assimilated into the sum of the price of its different elements. Karpik makes the difference between a flat, for which a price can be calculated from the surface, the number of rooms, the parking, garden, location, and so on and a great wine, for which the components of the product are interdependent (Karpik, 2009, pp. 167–8).
26. This refers to the impossibility of comparing goods. For example, it cannot be said once and for all that the music of Wagner is 'better' than the music of Mozart.
27. The quality of the good cannot be known at the time of its purchase. It can, at best, be assessed during the time of consumption (*ibid.*, p. 168).
28. See the website of the project (and of Eighth Wonder), http://www.heirloomrice.com/index.php?p=project&n=terraces, date accessed 15 August 2011.
29. Interview with one of the members of BPKIFA in Ibayong, 31 July 2008.
30. Interview with Emilio H. Abayao, 30 July 2008. He is an agriculturist at the Department of Agriculture of Banaue and a contributor to a comprehensive book on agriculture in the Cordillera region.
31. Mr Camhit, the former Principal of the elementary school in Banaue, described agriculture as follows. 'Agriculture in Ifugao is not attractive. Despite the many benefits that can be derived from this activity, the new and coming up generation do not have interest in going to farm schools. Young Ifugaos tend to go to the schools of education, medicine, technical traders, and engineering. Only a few of them are left to manage the rice paddies. Due to this lack of manpower, production of rice is declining' (Interview, 1 August 2008).

References

Akerlof, G. (1970) 'The Markets for "Lemons": Qualitative Uncertainty and the Market Mechanism', *Quarterly Journal of Economics*, 84, 488–500.

Appadurai, A. (ed.) (1988) *The Social Life of Things: Commodities in Cultural Perspectives* (Cambridge: Cambridge University Press).

Arnot, R. and J. E. Stiglitz (1988) 'Randomization with Asymmetry of Information', Working Paper 2507, NBER.

Augustin-Jean, L. (2008) 'The Food Crisis and the Regional Cooperation in Asia', Conference of Hong Kong Committee for Pacific Economic Cooperation and the Hong Kong Federation of Youth Groups, Hong Kong, 19 December.

Augustin-Jean, L. (2010) 'The "Social Construction of the Market" in a Transitional Economy: The Sugar Industry in China in the Context of Globalization', *Economic Sociology – The European Electronic Newsletter*, 11(3), 33–42.

Boltanski, L. and L. Thévenot (2006) *On Justification: Economies of Worth* (Princeton, NJ: Princeton University Press).

Chan, C. S. (2010) 'Imagining and Consuming Cultures. Nostalgia and Domestic Tourism Development in Taiwan', in L. Augustin-Jean (ed.), Entrepreneurship and Development in Asia, Special Section, *The Canadian Journal of Development Studies*, 31(3–4), 367–80.

Cappleman, L.D. (2006) 'Characterization of Stains of the Traditional Rice Variety "Tinawon" from Amganad, Banaue. Ifugao', unpublished dissertation, University of the Philippines Los Banos.

Chaudhary, R.C., D.V. Tran, and R. Duffy (eds) (2001) *Speciality Rices of the World: Breeding, Production and Marketing* (Enfield, NH: Science Publishers; Rome: Food and Agriculture Organization of the United Nations).

Daviron, B. and S. Ponte (2005) *Coffee Paradox: Global Markets, Commodity Trade and the Elusive Promise of Development* (London: Zed Books).

Druguet, A. (2009) 'La commercialisation du riz Tinawon, Ifugao (Philippines). Vers une Recomposition Sociale et Territoriale?', Localiser les Produits, International Conference, UNESCO, 9–11 June.

Dubuisson-Quellier, S. and J.-P. Neuville (eds) (2003) *Juger pour échanger* (Paris: Maison des Sciences de l'Homme, INRA).

Dulawan, L.S. (2001) *Ifugao Culture and History* (Manila: The National Commission for Culture and the Arts).

Eighth Wonder Inc. – RICE Inc. (no date) *Heirloom Rice from the Philippines: Social Entrepreneurship Beyond Fair Trade*, http://www.heirloomrice.com/index.php?p=project&n=terraces, date accessed 22 August 2011.

Fligstein, N. (2001) *The Architecture of Markets: An Economic Sociology of Twenty-first-century Capitalist Societies* (Princeton, NJ: Princeton University Press).

Garcia-Parpet, M.F. (2007) 'The Social Construction of a Perfect Market: The Strawberry Auction at Fontaines-en-Sologne', in D. MacKenzie, F. Muniesa, and L. Siu (eds), *Do Economist Make Markets? On the Performativity of Economics* (Princeton, NJ: Princeton University Press), pp. 20–53.

Intal, Jr., P.S. and M.C. Garcia (2005) 'Rice and Philippine Politics', Discussion Paper Series No. 2005-13 (Manila: Philippine Institute for Development Studies).

Juliano, B.O. (2003) *Rice Chemistry and Quality* (Manila: Philippine Rice Research Institute).

Kainuma, E. (2003) 'Geographical Study on Regional Differentials of Family Income in the Philippines', unpublished dissertation, University of Tsukuba, Japan.

Kaplinsky, R. (2000) 'Spreading the Gains from Globalization: What Can Be Learned from Value Chain Analysis?', Institute of Development Studies Working Paper No. 110.

Karpik, L. (2009) 'Elements de l'économie des singularités', in P. Steiner and F. Vatin (eds), *Traité de Sociologie Economique* (Paris: Presses Universitaires de France), pp. 165–208.

Karpik, L. (2010) *Valuing the Unique: The Economics of Singularities* (Princeton, NJ: Princeton University Press).

Keesing, F.M. (1962) *The Ethnohistory of Northern Luzon* (Stanford, CA: Stanford University Press).

Osman, A.M. (1990) 'Changing Ifugao Agriculture: Roles of Cultivators and Agro-technologists in Developing Terrace Rice Cultivation in the Philippines', unpublished dissertation, Department of Rural Sociology of Developing Countries, Wageningen Agriculture University, Netherlands.

Philippine Star (2007) 'Possible Delisting of Ifugao Terraces as World Heritage Site an Empty Threat', 13 September.

Philippine Star (2011) 'Philippines to Greatly Cut Rice Imports in 2012', 23 May.

Philippines Peasant Institute (1994) *Rice Marketing in Luzon: The Foodwatch Research* (Quezon City: Philippines Peasant Institute).

Polanyi, K. (1944) *The Great Transformation: The Political and Economic Origins of Our Time* (Boston, MA: Beacon Press).
Schumpeter, J. (1934) *The Theory of Economic Development: An Inquiry into Profits, Capital, Credit, Interest, and the Business Cycle* (Cambridge, MA: Harvard University Press).
Securities and Exchange Commission (Republic of the Philippines) (no date) http://www.sec.gov.ph/, date accessed 28 January 2008.
Sekimoto, S. (2009) 'The Reconstruction of Quality in Regional Specialty Food Production. A Case Study of Tinawon Rice from Ifugao Province, Philippines', unpublished dissertation, University of Tsukuba, Japan.
Simon, H. (1997) *Administrative Behavior: A Study of Decision-making Processes in Administrative Organizations*, 4th edn (New York: The Free Press).
Tenryo, U. (1993) *Dictionary of Geography* (Tokyo: Daimeido).

10

Geographical Indication and Institutional Organization of Food Market in China: A Case Study of Jinhua Ham*

Wang Guihong

Introduction

Many studies show that the characteristics of Geographical Indication (GI) products are a symbol of territory (Casabianca et al., 2005), or wealth and authenticity (Bérard and Marchenay, 1995). The system of GI is an integral part of quality signs and know-how; it indicates both the quality and origin of production in order to provide clues about the warranty, the know-how and special characteristics of the product. The system fits well in periods of economic history in which long-distance trade requires the geographical origin to be identified (Allaire and Daviron, 2006; Sylvander et al., 2007). It also plays an important role in agricultural policy which is a tool for market regulation. It enhances the quality of products (Valceschini and Maze, 2000) and is involved in rural development, the protection of know-how, and even the protection of biodiversity (Sylvander et al., 2005). This is also why this is an important issue in world trade negotiations.

---

*The author gratefully acknowledges from the European Community financial contribution under the Sixth Framework Programme for Research, Technological Development and Demonstration Activities, for the Specific Targeted Research Project SINER-GI SSPE-CT-2005-006522 (coordinated by Bertil Sylvander and Gilles Allaire). The field survey and the sinerg-gi case study on Jinhua ham was conducted with Bertil Sylvander and Frederic Wallet.

The views expressed in this chapter are the sole responsibility of the author and do not necessarily reflect the views of the European Commission. Neither the European Commission nor any person acting on behalf of the Commission is responsible for the use which might be made of the information.

The implementation of GI systems is regulated by several stakeholders who are involved at different levels: state, local authorities, associations of producers, and so on. They are also subject to regulations established by international organizations like the World Trade Organization (WTO). However, all of the regulations on the GI systems vary according to cultures and traditions. Many laws and regulations have been established at national level and also at international level to define the scope of protection. Internationally, the GIs are regulated under the Trade-Related Aspects of Intellectual Property Rights (TRIPS) Agreement, which provides a relatively broad definition which matches with the diversity of designs and can be adapted to national strategies. In this context, GIs are associated with intellectual property rights and the WTO has given a clearer picture of GIs: the quality, reputation or other characteristics of a product can be determined by its origin. Geographical indications are geographical names (or, in some countries, words associated with a location) used to identify products coming from these places and their characteristics.[1]

For this reason, the applications of the GI systems in different social contexts are not always the same: they keep their main characters while adapting to the local environment. Two main options for protecting the geographical indications may be adopted (Sylvander et al., 2007). The first is a protection of GI products by legal means, through laws on trademarks (trademarks, collective marks or certification marks), while the second is a more restrictive *sui generis* system which guards against the direct commercial use of a GI (Dolphins, 2003 and SINER-GI, 2008). In some countries, other administrative measures might be in place for protecting GI products.

From the 1990s, China embarked on the gradual establishment of mechanisms to protect intellectual properties and GIs in preparation for its entry into the WTO. China's accession has forced its government to accelerate reforms and modernize the institutions to respect international rules, particularly in the context of agricultural policy. The main question is to understand how China responds to these international requirements while supporting the emphasis on rural development that appears to be its first priority.

This contribution will study the relationships between the stakeholders of the Jinhua ham industry, in order to analyse the strengths and weaknesses of the application of the GI system in China. The aim of this chapter is to clarify in some ways the organization of the GI system by considering the links between the institutions involved in GI product protection.

In the first part, I detail the institutional framework in the implementation and management of the GI system in China. This framework, while shaped by overlapping economic and political forces, is influential in explaining the social construction of the product; at the same time, it is also justified by this very same social construction. In the second part, I illustrate, with a case study of Jinhua ham, the interactions that occur between the different institutions and attempt to gain some insights into the changes that are needed at the institutional level for a successful implementation of the GI system.

The case of Jinhua ham has been chosen because it is one of the first products selected for GI protection in China. However, the technical and legislative environment has not been quite complete for its implementation, which is also a good reason for this study.[2] In addition, Jinhua is located in Zhejiang province, in south-eastern China, a region that boasts a relatively high level of economic development compared to the average level of the country. This study can show the contributions of GI systems in economic development and preservation of biodiversity. It analyses the impact of the implementation of the GI protection system on the entire Jinhua ham industry and the links created between all the economic and social actors in the production chain of Jinhua ham. It also highlights the role of the institutions in the implementation of this policy and the issues that remain to improve the management system.

10.1 Background and implications of the GI protection system

Quality is not absolute; it is relative and changing. It is closely related to changes in industrial and economic movements in the history of societies (Nicolas and Valceschini, 1995). The minimum criteria of quality that allow consumers to choose consist of a good product (in terms of its taste and appearance), healthy (with its composition and compliance with manufacturing standards) and respectful of the manufacturing traditions and the origin (*terroir* and specifications). This notion is built endogenously through the interplay among economic actors (Sylvander, 1995). In the food production sector, the search for quality has as much influence on agricultural public policy as on the strategies to integrate the market. A consequence is the need for readjusting the forms of institutional governance accordingly.

The defining of a sign of quality grants, in practice, the producers and/or processors of the product a collective competitive advantage in an internationalized market. It is a reflection of a collective will as well as a choice of self-management at the local level in order to influence local development (Pivot, 1998).

The initial character of the GI is in fact a sign of quality that provides direct information to consumers and thus avoids the risk of asymmetric information. 'Quality', '*terroir*' and 'local and traditional knowledge' are the main indices that the sign confers. The concept has gradually evolved over time to include nowadays anti-counterfeiting and anti-fraud regulations and resource conservation.

This system is at once an instrument of public policy (Sylvander et al., 2006) because of the need for government intervention to balance the roles of market players, a means to enhance local knowledge and typicality (Lacroix et al., 2000) and a method of organizing groups of local producers.

The application of GI systems in China is, however, subject to the context of economic transition. The advantages and disadvantages of different modes of application and protection of GIs coexist and are all subject to the influence of the institutional environment. Huchet and Yan (1996) shows that economic reforms in the countries of South-west Asia are framed by government intervention and regulation. Zhang (1997) highlighted the indispensable role of government authority for economic development; he has studied in particular how China uses the power of the state and the regulations as a development strategy to promote its rapid growth. The World Bank report stresses that the state has a major responsibility in building the institutions necessary for the establishment of the market (World Bank, 1993). However, the state cannot be fully instrumental in stimulating development (Boyer, 1999), because the political actions which aim to correct the inequalities generated by the market may in turn generate other sources of inequality through the distribution of privileges and conditions of access to power. Yet in a planned economic system, the dominance of state ownership can take the form of a control of the economic and social activities and the decisions thereof (Andreff, 2005).

There are several variants of GI systems in China. This situation results from the complexity of the institutional structures inherited from the past. The phenomena of the transformation of production systems and forms of coordination consist of institutional hybridization that results from a dynamic and gradual dissemination of conflicting organizational principles (Allaire, 2002). I will study the implications of this through the actions of the different political and economic forces responsible for the organization of the institutions. The objective of this study is to clarify in some way the organization of the GI system in China by designating the institutions as the product of an ongoing social construction in which we see the result of overlapping in political and economic power.

10.2 The institutions for protecting GIs in China

Many Chinese products have acquired a strong identity based on a geographical origin and a good reputation over long periods of marketing, sometimes up to 2,000 years. Producers and traders did not use the brand system marketing but rather some designation. This method of sharing the same name results in creating de facto a true designation of origin, such as Jinhua ham, Qingdao beer, Longkou vermicelli. Before the establishment of a basic protection for origin products, some Chinese companies registered the common names of these traditional products as their own brand, which undermined the interests of the traditional producers and the consumers and destroyed the balance of the competition.

Economic reforms began in China during the 1980s and continued through the efforts to ensure the compliance of Chinese law to international rules during its period of candidacy for the WTO. In the period since China joined the WTO in 2001, the government has stepped up the reforms in the implementation of a GI protection system, demonstrating its intention to answer the demands of the WTO and to respect intellectual property rights. The right of property is an effective tool for economic development and is also a way to protect and develop the agricultural economy; in that sense and considering the richness of the Chinese agricultural heritage, the use of the Geographical Indications as a part of intellectual properties, could play an important role in rural development in China. The Chinese state has implemented some new laws and regulations that correspond to the international standards and has amended its legislation on intellectual property in order to comply with TRIPS.

Compared with the GI protection systems adopted by other members of the WTO, China has opted for an original solution which allows for the coexistence of different models of recognition and protection. Currently, there are three main systems of GI protection in China. The first one is under the supervision of the State Administration for Industry and Commerce (SAIC) and is regulated by the specific trademark law. The second is a special protection handled by the General Administration of Quality Supervision Inspection and Quarantine (AQSIQ). Finally, the third system has been established by the Ministry of Agriculture (MOA) since 2008 and is more raw agricultural products oriented.

10.2.1 GI protection system by the trademark law enforced by SAIC

SAIC is responsible for market supervision and regulation, and protecting the legitimate rights and interests of business and consumers by carrying out regulations in the fields of enterprise registration, competition, consumer protection, trademark protection and combating economic illegalities.

The Trademark Law in China was first passed on 23 August 1982 and was subsequently amended in 2003.[3] It prohibits the registration of a geographical name as a usual trademark since 1983. Yet many of the known '*terroir*' products (such as Jinhua ham and Qingdao beer) were still registered as trademarks. At that time, China had not yet established a clear definition of the Geographical Indications based on the property rights, resulting in some dissensions directly related to this point. This is exactly the case for Jinhua ham (SINER-GI, 2008).

It was only in 1986 when a desire to protect the Geographical Indications products emerged. In one of its publication, the SAIC notes the contradiction in protecting the name of a district as a private mark. The concept of geographical indications has not yet been defined clearly, but the document refers to three specific points that correspond to the main characteristics of GI products:

- GIs have all of the characteristics of brands.
- The GIs are a part of public property, and may not be registered as a trademark by a company or individual, as this would affect the rights of others.
- GIs can be considered protected by law.

Article 16 of the Trademark Law specifies the subject and gives the definition of Geographical Indication: 'The geographic indications mentioned in the preceding paragraph refer to the signs that signify the place of origin of the goods in respect of which the signs are used, their specific quality, reputation or other features as mainly decided by the natural or cultural factors of the regions.'[4]

Under this law, GI products are registered as a certification mark. The definition of the geographical signs by the Trademark Law is consistent with the definition of the GI as given in the TRIPS Agreement.

10.2.2 GI protection system enforced by AQSIQ

The AQSIQ office is a ministerial administration office directly under the State Council of the People's Republic of China. It functions as a law enforcement agency and owns many administrative roles. It is in charge of national quality, import/export, health quarantine, food safety of import/export goods, and certification, standardization, and so on.

Once China had opened its market at the beginning of the 1990s, the country saw the appearance of fake products and the misuse of appellations. It was mainly traditional products that were targeted. In addition, people barely knew the concept of intellectual property. To protect the interests of economic actors and regulate the order of the market, AQSIQ has reinforced exchanges since 1994 with foreign countries like France that have substantial experience in protecting traditional products.

In 1999, AQSIQ enforced a system of designation of origin to protect the know-how and interests of all stakeholders and to promote rural development in China. In June 2005, AQSIQ published a new decree entitled 'The Rule of the Protection of Geographical Indication Products' (Decree No. 78) to further harmonize its content with other laws in force in China. Moreover, in Article 2 of this Decree, it gives for the first time its own definition of GIs:

> GIs are special products that come from specific areas. Their quality, reputation and characteristics depend on the human and natural factors. GI products are cultivated or animal products which are manufactured in the region with traditional methods and raw materials originating fully or partially from the region.

The decree has dramatically improved the system's efficiency compared to 1999. It is more focused on the control of product quality and fighting against counterfeiting, and the standards of GI products should now reach international standards. For each product, precise specifications have been set up that are more detailed than in the past and are linked to the economic needs of the country.

This definition of GI products is different from that of the Trademark Law administered by the SAIC. This definition, based on the TRIPS Agreement, resembles some aspects of the European Regulation on protected Geographical Indications. It has even promoted the rapprochement between the authorities responsible for the protection of origin products in Europe and China.

10.2.3 A new system for GI protection enforced by MOA

The third system for protecting GI products has been promulgated by the MOA in 2008 by means of an administrative measure, 'Measure of Management in Agricultural Products of Geographical Indication'. This system is oriented towards the protection of raw materials on the basis of the Law on Agricultural Product Quality Farming and the Law of the Ministry of Agriculture. The entire registration process is managed by the Centre for Quality and Safety of Agricultural Products in MOA.

Based on its experience on organic products and green food products, the MOA planned to develop a system capable of promoting the environmental protection, the production methods and the quality of the raw farming materials. The MOA emphasizes aspects similar to

Table 10.1 The three types of legal systems for protecting the traditional and origin-linked food products in China

	AQSIQ	SAIC	MOA
GI Definition	Grown products, livestock and aquatic products come from the defined area. The raw materials are originated entirely or partially within this defined zone, and then processed in this area to comply with the specifications.	A GI product is from a specific region with its quality reputation and other features that are determined by natural or cultural elements of the region	GI agricultural products are named after a geographical area indicating that it is produced within that area and their quality and characteristics are depended on natural, historical and cultural factors
Level of Protection	Decree No. 78, based on the "Product Quality Law" and "Standardization Law"	Trademark Law, regulations and measures. The GI protection is made compatible with TRIPS.	Administrative measures which came into effect on 1 Feb 2008
Type of Protection	Specifically for GI products	GIs can be registered by SAIC/CTMO as a certification mark or a collective mark.	Specifically for raw agricultural products
GI systems logos			

Source: Wang (2009).

those of European GI products, intending to meet the expectations of the sustainable development of rural areas.

The following sections will explore in a more concrete way how the GI protection systems as defined by the AQSIQ and the SAIC are implemented and demonstrate from the case study of Jinhua ham the strengths and weaknesses of each of them in turn.

10.3 The differences in the protection systems of Jinhua ham between standard products and GI products

Like many GI products in China, Jinhua ham is protected by both the GI system set up by the AQSIQ and also the system of protection for origin products introduced by the SAIC. This is the result of nearly 20 years of legal battles over the ownership of the appellation 'Jinhua Ham' between a public company at the provincial level and the association of local ham producers in the region of Jinhua supported by local authorities. This conflict has become quite symbolic, illustrating as it does the types of disputes that may arise between trademarks and geographical indications, and highlights the contributions of GI systems in resolving such conflicts.

Although producers have now more choices in protecting their interests, most of them have opted for a dual registration with the AQSIQ and SAIC to ensure maximum coverage. It is also a simpler and more efficient way to find business opportunities for their products. This is not just the case for Jinhua ham, but also for other types of GI products.

10.3.1 History and reputation of Jinhua ham

The tradition of making Jinhua ham goes back almost 1,200 years. In 1915, Jinhua ham won the gold medal at the Panama International Exposition in San Francisco. Jinhua ham is a traditional regular dish for the local people, but is also considered a symbol of cultural heritage. Since 2008, it has been registered and protected as an intangible cultural heritage by the Chinese state.

Jinhua ham is served in daily meals or as an essential ingredient in some fine cuisine in China. The local population has also discovered its therapeutic value, for instance, for the frail elderly and women after childbirth (Gong, 1987). Indeed, scientific analyses have revealed a good variety and substantial amount of amino acids in Jinhua ham – with levels as much as thirty times as high as in fresh pork. Because of its reputation, it is renowned in Japan and throughout Southeast Asia.

During the preparation phase and owing to its traditional production method, Jinhua ham is shaped like a bamboo shoot or a Chinese lute. It is hard and dense and thus different from traditional western hams that are tender and sophisticated and often served raw in thin slices. Such a difference in the traditions may explain why the reputation of Jinhua ham prevails only in the neighbouring Asian countries.[5]

Since the 1970s, the Chinese government has encouraged farmers to adapt to the new market conditions and invest in modern technology to cope with strong competition and reduce the risks. This period has been remarkable, and, in 1979, at the beginning of the economic reforms, the market became open, which allowed companies with private investment, not necessarily from the local region, to enter the scene. Consequently, the number of new producers has increased rapidly over time, but the local element of the product has been compromised.

10.3.2 The registration as a standard mark – 'Jinhua Ham' – at SAIC since 1979

The registration of the 'Jinhua Ham' standard trademark reflects the historical change at the beginning of the economic transition and reforms. In the early 1980s, Zhejiang Food Co. was a public company in charge of every agrofood company in the province. A local company, Pujiang Food, was the owner of the trademark 'Jinhua Ham' registered at the SAIC in 1979. At the time, there was no restriction in using a geographical name as a trademark. In 1984, following the economic reforms, Zhejiang Food Co. decentralized some of its operations but it retained the ownership of the trademark. It is this particular context of economic transition and reforms in the agricultural system that is the origin of the conflict between local Jinhua ham producers and the Zhejiang Food Co. Ltd.

The Zhejiang Food Co. did not produce the ham directly; instead it delegated the production to some hundreds of enterprises. These enterprises were not necessarily located in the traditional production area and did not have to adhere to any particular constraints on the origin of the raw materials (see Table 10.2). They were only required to pay a fee for using the designation, according to the trademark laws, which applied also to those producers located in the historical Jinhua ham production area. The local producers argued that the Zhejiang Food Co. had misled the consumers about the origin of its products and caused significant damage to the quality and reputation of Jinhua ham. They therefore sought ways to protect and enforce their know-how and traditions. This initiated a long period of conflicts between the local producers and Zhejiang Food Co.

Table 10.2 Comparison of the characteristics between the three systems of the protection of Jinhua ham – specific protection GI, GI certified brand and generic brand

Control organization	'Jinhua Ham GI' committee with the producers professional association	'Jinhua Ham of Jinhua City' committee with the producers professional association	SAIC and AQSIQ
Duration of validity of protection	Unlimited	10 years, to be allowed to use the designation, companies must apply for renewal each year	10 years, renewable at SAIC
Specifications	National Norm (GB19088-2008)	None (based on the Trademark Law), but the committee verifies the quality of the product before granting the right to use the certification mark	None, National Standard of China Ham (SB / T 10004-92) Business Standard (Q / ZS 001-2004)
Protection area	Jinhua and Quzhou	Jinhua	No geographical limit
Origin of raw material	Jinhua Pigs and Hybrid Jinhua Pigs	No restriction	No restriction
Production season	Winter	Winter	Year long
Market outlets	Supermarkets, hotels and restaurants; exported to other Asian countries	Supermarkets, hotels and restaurants; exported to other Asian countries	Supermarkets; exported to Southeast Asia
Numbers of producers	30 enterprises are allowed to produce in 2009[1]	39 enterprises are allowed to produce in 2009[2]	Several hundreds of enterprises

Notes:
[1] http://www.jhbts.gov.cn/bulinfo.jsp?id=38, dated access 5 December 2009.
[2] http://www.jhhtzmsb.com/ShowArt.aspx?News_ID=193, dated access 5 December 2009.
Source: Wang (2009).

10.3.3 A specific GI protection by AQSIQ – 'Jinhua Ham GI' – since 2002

The benefits and protection provided by the AQSIQ system correspond to the demands of the local producers of Jinhua ham who wished to provide for the consumers a distinctive sign for differentiating their products from those of the registered trademark 'Jinhua Ham'. Local producers hoped to demonstrate a qualitative advantage and the local origin of their products compared with the generic ham made from products that might originate from outside the Jinhua region.

In 2001, the professional association of Jinhua ham producers launched the application process at AQSIQ for its registration as a GI product, in the hope of protecting their interests. The local government of Jinhua had liaised with the local AQSIQ and SAIC, the local MOA office and the producers to create a Management Committee Office for the GI Jinhua Ham. The following year, the Jinhua ham producers obtained from the AQSIQ the GI protection. Based on their production criteria, 15 cities and districts around Jinhua and Quzhou have been included in the area of protection of the product. In 2009, 30 companies were authorized by AQSIQ to use the GI 'Jinhua Ham' and the GI logo (Wang, 2009).

With this official recognition as a GI product, the producers of Jinhua ham legitimately believed that they could use the designation of origin for their products. But two distinctions continued to coexist for the same product: the brand 'Jinhua Ham' registered at the SAIC and the 'Jinhua Ham – GI' which was managed by the AQSIQ. In 2003, Zhejiang Food Co. Ltd. filed a lawsuit against the local businesses for counterfeiting and usurpation of the name 'Jinhua Ham'. The dispute over the legality of retaining the appellation had continued for years before the City Council and Zhejiang Food Co. Ltd. began to open discussions with SAIC, in the hope of finding a solution.

10.3.4 The registration as a certification mark – 'Jinhua ham from Jinhua City' – at SAIC since 2008

The SAIC implemented the system of designation of origin in 1994; origin-based quality products may be protected as a certification mark.

While the company, Zhejiang Food Co. Ltd, officially held the trademark 'Jinhua Ham', Jinhua City Council had liaised with SAIC, AQSIQ, MOA and the local producers' association to establish a special committee in 2003 to register the Jinhua Ham GI as a certification mark at SAIC under the name 'Jinhua Ham of Jinhua City', in order to distinguish it from the standard brand 'Jinhua Ham'. In 2008, the Central Office of

SAIC registered 'Jinhua Ham of Jinhua City' as a certification mark and Zhejiang Food Co. had officially declined to appeal the decision. In 2009, 39 companies had obtained from SAIC the permission to use the certification mark (Wang, 2009).

10.4 The specification for the two systems of GI products protection

Measuring quality is not easy, as the definitions and representations of quality among actors strongly differ (Nefussi and Philippot, 1995) and because qualities are formulated by multiple dimensions and complex quality profiles.

Every GI protection system has a standard set of norms that define the criteria for production and protection, that is common rules of production to which producers should adhere strictly, in order to obtain and preserve the right to use the name and logo.

In the case of Jinhua ham, quality criteria are based mainly on the experience of subject matter experts who are very often professionals. For the experts, the most difficult to measure is the scent of ham, and this will depend on the experience they have earned over the years.

When one compares the production specifications between the certification marks 'Jinhua Ham of Jinhua City' and 'Jinhua Ham GI', it seems that the criteria in AQSIQ are more stringent.

According to the tradition and in order to give the consumers a clear indication, the new standard 'Jinhua Ham' (GB/T/19088-2008) emphasizes that the pig's legs used as the raw material of the GI product must come specifically from the 'Jinhua Pig' race or hybrid races. This ensures the traditional product quality and respects the interests of the consumers along with the whole production chain. It clearly defines the area of production and the manufacturing conditions (climate, season of production, and so on), the criteria for selecting the raw materials (such as race and weight) and provides some technical parameters such as the percentage of fat on fresh legs, the weight, the humidity, and additives such as salt and oil. It details the preparation process, dividing it into several stages and specifying their duration.

In the system as implemented at SAIC, there is no real 'code of practice' or common rules of production; the production process must follow the National Standard of China Ham (SB / T 10004-92) and there is a control on the final quality, evaluated by experts. To be allowed to use the certification mark, a producer must apply to the committee.

10.5 The stakeholders of the Jinhua ham supply chain and the market

The implementation of the Jinhua ham Geographical Indications systems is regulated by various stakeholders involved in the market. Each one plays its own role in the application of the GI system.

10.5.1 Farmers and breeders

Because of the lack of financial resources and the level of social development, the existence of small farmers, especially in family units, is still prevalent today in the rural areas in China. In Jinhua and some parts of Quzhou, the rural population has the tradition of raising the Jinhua pig to increase their income. Although the economy of Zhejiang is more developed than elsewhere in China, many farmers from the mountainous areas still live on an income below CNY2000 per year (€200), most of them depending on livestock and poultry as their main sources of income.

Very little information about the farmers has been collected in the field, in particular in respect of small farmers who live in remote areas with limited means of transport and a low level of practice in new technology. Even though the keeping of livestock might increase their income, it appears they have limited possibilities to do so.

The advantages of small units are a greater ease and flexibility in adapting to market circumstances, but these small farms are also more susceptible to be influenced by changes in the market structure.

With the economic reforms, people are increasingly aware of new opportunities to make profits. The livestock breeding is better organized. At the industrial stage, some farmers have diversified into producers of animal products while others continue in the classic way – keeping breeding as a sideline activity.

According to the data of the Livestock and Veterinary Bureau in Jinhua, in 2009 some 3,738,200 pigs were raised. The pig farming industry in the region of Jinhua applies a model which includes some larger-size industrial units. In this region, 510 of the farms have more than 500 pigs each; and, of these, 22 house more than 10,000 pigs. There is a strong tendency to move from a traditional farming model to modern methods which are more centralized and on a larger scale. Small farming households and small enterprises are now leaving the business because of the strong competition from larger companies. Despite this trend, the lack of capacity in managing market risks still exists in the new organization.

Establishing a brand is one main solution for large barns to boost their market share and create a company image. Large piggeries cooperate with small farmers and breeders to reduce the risks and enhance their competitiveness. They also create some links with the processors in order to produce a range of different products. These interest networks allow producers to avoid fluctuations in the prices of fodder and meat.

The environmental and sustainable development of the livestock sector is increasingly discussed in the state policy and reinforced by the policies of local governments; this is now an inevitable trend. The farmers have received financial support to invest in technology to recycle the animal wastes and implement a prevention mechanism against animal epidemics. The government also encourages the cooperation between the livestock sector and other sectors[6] (crop, forest, fisheries, and so on) on environmental protection and sustainable development and on furthering the social and economic development.

10.5.2 The ham producers

Even though both GI systems coexist in the Jinhua area, the methods of production remain the same. The main difference is in terms of the breeds of pig selected as raw materials. When they have the appropriate raw material, companies may proceed with the type of production as demanded by the market; thus, many companies might produce at the same time some 'Jinhua ham GI' and some 'Jinhua Ham of Jinhua City' certified mark.[7]

Producers organized themselves to create the 'Jinhua Ham Producers Professional Association' and assist in implementing the new systems. The members of this association consist of producers of Jinhua ham and advisors from public offices, such as the local AQSIQ, SAIC and MOA offices, and the Public Health Office whose role is to explain the policies and regulations. The purpose of this association is to enable the greater participation of producers in creating alliances and to keep in touch with the administration. The primary functions of the association are to establish the norms concerning the Jinhua ham, facilitate the exchange of technical information, promote the products, and organize product quality contests. Moreover, this association acts as a bridge between the government and the producers in conveying opinions and grievances, and facilitating the implementation of new regulations. It acts directly on the market by participating in anti-counterfeiting control operations and provides legal information to their members.

10.5.3 The strong consumer demand

Since the introduction of economic reforms, there have been dramatic changes in the consumption pattern. Those Chinese people who used to be on a vegetable-based diet are now consuming increasing quantities of meat. The trend of demand for meat products has increased rapidly in recent years. Traditionally prepared meats, such as salted, pickled or smoked ones, are becoming distributed widely on the tables of Chinese consumers.

Today, Jinhua ham is traded in the country by many large retailers. It is relatively expensive compared with other Chinese traditional hams, but it is a niche product and has a great reputation. The average price of a Jinhua ham GI is around 500–600 RMB, whereas a standard ham is priced at 200–300 RMB. This large gap in prices has attracted more and more investment into the livestock and production sectors.

Despite its relatively high price, the demand for Jinhua ham is growing rapidly and consumers are willing to accept to pay a premium for such products. Companies have also developed new product lines on the basis of Jinhua pigs and created new delicatessens to adapt to the new ways of consumption of the urban population. The population of the region uses Jinhua ham as an ingredient in traditional dishes, and in large restaurants and hotels, it has become an essential ingredient in fine cuisine. Some companies are targeting in particular on customers with substantial purchasing power. They have opened shops in Hangzhou, the capital city of Zhejiang province, that are dedicated entirely to products made from Jinhua pigs. Some companies have also set up shops in the Pearl River Delta region in southern China in cities like Guangzhou, Hong Kong and Macau, and even in various parts of Southeast Asia which offers good potential for market development.

One of the main difficulties for consumers of Jinhua ham is to ensure the quality of the product. In this sense, the proliferation of signs, labels and trademarks which were purposed originally to enable a distinction of qualities has become a real source of confusion. In this sense, not only the producers, but also the state must play a more specific role in regulating the marketing for these products and educating consumers to better understand and appreciate their characteristics.

10.6 General summary: lessons regarding the overall functioning of the GI system in China

Stoker (1998) has shown that in a modern society, the state transfers its responsibilities to social actors. Private services and groups gain as much importance and roles as a public service. There is interdependence in the power between these structures. They must establish reciprocal links in order to achieve the most effective results possible.

10.6.1 Insights from both GI protection systems

Through our analysis of the case of Jinhua ham, we find that different applications of the GI protection systems have similar and specific features. To be registered as a Geographical Indication in China at SAIC, it is stipulated by the law that the product cannot be registered as a trademark, but rather as a collective mark or a certification mark.

Although the preliminary registration of certification marks may be found, for example, in the American system, it is worth noting the similarity of the procedures and principles of the SAIC with those of the European Union. For example, the SAIC procedures prevent the use and sale of the certification mark outside the designated geographical area of the GI. This point contradicts the logic of certification trademarks, but is in accordance with the regulations in force within the European Union.

This example shows that the originality of the Chinese system of the protection of quality in regard to origin is not only the coexistence of several modes of recognition based on different principles of intellectual property, but also a process of institutional 'hybridization', based on the combination of diverse principles and procedures (Gilly and Wallet, 2005).

AQSIQ has expanded its role in the implementation of its own system: their priorities are now how to increase the value added and how to use this system to promote rural development. Its GI protection system is no longer only a legal protection, but it also enhances product quality by supporting the research and development in technology. AQSIQ also helps producers develop new market opportunities. Thus, at the local level, its role now surpasses its original objective of facilitating the implementation of the GI system. For example, the Shanxi Province has promulgated regulations for the management of GI products. More and more, local governments are taking the lead in the management of the GI system.

AQSIQ protects GIs according to Decree No. 78, while SAIC is using the Trademark Law to manage GI products. The use of the Trademarks Act and its complementary rules allowed SAIC to obtain some results in the protection of know-how and rural development in China, and the number of registered products is growing rapidly. As at the end of March 2009, 496 products were registered with the SAIC, 465 of which were Chinese products and 31 foreign products. The categories of these products are relatively varied: 90 per cent come from the agro-food sector, but they also include the Yixing potteries (Jiangsu Province), the woodcarvings of Dongyang (Zhejiang Province), and plants such as the Nanjing orchid (Fujian province) that are registered as GIs; as traditional Chinese medicines have a lot of influence in the country, they account for nearly 4 per cent of the products that are registered. Other typical products, including Songyang tobacco (Zhejiang province) and Nanjing tissue (stifles) (Jiangsu province), are also protected under the SAIC system.

10.6.2 Industrial management and strategic orientation of the industry

Business management and development strategies are crucial for the vitality of enterprises. Although they have achieved economic success in the short term with the economic reforms, most companies still use a traditional method of management.

Companies that have more resources put more emphasis on scientific research and modern management methods to create new product lines in order to ensure sustainable development. This trend is becoming stronger.

Food quality issues in China are overseen by a dozen of administrative offices; for a health-related issue, it might involve the AQSIQ, SAIC, the Bureau of Agriculture, the Bureau of Customs, Office of Trade, Administration for Food and Drugs, and so on. As a consequence, we notice that for some of the tasks, the management is covered a number of different administrations, while for other tasks the demarcation is unclear. Also, one major problem that persists is the inaccuracy in the statistics and sources and the lack of management of the food products databases.

Many products with an indication of origin are registered as GIs, but most of them are located in underdeveloped areas. They are produced using obsolete methods and the producers receive no real support from any administrative level of the government. As a result, the low level of production remains. Administrative offices at a local level have little awareness of the importance and value of GI products. The lack of communication between the different administrations often creates gaps in the management, which causes quality problems and unfair competition.

The state has spent personnel and financial resources to reform the market and fight against unfair competition through the implementation of policies, laws and regulations. However, the lack of involvement of the professional organizations has a direct influence on the results. These associations are often important in a GI system, as they act as an intermediary between the institutions and the producers, but, in most cases, they do not have sufficient financial and administrative autonomy to become more involved in managing the production and the quality control of products. More time will be needed to allow for changes in the management capabilities across sectors.

10.7 Conclusion

GIs are a sign of quality, a sign of product origin and an intellectual property. Yet governments, agencies and producers have only a partial understanding of this (Feng et al., 2007). Training sessions on GI products management should be promoted among stakeholders.

Consumers have lost confidence in product quality and do not trust the value of the GI logo. They do not have enough knowledge about the value of the GIs, mainly because they are distracted by the number of quality signs that are attributed (such as organic products, green products, no-examination product, and 'safety label'). Before they can learn about product quality through GIs, it is necessary to instil their confidence through balanced information.

GIs have the potential to be a useful tool for the Chinese authorities to accelerate the increase of incomes in some rural areas. Given the situation in China, the point is to understand how the different systems can be used jointly while at the same time avoiding duplication and administrative conflicts. The example of Jinhua ham shows that this equation is difficult to solve.

The state must change the institutional arrangements that rule the market and develop more efficient instruments to control and invest in ways that will encourage all stakeholders (consumers, producers, distributors, decentralized authorities, administrative offices, and so on) to adopt behaviours and regulations to address the issues of GIs.

The different rules established by the agencies (SAIC and AQSIQ) are now well developed after several years of improvement. It is not necessarily a problem that there are two GI protection systems in China, both systems considering GIs as common heritage and tradition. Each administration has its own prerogatives: the SAIC is dedicated to market regulation, while the AQSIQ is oriented towards quality and food safety. But it is necessary to improve the collaboration between both institutions to clarify and ease the registration process for the producers, and give clear identification signs to consumers.

The priority of the government should be to enhance cooperation among the institutions in order to avoid conflicts and wastes of resources, and to improve the effectiveness of the Intellectual Property protection.

GI products are the crystallization of thousands of years of culture and tradition of Chinese populations. Their special features give them strong potential for competition, but most of them have difficulties in gaining market share. The market in China is enormous and is influenced by brand images that are synonyms of quality. It is therefore necessary to strengthen the image of the GI logo while reinforcing the special characters of GI products such as local know-how and the concept of '*terroir*'.

Notes

1. See Hélène Ilbert, in this volume.
2. Jinhua ham was chosen as a case study for the SINER-GI project (2008) and was the subject of a presentation at the Asia FAO conference in 2009 (Wang, 2009). The field survey was conducted in China in 2007 for the SINER-GI project. Intensive investigations were carried out on the basis of a detailed interview guide. Given the specificity of local conditions in China, it has not always been possible to observe the process in the strict sense, thus important issues of the interview guide could not be addressed, due to the time constraint and sometimes perhaps also the lack of adherence to the research process (SINER-GI, 2008). Additional data were collected by consulting the databases available on the Internet.
3. SAIC: http://sbj.saic.gov.cn/flfgl/flfg/200501/t20050104_53010.html, date accessed 12 September 2007.
4. 'Trademark Law of the People's Republic of China', http://202.108.90.115/english/show.asp?id=47&bm=flfg, date accessed 2 November 2011.
5. Some researches were conducted to compare the taste of different hams, including Jinhua ham (Bolzoni et al., 1996; Sabio et al., 1998; Zhu et al., 2001). The taste and quality of products depends partly on how the ham is processed and partly on the specific quality of the raw material (e.g. slow-growing breed). In the case of Jinhua ham, a specific climate and the experience of the producers directly determine the quality of the product.
6. http://www.zjahv.gov.cn/html/main/zw_jcxxView/8102.html, dated access 5 December 2009.
7. There is no accurate data on the amount of production and distribution since productions have different logos.

References

Allaire, G. (2002) 'L'économie de la qualité, en ses secteurs, ses territoires et ses mythes', *Géographie, Economie, Société*, 4, 155–80.

Allaire, G. and B. Daviron (2006) 'Régimes d'institutionnalisation et d'intégration des marchés: le cas des produits agricoles et alimentaires', in *Journée d'études du GDR Economie et sociologie 'les nouvelles figures des marchés agro-alimentaire, apports croisés de l'économie, de la sociologie et de la gestion'* (Montpellier).

Andreff, W. (2005) 'La new comparative economics: nouvelle analyse ou cosmétique institutionnelle du "mainstream"?', 3ème colloque, 'La transition: quelles relations entre économie de marché et démocratie politique?' Université de Paris 1.

Bérard, L. and P. Marchenay (1995) 'Lieux, temps et preuves. La construction sociale des produits de terroir', *Terrain*, 24, 153–64.

Bolzoni, L., G. Barbieri and R. Virgili (1996) 'Changes in Volatile Compounds of Parma Ham During Maturation', *Meat Science*, 43(3–4), 301–10.

Boyer, R. (1999) *Entre l'Etat et marché, les innovations institutionnelles, condition du développement au XXI siècle* (Paris: CEPREMAP, CNRS, E.H.E.S.S.)

Casabianca, F., B. Sylvander, Y. Noël, C. Beranger, J.B. Coulon and F. Roncin (2005) 'Terroir et Typicité: deux concepts-clés des Appellations d'Origine Contrôlée. Essai de définitions scientifiques et opérationnelles', Communication au Symposium international: 'Territoires et enjeux du développement régional', Lyon, 9–11 March.

Dolphins (2003) 'Concerted Action DOLPHINS: Development of Origin Labelled Products: Humanity, Innovation and Sustainability', http://www.origin-food.org/cadre/cadol.htm, date accessed 2 November 2011.

Feng, Z.Z., S.H. Sheng, and M.F. Zhang (2007) 'Zhongguo nongchanpin dili biaozhi guanli zhidu fazhan fanglue sikao' (A analysis of the development strategies of the geographical indication management system for Chinese agricultural products), *World Agriculture*, 2, 16–18 (in Chinese).

Gilly, J.P. and F. Wallet (2005) 'Enchevêtrement des espaces de régulation et gouvernance territoriale', *Revue d'Economie Régionale et Urbaine*, 5, 699–722.

Gong, Y.L. (1987) *Jinhua Ham Processing Technology* (Beijing: Popular Science Press) (in Chinese).

Huchet, J.F. and X.J. Yan (1996) 'Les entreprises d'État chinoises à la croisée des chemins', *Revue Tiers-Monde*, 37(147).

Lacroix, A., A. Mollard, and B. Pecqueur (2000) 'Origine et produits de qualité territoriale: du signal à l'attribut', *Revue d'Économie Régionale et Urbaine*, 4, 683–706.

Nefussi, J. and J.P. Philippot (1995) 'Agro-alimentaire: une économie de la qualité', in F. Nicolas and E. Valceschini (eds), *Agro-alimentaire: une économie de la qualité* (Paris: Economica).

Nicolas, F. and E. Valceschini (eds) (1995) *Agro-alimentaire: une économie de la qualité* (Paris: Economica).

Pivot, C. (1998) 'Signe de qualité et développement rural', *Revue Région et Développement*, 7, 135–63.

Sabio, E., M.C. Vidal-Aragon, M.J. Bernalte and J.L. Gata (1998) 'Volatile Compounds Present in Six Types of Dry-cured Ham from South European Countries', *Food Chemistry*, 61(4), 493–503.

SINER-GI (2008) 'SINER-GI Project', http://www.origin-food.org/2005/base.php?cat=30, date accessed 2 November 2011.

Stoker, G. (1998). 'Governance as Theory: Five Propositions', *International Social Science Journal*, 50(155), 17–28.

Sylvander, B. (1995) 'Convention de qualité, marché et institutions: le cas des produits de qualité spécifique', in F. Nicolas and E. Valceschini (eds), *Agro-alimentaire: une économie de la qualité* (Paris: Economica).

Sylvander, B., G. Belletti, A. Marescotti, G. Allaire, D. Barjolle, E. Thevenod-Mottet and A. Tregear (2005) 'Evolution des dispositifs français et européens de protection de la qualité et de l'origine dans le contexte de l'OMC: les apports du projet', *Dolphins, Symposium international, Territoires et enjeux du développement régional.*

Sylvander, B., G. Allaire, D. Barjolle, E. Thévenod-Mottet, G. Belletti, A. Marescotti and A. Tregear (2006) 'Qualité, origine et globalisation: justifications générales et contextes nationaux, le cas des Indications Géographique', *Canadian Journal of Regional Science/Revue canadienne des sciences régionales*, 29(1) (Spring), 43–54.

Sylvander, B., L. Lagrange and C. Monticelli (2007) 'Les signes officiels de qualité et d'origine européens', *Economie rurale*, no. 299, 7–23.

E. Valceschini and A. Mazé (2000) 'La politique de la qualité agro-alimentaire dans le contexte international', *Economie rurale*, 258, 30–41.

Wang, G.H. (2009) 'Application of Geographical Indication Systems in China: Jinhua Ham Case Study', in *Quality Linked to Geographical Origin and Geographical Indications, Lessons Learned from Six Case Studies in Asia* (Rome: Organisation des Nations Unies pour l'alimentation et l'agriculture).

Wang, G.H. (2011) 'La mise en place d'un système de protection des Indications Géographiques dans une économie en transition: l'exemple de la Chine. Les cas du thé de Longjing et du jambon de Jinhua', PhD dissertation, Université de Toulouse.

World Bank (1993) *The East Asian Miracle: Economic Growth and Public Policy* (Washington, DC: The World Bank).

Zhang, G.Q. (1997) ' "Dongya jingji qiji " de xitong fenxi: guanyu "Dongya zhengzhi jingjixue" de chanshi' (A Systematic Analysis of the 'East Asian Economic Miracle': From the Perspective of 'East Asian Political Economics'], *Journal of Nanjing University (Philosophy, Humanities and Social Sciences*, 1, 24–34 (in Chinese).

Zhu, S.S. (1993) 'Jinhua Ham Flavour Volatile Research', *Food Science* 158(2), 16–18.

11

Terroir and Green Tea in China: The Case of Meijiawu Dragon Well (*Longjing*) Tea

Selina Ching Chan

The concept of *terroir* has been widely associated with evaluating agricultural products, especially wine, tea and coffee. *Terroir* is often translated as 'a sense of place', seen from both physical and cultural perspectives. In terms of the physical aspect, *terroir* entails how a number of factors such as environment, territory, microclimates, soil aptitudes, and ecology affect the quality of agricultural products (Guy, 2003, pp. 41–2; Fanet, 2001, p. 10). The cultural aspect of *terroir* is involved with how the subtle interaction of environmental factors with human skills determines the quality of products (ibid.). In other words, the traditional knowledge and skills in the local place is of particular importance to the understanding of *terroir* (Amilien, 2005, p. 6). *Terroir* also determines quality and typicality, which characterizes a collective taste memory of specific products in a particular place (Charters, 2010, p. 5). It may include how different agents reinterpret the past, narrate and imagine the history of a place (Demossiers, 2004, cited in Charters, 2010, p. 3). It is an indicator of reputation and quality assurance and it has often been well promoted through place branding because it involves an articulation of 'history and heritage, efficiency and quality, reputation and status' (Rausch, 2008, p. 139).[1] Indeed, the cultural aspect of *terroir* has been enhanced through different promotional and marketing strategies.

Longjing tea is taken as a case study to examine the importance of *terroir* in this agricultural product. *Longjing* is one of the most prestigious hand-roasted green teas in China. It has been favourably consumed by many emperors since the imperial days. The colour of the tea is bright green and the tea is famous for its unique fragrance and favour. This chapter examines *longjing* tea, one of the most prestigious hand-roasted green teas in China, with reference to the discourse of *terroir*. Following Foucault (cited in Hall, 1997, p. 6), discourses will be taken as groups of ideas, images and practices, which define the scope of knowledge, the ways of discussion, and the methods to appropriate a particular subject or practice. And it is in multiple discourses that power and knowledge are joined together (ibid.). *Terroir* will be taken as a discourse to understand how various groups of actors and institutions interpret it. I will examine how the state, the village government, entrepreneurs, the media and the villagers draw knowledge, authority and credibility from discourses based on historical, legal, and labour sources in arguing for the genuineness of *longjing* by referring to the physical and cultural aspects of *terroir*. The way in which public institutions and different individuals in China claim, through multiple discourse, that the locally produced *longjing* in Hangzhou is the original and 'authentic' version will be investigated.

The first section will examine how the Chinese government defines *longjing* through legal order by paying attention to the physical aspect of *terroir*, the geographical location, soil, water, climate and environment. The second section investigates how the articulation of history and heritage determines the *terroir* of *longjing*. The third section examines the importance of local knowledge and skills in making *longjing*. It investigates how the traditional tea-roasting technique is perceived as a component of *terroir*, especially if it is identified as national-grade intangible cultural heritage. The final section considers how the media discourse illustrates a product by emphasizing on the reputation of its place of origin.

This chapter considers the case of Meijiawu village in Hangzhou, the capital city in Zhejiang Province in eastern China, to examine the importance of '*terroir*' in the case of *longjing* tea. Meijiawu is a village within the West Lake area, about 15 miles from the city centre of Hangzhou. West Lake is a famous freshwater lake located in the historic centre of Hangzhou. The village is more than 500 years old and has a long history of growing *longjing* tea. It has around 153 hectares of tea farms and their annual produce forms a significant fraction of the total *longjing* output in Hangzhou.[2] Data in Meijiawu were collected in separate two-week visits in August 2005, July 2006 and April 2008. In-depth interviews were carried out with sixty informants, including fifty local villagers, six village cadres and four government officials from the Tourism Bureau at the Provincial level.

11.1 Historical discourse and place-branding: West Lake *longjing* as a tribute for emperors and leaders

'*Terroir*' does not merely imply a physical concept relating to place, but also conveys a historical and cognitive concept of place (Charters, 2010,

p. 3; Aurier, Fort and Sirieix, 2005, p. 3). This historical and cultural meaning of '*terroir*' carries 'attributes, information, imagination, expectations, social, emotional and symbolic value' (Hankinson and Cowking, 1993, p. 10, cited in Rausch, 2008, p. 137; Philip and Gertner, 2002, pp. 249–50) and is important for us to understand the discourse of *longjing*. In the following, I am going to demonstrate how the general public defines 'authentic' *longjing* as West Lake *longjing* by interpreting the past and remembering the history of a place.

Longjing seedlings were said to be first planted and consumed by the monks at the famous temples of Tianzhu and Lingying along the West Lake (Xihu) area in Hangzhou (the capital city of Zhejiang province) during the Northern Song dynasty (960–1127), and was officially named as Hangzhou West Lake *longjing* tea only in the Southern Song Dynasty (1127–79) (Dewar and Li, 2007, p. 185). Since the Ming dynasty (1368–1644), the tea has also been grown in other areas along West Lake and consumed by ordinary people. In the Qing dynasty (1644–1911), Emperor Qianlong (1736–95) visited tea farms at a place called Longjing in the West Lake area for four times during his six trips to the Lower Yangtze Delta. According to locals, Qianlong even handpicked 18 trees and named them as 'emperor's *longjing*'. West Lake *longjing* tea in Hangzhou became the emperor's tribute and its value increased significantly. West Lake *longjing* has been referred to as 'emperor's tea' (1662–1722) period in the Qing dynasty.

The term West Lake *longjing* increased in popularity during the planned economy period as it was highly regarded by Chairman Mao Zedong and other leaders. There is around 363 hectares (around 5,500 *mu*) of tea gardens around the West Lake area reserved for growing *longjing* Tea (http://whc.unesco.org/en/tentativelists/5329/). As my informants pointed out, these tea gardens are located mainly in five places within the West Lake District in Hangzhou: Shifeng, Longjing, Yunxi, Hupao and Meijiawu. West Lake longjing was exclusively produced for the consumption of senior government officials working in the central government at that time.

While defining their homegrown *longjing* tea as West Lake *longjing*, Meijiawu villagers also promoted their own tea through monumentalizing memories of its consumption by powerful leaders during the pre-reform period. The linkage between the locally made tea in the rural periphery and those powerful men in the central authority is an important way of boosting the status of Meijiawu *longjing*. During my fieldwork, I was often told by the villagers that Zhou Enlai, the first premier of the PRC, took a particular interest in Meijiawu and visited it five times during the period between 1953 and 1962.[3] Many old villagers narrated fondly how they saw Zhou Enlai coming to the village when they were children. Several villagers told me that Zhou Enlai appreciated the tea a lot and he even ate some of the tea leaves. A Memorial Hall dedicated to Zhou Enlai was built by the villagers together with the village government in 1991.

Today, pictures were displayed in the Hall to narrate the visits of Zhou with other international leaders to Meijiawu. Indeed, many of these pictures were also put up in other tea stores in the village. These pictures have become spectacles which bear exhibitionary meanings and are proof of the historical reputation of Meijiawu *longjing*. The fact that leaders from Russia, America, Romania, Cambodia and other countries were brought to see the tea-producing process in Meijiawu also implies that the village has an established national and international reputation in producing *longjing* tea. In some other tea stores, photographs of the recent former president Jiang Zemin during his visit to Meijiawu were also found. The attention given by these important leaders in tea-growing here has itself also become a kind of quality assurance for Meijiawu's *longjing*. Indeed, *longjing* in Meijiawu has been identified as *guojia lipin cha* – national gift tea – and was not available in the market before the reforms. It was considered by senior national and international leaders to be a superior gift. Farmers recalled fondly that the tea was for important leaders: even they themselves were deprived of tasting their own tea in those days. Narrating these leaders' liking for *longjing* tea in various forms and in public space entails a process of monumentalizing their visits to the rural village, which enshrines the value of *longjing*. Kopytoff's (1986, p. 66) biographical approach is particularly useful here for further understanding how the exceptional value of *longjing* in Meijiawu is enshrined. The historical biography of *longjing* relates its ownership to the society's class structure. The fact that *longjing* was a luxury and a celebrated gifted item circulated exclusively among leaders marked its status as a singularized object and not an ordinary commodity. The monopoly and its cultural prohibition during the pre-reform period has added value to *longjing*.

More interestingly, the memorial hall is now an official site for 'patriotic education'.[4] Schoolchildren and work units from different parts of China visit this site. I was told by the guard of the memorial hall that these visitors have often come during their sightseeing trips to Hangzhou. The official objective of the visit to this site is to learn about the concern shown by top leaders for the poor, rural villager. Nevertheless, what most people are impressed is that Meijiawu has produced exceptional-quality *longjing* which attracts the attention of top leaders from different places. Thus, while this site for the patriotic education may not be very effective in actually promoting patriotism, it could be fairly successful in promoting Meijiawu's *longjing* as the prestigious West Lake *longjing* through narrating its 'imperial' connections.

11.2 Soil and place: 'authentic' *longjing* in the legal discourse

Since the market reforms in 1978, there has been rapid growth in the demand for *longjing*. As there is limited tea farmland along Hangzhou, *longjing* started to be widely cultivated by many farmers in other counties within Zhejiang. In fact, some tea farmers in Hangzhou were invited to teach farmers at Xinchang county in Zhejiang Province to grow *longjing* tea, and to roast the tea leaves. Thus, the local tea-planting and tea-roasting techniques spread quickly to many other places. Today, *longjing* tea is well-known to be grown along the West Lake area in Hangzhou, other nearby counties within Zhejiang Province, as well as other provinces. My informants told me that *longjing* is now grown in as many as 50 counties in certain provinces, including Zhejiang, Yunnan and Guizhou.

Although the peasants in Yunan and Guizhou are able to pick up the farming and roasting skills for producing *longjing* tea and their tea may appear to be the same as the *longjing* farmed and roasted in Zhejiang, the difference in quality and taste is significant. It is in this context that the term 'authentic' *longjing* arose in the public sphere to draw a distinction between *longjing* grown in the West Lake and Zhejiang and that grown elsewhere. As the tea experts highlighted, differences in soil and water have a great impact on the quality of *longjing*. They believe that the physical environment in the West Lake region in Hangzhou is the best for growing *longjing*, while those grown in other areas in Zhejiang province is of lesser quality, and others planted in other provinces is simply unacceptable. The climate in West Lake region is moderate, averaging around 16 degrees Celsius with annual rainfall of around 1,500 milimetres a year, and is considered to be the best for planting *longjing* (Amazing Green Tea 2011). Indeed, the geographical space around the West Lake and Zhejiang forms an important component of *terroir*. The reference to the physical aspect of '*terroir*' has therefore become an important indication of 'authentic' *longjing* for the general public.

In 1997, Hangzhou Xihu (West Lake) Agricultural Bureau began toying with the idea of having West Lake *longjing* as a registered brand, although the application was initiated only in August 2006. The place, West Lake, has become the centre of this brand of tea as it is believed that the physical environment is the best for growing *longjing*. This legal action has officially granted prestige to *longjing* grown in the West Lake region. Since 2007, Hangzhou Xihu (West Lake) Agricultural Bureau stipulated that only *longjing* produced within the West Lake region is eligible to be named as West Lake *longjing*. A predetermined number of labels is given by the Hangzhou Xihu (West Lake) Agricultural Bureau to each tea farmer according to their estimated productivity of the land owned by them. Four labels will be issued for each catty of *longjing* grown.[5] As West Lake villagers, Meijiawu tea farmers obtained a particular number of labels according to the size of their farms. These labels authorize them as legitimate farmers and sellers of *longjing* in Meijiawu. The code of the tea farmers is found in the website of Hangzhou Xihu Agricultural Bureau and the telephone number of the Bureau is provided in each label. Consumers could go to the website operated by the Xihu Agricultural Bureau and key in the code of a tea farmer to check whether or not particular producers are authorized farmers of West Lake *longjing* at Meijiawu.[6]

Not only has the term West Lake *longjing* been registered for exclusive use by the Hangzhou Xinhu (West Lake) Agricultural Bureau; the Agricultural Bureau of Zhejiang has also further registered the brand *longjing* with the State Administration for Industry and Commerce in 2009. Since then, the term *longjing* is legally allowed to be labelled on tea grown from a restricted area within Zhejiang province. *Longjing* tea is now eligible to be named as *longjing* only if it is grown in 18 counties within West Lake, Qiantang and the Yuezhou regions within Zhejiang Province (China Web 2009). Thus, all other farmers from Anhui, Guizhou, and Yunnan cannot claim that they produce *longjing* despite using the same tea seedling and roasting technique (ibid.).[7] Farmers and enterprises who want to use the brand *longjing* have first to obtain permission from the Agricultural Bureau of Zhejiang. This branding of the tea forms a legal discourse of identifying what is 'authentic' *longjing* through an institutionalization process. Though the region of growing *longjing* has been expanded from 'West Lake' area to other nearby places in Zhejiang Province, the expanded geographical region is still a small area near Hangzhou. Here, the physical aspect of *terroir* is most helpful as its emphasis was on 'the soil of a more or less understood yet vague area'.[8] Indeed, the soil, water and climate within this defined area in Zhejiang province is similar and is most suitable for breeding good-quality *longjing*.

11.3 Intangible Cultural Heritage: labour discourse and performance politics

Meijiawu villagers also attribute the high quality of authentic *longjing* to its complex local handmade procedures. Handmade procedures are indeed an important component of *terroir* in which local knowledge and experience are utilized. This has become an even more important item as *longjing*'s tea-roasting technique has been officially recognized as a national grade intangible cultural heritage in 2008. According to UNESCO, intangible cultural heritage includes oral traditions, performing arts, social practices, rituals, festive events, knowledge and practices concerning nature and the universe or the knowledge and skills to produce traditional crafts (United Nations, Educational, Scientific and Cultural Organization 2011). These knowledge and skills are often recognized by members in the communities and they also help reinforcing social cohesion and identity (ibid.). Following the definition of intangible cultural heritage identified by UNESCO, the Chinese government identified the knowledge and skills to produce *longjing* tea as an intangible cultural heritage. Indeed, the tea-roasting technique involves sophisticated procedures that are well recognized by local farmers – something that also provides them with a sense of identity. On 29 March 2009, the Ministry of Culture of the People's Republic of China conferred this award on the West Lake region for its 'West Lake *Longjing* Tea-roasting Technique' at the opening of its annual tea-picking ceremony (China Web 2009). The processing of *longjing* leaves involves several lengthy steps that require handling by workers rather than the tea being fed into machines. It includes drying the freshly picked green tea leaves and the initial round of roasting these leaves. After cooling off the roasted tea for a day, the tea needs to be roasted again. Finally, one has to sort out the tea, removing the broken tea leaves. All of these procedures are to be executed by hand. Experience in roasting tea is important as it affects both the shape and taste of the tea leaves. Although the use of machines would make the production process three times faster, many villagers admitted that it affects the level of moisture in the leaves, thereby changing the taste of tea. With the manual-roasting method, the moisture from one's palm prevents the tea leaves from becoming too dry and hence preserves the fragrance. The villager-cum-entrepreneur and husband of the female boss of Lu Zhenghao stressed the value of *longjing* in its artistic production method. He told me that tea leaves look, smell and taste differently if they are roasted by different people. He prides himself on being able to identify the person who had carried out the roasting simply by looking at the shape of the tea leaves.

An interesting dialogue between Zhou Enlai and a foreign visitor was also displayed in the Zhou Enlai Memorial Hall at the village to commemorate the prestigious hand-roasting procedures. The content of the conversation between Zhou and a foreign visitor was to highlight the importance of human labour in tea roasting. When asked by the foreign visitor why *longjing* has to be hand-roasted in such a time-consuming way, Zhou replied, '*Longjing* tea is not merely a kind of drink, it is an artwork. It bears good color, scent, taste and shape. It has to be made by hands which embody several decades of accumulated experience. It cannot be replaced by a machine.' The appreciation by one of the most favourably regarded national leaders for Meijiawu's *longjing* as an art resulted from local knowledge and experience highlighted the importance of cultural aspect of '*terroir*' in defining *longjing*. It is the local tea-roasting practices associated with the particular soil, climate along the local place of West Lake region that creates the uniqueness of *longjing*. Indeed, the emphasis on local knowledge and experience and the refinement of this home-made agricultural product into a cultural object involves a conscious and active social construction of the present by important leaders, villagers and entrepreneurs.

During the tea-collecting season in late March and early April, visitors are always impressed by the smell and beautiful scenes of tea roasting. Indeed, tea-roasting work is a performance for the audience who are potential customers. On the streets, one could easily spot tea-collecting women walking in groups of six or seven, with their tea baskets hanging on their backs. Tea leaves were dried outdoors in the sun, being laid evenly over rattan mats. Tea farmers were seen here drying their freshly collected tea leaves and operating woks that were used to roast tea leaves.

Along the main road, many villagers are performing tea roasting in front of their houses while trying to sell tea to the tourists at the same time. In addition, coercive technologies and practices are used to ensure that *longjing* is 'handmade'. Many informants showed me how their hands were burnt after roasting continuously for long hours during the peak season. In fact, tea leaves have to be quickly collected once they are ready. Otherwise they would turn old and big, which would affect their market value. The freshly collected tea leaves have to be dried immediately and roasted soon afterwards, otherwise they would be spoiled. During the peak season, many workers have to roast tea for long hours day and night. A full day and night of work by one person might only result in four to five catties of *longjing*. The use of machines would be able to speed up the production process three times.

Today, while most villagers use electric woks, some individual farmers in the village use wooden fires to roast tea. This practice is reflective of the nostalgia for the past. In addition to reducing the electricity bill, the use of a wood fire can be viewed as a performance which re-enacts the tea-roasting scenery in the old days. A villager told me, 'the officials said that wooden fire causes pollution, but they forgot that it is a beautiful picture for tourists'. Indeed, tea roasting is now partly work and partly an important performance in which sights, smells and sounds are key features in evoking pleasurable associations with tea consumption.

Apart from individual performance launched by the individual teahouse owners – also the tea farmers – a more well-planned performance was also organized by professional businessmen at tea stores in the village. The performance of tea roasting at its place of origin grants tourists a good sense of authenticity, in which fresh *longjing* was collected at the local tea farm, purely hand-made, fried on the spot, and sold at the store.

The fact that tea roasting is conducted in public commercial space together with the sale of tea is consistent with what Goffman (1971) said about the presentation of images becoming part of exchange and of the consumption experience. Firstly, the roasting of tea in front of the teahouses by the villagers is a visual relic in theatrical terms, which pleases the audience through their tourist gaze. This tea-roasting performance is a spectacle put on by tea-sellers and entrepreneurs to recapture the social imagination of the tea village – an authentic hometown of *longjing* tea handmade by local villagers. Secondly, the public performance of tea roasting is important in reaffirming the status and identity of Meijiawu village as an authentic *longjing* production centre. Thirdly, the performance of hand-roasted *longjing* presents the unique art of making tea. Indeed, this public performance is a self-managed series of façades intended for the tourists at the front stage.

11.4 Discourse of media and the market value of *longjing*

In addition, the media has reported widely on the market value of local *longjing* by highlighting its historical legacy, handmade craftsmanship, and medical value. It is the businessmen who worked closely with the media to make all these reports. *Longjing* is widely reported by the media as being one of the best green teas which has protective effects against cancer. *Longjing* is known to have epigallocatechin gallate (EGCG), which is a stronger antioxidant than either vitamin C or E. It has also been identified as a 'golden name card' in Hangzhou for its medical value and historical legacy (http//222.lotour.com/snapshot/2007-3-27/snapshot_60494.shtml).

Every year, the highest price of first-grade *longjing* is reported by the media and it is often as high as four to five thousand RMB per catty.[9] During the spring tea season, when the picking and roasting of *longjing* leaves begin, there are regular media reports on different events such as the West Lake International Tea Culture Exposition and the China Hangzhou West Lake *Longjing* Tea Picking Festival. Crews from different TV stations take videos of the tea-roasting procedures carried out by the tea farmers in different villages within the West Lake district. Not only are hand-roasting performances regularly shown on TV, but tea-picking and tea-roasting competitions are also conducted and reported. In 2008, 16 tea-roasting masters were selected for their outstanding tea-roasting skills (Hangzhou Web 2011). They were introduced to the public and the eventual winner was a 36-year-old tea farmer who learned the technique from his grandfather. He began learning when he was 16 and managed to roast tea independently when he was 21. His family owned a tea farm of 0.132 hectares and their total annual income from selling tea was around 100,000 RMB.[10] In 2006, he was also the winner of the 'king of young tea-roasting masters' contest. The tea which he roasted was taken to an auction and was sold at the price of 110,000 RMB per 100 gram.[11]

11.5 Conclusion

The term *terroir* involves the 'refinement of the agricultural product into a cultural object with the label of authenticity in the form of national heritage' (Barham 2003, p. 132). The importance of *terroir* in defining *longjing* is highlighted through explaining both physical and cultural aspects. From the physical perspective, the legal discourse of *longjing* has been defined by various government organizations with reference to the importance of soil in the local place. As for the cultural aspect of *terroir*, it involves a complex process of interaction between people, climate and soil. This entails narrating the historical background of *longjing* tea as local heritage, as well as highlighting the tea-roasting skill as an art and intangible cultural heritage by local farmers and businessmen.

'*Terroir*' is contested and discourses from history, legal, media and labour sources are sites of contestation because they are ambiguous and plurivocal. All of these discourses pinpoint the importance of products of origin, the local knowledge and experience of tea roasting. While the historical discourse emphasizes that authentic *longjing* was produced within the West Lake region in Hangzhou, the legal discourse suggests that the place of origin could be more diversified and may go beyond West Lake region to other areas within Zhejiang Province. However, these two discourses are not totally incompatible. Based on these two discourses, the general public acknowledges authentic *longjing* as defined by the stringent historical discourse as top-grade West Lake *longjing*, while *longjing* grown in other areas within Zhejiang province – as accepted by legal discourse – as less prestigious authentic *longjing*. With the help of the media discourse, the hegemony of historical discourse has become more dominant than others in defining *longjing*'s market value. Indeed, West Lake *longjing* is much more expensive than Zhejiang *longjing* as it is widely believed by the public to be of better quality.

Notes

1. Place-branding is widely found in the contexts of nation-branding, regional-branding, city-branding, and rural branding (Bilkey and Nes, 1982; Kotler and Gertner, 2002; Rausch 2008).
2. There is no reliable source that accounts for the total production of *longjing* tea in Meijiawu because there are many fake teas claiming to be from that area.
3. Zhou Enlai was a native from Shaoxing in Zhejiang province.
4. Just as other modern nation states have been active in cultivating nationalism and conducting national education, China is no exception. China is famous for its national education, often termed it as 'patriotic education'.
5. One catty is 500 grams.
6. One could file a report to the police if the producers are not authorized farmers. Nevertheless, this legal system of labelling is not effective in actual practice. Firstly, regular customers who buy tea from farmers do not ask for labels because they trust the tea farmers. Secondly, it is easy to make and buy fake labels which contain the name of real producers. It is difficult for the police or others to keep track on how many catties of *longjing* each producer sold. My fieldwork in Meijiawu during the tea-roasting season in 2008 made me quite sceptical about the efficacy of the labelling system and the implementation of the newly established branding law. Tea sold to customers was not packed beforehand, and would only be packed and labelled after the customers had decided on the type of tea to buy after viewing and tasting it. Farmers would then quickly buy boxes and labels from across the street at a temporary specialist stall which only sells these packing products. Different types of sealing bags, labels and boxes are sold with various names, such as Meijiawu *longjing* or West Lake *longjing*. The price varies according to the design and quality of the boxes sold. Typically, these boxes cost between

15 and 80 RMB. Customers could choose whatever packaging they like and at whatever price they prefer. During the spring tea season, these temporary stalls selling boxes usually enjoy brisk business.

7. Farmers outside the Zhejiang area sometimes produce tea which shares the same tea seedling and roasting technique as farmers in Zhejiang. These teas will be considered counterfeit tea by the government and the public. One could file a report to the relevant department but the prosecution process is lengthy and tedious. In practice, it is difficult to stop counterfeit products in China.
8. Since the end of the thirteenth century, *terroir* has been used to 'designate the aptitudes of various soils' (Guy, 2003, p. 42).
9. 100 RMB is around US$15.6 at current rates.
10. It is around US$15,600.
11. It is around US$17,160.

References

Amazing Green Tea (2011) 'Xihu Longjing Tea: An Insider's Guide', http://www.amazing-green-tea.com/longjing-tea.html, date accessed 10 October 2011 (in Chinese).

Amilien, V. (2005) 'Preface: About Local Food', *Anthropology of Food* (online) May (4).

Aurier, P., F. Fort and L. Sirieix (2005) 'Exploring *terroir* Product Meanings for the Consumer', *Anthropology of Food* (online), May (4).

Barham, E. (2003) 'Translating *Terroir*: the Global Challenge of French AOC Labeling', *Journal of Rural Studies*, 19, 127–38.

Bilkey, W. J. and E. Nes (1982) 'Country-of-Origin Effects on Products of Evaluations', *Journal of International Business Studies*, 13(1) (Spring–Summer), 89–99.

Charters, S. (2010) 'Marketing *Terroir*: A Conceptual Approach'. Paper presented at 5th International Academy of Wine Business Research Conference, Auckland, 8–10 February.

China Web (2009) 'The Award of West Lake Longjing Tea Roasting Technique of National Grade Intangible Cultural Heritage', http://www.china.com.cn/culture/txt/2009-03/31/content_17528451.htm, date accessed 4 April 2009.

Dewar, K. and Li Wen Mei (2007) 'Hangzhou: China's Green Tea City', in L. Jolliffe (ed.), *Tea and Tourism: Tourists, Traditions and Transformations* (Toronto, Buffalo and Clevedon: Channel View Publications).

Fanet, J. (2001) *Great Wine Terroirs* (tr. Florence Brutton) (Berkeley, Los Angeles and London: University of California Press).

Goffman, E. (1971) *The Presentation of Self in Everyday Life* (Edinburgh: University of Edinburgh, Social Sciences Research Centre).

Guy, K. M. (2003) *When Champagne Became French: Wine and the Making of a National Identity* (Baltimore and London: Johns Hopkins University Press).

Hall, S. (1997) *Representation: Cultural Representations and Signifying Practices* (London: Sage in association with the Open University).

Hangzhou Web (2011) 'Tea Roasting King' http://www.hangzhou.com.cn/20080401/ca1478538.htm, date accessed 2 August 2011 (in Chinese).

Hankinson, G. and P. Cowking (1993) *Branding in Action* (London: McGraw-Hill).

Kopytoff, I. (1986) 'The Cultural Biography of Things', in A. Appadurai (ed.), *The Social Life of Things: Commodities in Cultural Perspective* (Cambridge: Cambridge University Press).

Kotler, P. and D. Gertner (2002) 'Country as Brand, Product, and Beyond: a Place Marketing and Brand Management Perspective', *Brand Management,* 9(4–5), 249–61.

Rausch, A.S. (2008) 'Place Branding in Rural Japan: Cultural Commodities as Local Brands', *Place Branding and Public Diplomacy,* 44(2), 136–46.

Oriental Daily (2009) 'Naming Zhejiang Longjing Tea', 11 January (in Chinese).

United Nations, Educational, Scientific and Cultural Organization (2011) 'What is Intangible Cultural Heritage?', http://www.unesco.org/culture/ich/index.php?lg=en&pg=00002, date accessed 10 July 2011.

Conclusion

Hélène Ilbert

This book analyses the rationales and the mechanisms at work for qualifying goods. In the global competition process, Geographical Indications (GIs) are one among many possible marketing tools. They are institutional devices anchored in the social construction of markets in the sense given by economic sociology. Philippe Steiner recalls, in Chapter 2, how institutions 'think' and 'control' food markets, which he analyses as 'special markets'. The historical architecture of food commodification is based on alimentary representations and daily practices contributing to the building of many organized markets. Fictitious goods and 'biopolitics' are at work in our modern way of life. Under this perspective, market regulations and regulations by the markets are embedded: social, economic and political practices and public or private norms constitute multidimensional architectures.

International driving forces: the strategic and international shift to the quality and origin regime in the 1990s

Strategic and institutional economics recalls how major players in the market are exacerbating competition through information control and marketing techniques. Jean-Louis Rastoin, in Chapter 6, analyses how the agribusiness sector shifts from a competition based on costs to the differentiation strategy. The distinctive uniqueness of a '*terroir*' takes the form of a network of firms focusing on the production of food products with a high level of quality. The local food model is organized into short value chains bringing agricultural production and agri-food processing closer together and which are rooted in the territories through a common history and socio-technical culture. The development of this quality food model requires the implementation of innovative public agricultural and food policies.

Major operators do integrate segments of innovation, authenticity and uniqueness corresponding to different client profiles. Multinational corporations and supermarkets have the marketing expertise to respond to food insecurity and the anxiety of the consumers with health products of an appealing nature and services (Omega 3, and so on). Gilles Allaire and Louis Augustin-Jean analyze how dominant actors extend the range and the scope of their 'products-services' (Chapters 3 and 4). This logic of innovation includes differentiation practices. The shift is not only strategic but corresponds to a shift in the economic driving forces: consumers ask for reliable origin and quality products and food chains have to adapt to this demand.

Thus, supply and demand combine with each other to reinforce a new international quality regime since the 1990s. The old Fordist industrial model includes new norms, principles and procedures to qualify a good. Emphasis is given to this new global quality regime as it contributes to strengthen attributes, classifications and codification practices. Competition is not only on prices, but also on the policies related to the social construction of the global quality market. Gilles Allaire, in Chapter 4, shows that this construction of quality is an institutional compromise which depends on judgements that are also cultural. The compromise is therefore not easy to reach. It is even more the case because the construction of quality also includes strategic and political dimensions at the states, the producers and the consumers' levels. The multiplication of standards and labels, both public and private, which are presented by the author can also be read from this perspective. The quality regime is complex and difficult to grasp.

At a macroeconomic level, Hélène Ilbert analyses how in the global knowledge economy, competitors interfere in an ongoing rivalry process (Chapter 5). Countries with high technological capacity such as Europe and the USA have been historically the leaders for protecting their food products, through specific signs and delimitation procedures such as the certification marks or the GI. The international intellectual property rights regime is concentrated in the hands of major players, both public and private. While trademarks are fully recognized by the world trade rules, GIs lack an international established registration system. Internal preferences are not valid outside domestic borders, unless new global institutional arrangements appear. Mutual commitments to make those signs credible for the consumer are at stake in the international negotiation forums such as the World Trade

Organization (WTO) and the TRIPS Agreement or the Biodiversity Convention.

Since the 1990s, a growing number of institutions and countries have been fighting for the recognition of exclusive monopoly rights at a global level. Major companies or local communities are acting through producers' consortiums such as oriGIn in order to organize the supply at a global level. Organizations from all over the world invest in order to clarify the qualification for GIs: the clearer the attributes are allocated, the less the transaction costs.

Fighting for wider monopoly rights at a global level and especially for GIs is a global trend, no longer limited to developed countries. Neantro Saavedra-Rivano, in Chapter 1, analyses how the potential stock of GIs based on traditional know-how is appropriated by New World countries as well as by developing countries. The market access issue, especially for famous and innovative agricultural products, is a major concern for countries, such as Brazil, China and India.

Potential growth of the world luxury markets in the near future highlights the role of GIs in international trade: new protected famous goods should continue to appear on the world market and match the demand for personalized and location-specific food products. The recognition of the mechanisms for protection is necessary for reinforcing market access and guaranteeing a global protection for high reputation goods for the growing elites worldwide.

The analysis of the Asian offensive or defensive strategies for seeking protection highlights the importance of market access as well as the issue of GI governance and its impact on prices.

Competition for monopoly rights: Asian strategies and global trends

Governments are not neutral players: they enforce protection in order to stabilize rents. Combining vertical and horizontal approaches through information monitoring, corporate agri-business and public stakeholders consolidate the global agro-food value through privileges and organizational forms. Governments intervene at the global level to gain market shares according to their domestic preferences. The analysis of the WTO panel on GIs (Chapter 5) is a testimony of this mercantile approach. Governance depends on coherence and loyalty to the global free trade arrangements, and intellectual property rights, such as GIs, follow the non-discrimination or the most favoured nation treatment principle. Competition norms match the global quality regime with the original legal framework: new differentiations orders are being implemented through geographical property rights and specific qualities.

This limited access order negotiated at a multilateral level requires definitions and enforcements of property rights. The process of commodification and of building specific devices, such as GI, depends on the criteria used to judge which delimitations are appropriate to specify the attributes of a good. The types of links defining the relations between the soil, the people and the product depends on how much the state, which is also a competitor, interferes to set up delimitations of exclusive rights. Louis Augustin-Jean analyses how definitions result from a political process in which actors compete to impose their own standards and their own views (Chapter 3). International competition is a competition not only on products, but also on their definition which can redesign the perception of comparative advantages. History matters and designs the relations between the soil, the people and the product in the commodification process and influences the type of interferences of the states in the international arena. The tense negotiation process between the European countries and the 'New World' is also a means for Europe to impose a form of competition based on traditions and historical values, while the USA and most Latin American countries reject the validity of the existence of such elements of comparative advantages.

The involvement of new players in the GI regulation, such as Asian countries, with their old products of origin may well change the current balance of power.

Japanese defensive strategy

Louis Augustin-Jean and Kae Sekine analyse the construction of GI for some emblematic products in Japan. Since 2006, Japan has established – under the Trademark Law – the regionally based collective rights for GIs: since then, 450 of them have been registered. This 'fast track' application and registration process is facilitated by easy territory definitions which often correspond to the prefecture delimitation (Chapter 7).

Internal Japanese preference for collective trademarks is close to the American certification approach. Flexibility is the major guidance and enterprises seek rent positions without having to establish a rigid code of conduct as in European countries. The comparison between Kobe and Matsusaka beef shows the specificity of the Japanese trademark system: the definition of criteria and membership conditions can change at any time. There is no code of practice, even though producers have to comply with general principles and the product must match with a strict definition corresponding to technical criteria, zone of production and strain. This definition is more restrictive in the case of Kobe beef than in the case of Matsusaka beef, reflecting different types of local organization and marketing strategies. Nicolas Baumert confirms this analysis by studying two regions of *sake* production. He shows how enterprises are working according to urban demand. The territorial dimension is a new factor for *sake* consumers as the firms' brands have been historically associated with this cultural emblematic product (Chapter 8). This case study is of specific interest, because it signals a shift for urban consumers and local producers from an emphasis on a brand to a GI system, with the valorization of know-how, tradition and history. Indeed, Japan has many local products for which consumers are showing an increasing interest. That might indicate that Japan may benefit from shifting to the valorization of these 'comparative advantages' based on history and the '*terroirs*'. Still, the reality is more complex, because the concept of '*terroir*' is not fully understood and adaptable to the Japanese situation. In one way or another, the strategy to protect GI should be extended, since both case studies conclude that a *premium* price is obtained for products protected by regionally based collective rights. Producers avoid price volatility and gain the ability to face high production costs.

This statement is also valid at the international level as Japan faces many counterfeiting cases. Japanese *sake* is widely imitated by Taiwanese, Southeast Asian and Korean producers which endangers local production. New appellations such as the *Hakusan* designation are a test case to extend the protection and propose easily recognizable local and original *sake*. However, international defence is not easy. Non-Japanese 'Kobe beef style' producers can prevent authentic Kobe beef producers from gaining market access in the United States, Australia and Canada, even though the possibilities of exports for Kobe beef are quite limited, because of the small volume of production. More importantly, without proper protection, Japanese producers have no way of stopping the production and the sale of non-genuine Kobe beef in European or American markets. According to the territoriality and the anteriority rules of trademarks, famous names have the right to be used by any private enterprise as long as they obey 'the first in time, first in right' principle. As in the case of 'Parma' ham, legal domestic protection is not valid overseas. And as in the case of 'Budweiser', private enterprises can export their products to its native geographical places and gain market access.

The Japanese choice for defining GI as a collective certification market can be interpreted as a 'soft power' choice: in this Japan is following the American strategy. It includes its cultural goods into the global commodities markets through private protection rules and differentiation methods. The governance is flexible, but the asymmetry of power is persistent because of the anteriority rule that prevails in trademark global management. Nevertheless, this situation can change. The existence of many traditional products and the interests of consumers for such products might affect the balance of power in Japan between the tenets of the trademark system and those of the '*terroir*'. The implications for the international negotiations and future regulations on GIs can be huge, but even if Japan follows its economic interests and decide to promote its '*terroirs*', it does not necessarily mean that the European system will be adopted straightforwardly, due to the different understanding of the concept in both places. The same can be said for China.

Chinese offensive strategy and European answers

China combines trademarks with GIs: the coexistence of both recognition systems enables the state to play at both the international and the local level. Guihong Wang explains how the trademark law amended in 2003 is consistent with the TRIPS agreement. GIs are recognized as a certification mark by the administration responsible for trade regulation (SAIC). Since 2005 they are also recognized as specific signs by the administration in charge of certification (AQSIQ) and as specific agricultural raw material by the Ministry of Agriculture (MOA). The national governance of property rights managed by three administrations is often conflictive as each administration adheres to its own rationale (Chapter 10).

Nonetheless, this governance system can also be interpreted as a way for the state to nurture durable institutional structures. The body of public laws is supported by a domestic top-down policy boosting the status of special markets. Central authorities enforce criteria and define the area of production and the processing conditions. The Jinhua ham case demonstrates how regulation covers a wide scope of possible delimitations in duration, expansion and control techniques. Permission to use the certification marks or GIs is granted if private organizations such as retailers or local producers act to protect their interests in the differentiation of public institutions. In the case of *Longjing* tea, the local and national authorities reserve the usage of the famous historical name to a definite number of hectares of tea garden located by the West Lake area in Hangzhou, as Selina Ching Chan analyses in Chapter 11. Other provinces or areas within Zhejiang province growing *longjing* are not officially entitled to use the distinctive name. Still, an extension of the original zone of production around the West Lake has been accepted, even though it remains unclear how this specific zone was designed.

At the international level, the official recognition provides methods to combine consistency with the global certification mark system and with the European GI model. *Longjing* tea benefits from a trademark certification protection and, since 2011, it is also protected through its inscription in the European GI register. Under a unique bilateral '10+10' pilot project, *Longjing* tea is one of the Chinese agricultural quality products that has been traded off with the famous European products.[1] This guarantees market access to the European market and autonomy from economic shocks. *Longjing* tea and other goods of special reputation coming from China, as well as from other Asian countries such as Thailand, India and Vietnam, are important emblematic products. Once recognized and registered in Europe, they can prosecute any private company using those national emblematic names under their own trademark.

The Chinese offensive strategy for seeking protection effectively establishes a limited entry that requires political connections. The political choices at the local level depend in the end on the goodwill of the central government. There is a balance of power between the state, the provincial and the local level that determine economic development. Those offensive policies have an impact on prices: the two case studies confirm the gap between the common price and the exclusive goods' *premium* price when they are driven by a national protection policy. The expansion of the protection in scope, nature, status and durability is sustainable as it is consistent with local and global arrangements.

The political process to restrict entry for definite types of products, such as the Chinese GI in the European register, increases potential contradictions between domestic and global interests. In the absence of appropriate institutions and in the presence of a deadlock at WTO negotiations, the European register is the unique regional systematic legal protection system. It works as an 'umbrella' trademark for GIs from all over the world. Bringing together GIs at a regional level in order to create '*terroir*-based products' can be presented as a theoretical alternative to global agro-industrial model (Chapter 6).

Nevertheless, in China, as in Japan, the word '*terroir*' has a different meaning than in the European context. The implementation of a plural system of protection, which leads to a confusion with respect to the exact level of protection, to legal conflicts and, in the end, to a poor perception of the product for consumers, illustrates this point. In a country that has changed its economic and legal system radically over the last thirty years, this is not really surprising, but it has also to be related to the fact that in China there are different perceptions of the concept of private property and property rights than are to be found in western countries. These differences are, first of all, cultural and are reflected in the way markets are organized. Again, if Asian countries have a major interest to adopt a GI system close to the European one (and the inclusion of Chinese products in the European Register demonstrate this interest), it does not mean that the European system will be *adopted*; more precisely, it might well be *adapted*.

Still, the European system has its own advantages. Mechanisms of protection in the European Union guarantee rights and privileges to outsider groups motivated by special quality and origin markets. But the recognition of the scheme and its symbol is not an easy matter. Once recognized by the European register, Chinese GIs, such as the Jinxiang Garlic (no. 285 of 01/11/2011), gain a direct market access. The local traditional French garlic produced by small farmers appears under the same European logo as the large-scale Chinese garlic-farming organizations. Under this perspective, it can be considered that the GI European logo, which is supposed to clarify the origin of the product, gives misleading information as it assimilates different origins in the same image.

It is confusing when distant products, defined under different authorities, and which may have little in common, are displayed under the same banner. This is aggravated by the low consumer perception of this sign. The 2011 European Court of Auditors special report (no. 11/2011) concludes that there is no clear strategy for raising awareness of the GI scheme amongst both producers and consumers. The design and the management of a regional European GI registry referring to the origin of the product is monitored by governments involved in the global competition: each national government carries out mercantile tradeoffs between valuable qualitative value chains. Exports and imports are calculated according to major commercial interests as in the bilateral '10 + 10' project between China and the European Union.

Intra-elite relationships at the global level institutionalize a limited access order in which GIs are bargained according to bilateral export negotiations. Under the influence of major agribusiness interests, compromises are concluded in favour of well-established reputation goods. State interference in markets management creates unfair competition dynamics and sustains a dominant coalition in which rules and schemes management are designed for export markets. Small farmers can hold their governments responsible for their commitments.

Equity, ethics, ecology, fairness, health and fitness: for sale

Corporate interests seek for differentiation and easy management schemes at the global and local levels. In order to avoid rigid delimitations, companies federate efficient tools in flexible architectures whose rules they control. The shift towards systematic private control is obvious in international global standards, such as global Gap or ISO. Private standards are de facto necessary for international trade: *Longjing* tea, Idaho potatoes or Roquefort cheese or any famous export quality food and product of origin respect the voluntary standards. Private international mechanisms regulated by private certification bodies have become standards for exports. Traceability procedures facilitate the identification of problems of liability in international trade.

In order to gain visibility and distinction, other layers of differentiation labels, such as fair trade or organic food, provide specific information concerning certain aspects of the good being produced. GIs are sometimes assimilated to these voluntary standards, as being a chance for the producers to build their own definition of local quality or local know-how. The legal conditions under which the GI is conferred and protected against imitation by national regulation are considered as additional guarantees that the quality set forth by a given label, such as organic farming. This wide range of differentiation tools and approaches contribute to enhance the offer strategies. The case of Tinawon rice, a speciality of Ifugao province in the Phillippines, is the subject of the chapter by Sekimoto and Augustin-Jean. It shows the importance of defining the standards and the marketing tools. Price *premium* is obtained through a sophisticated social and technical management. Sold as an exceptional product to overseas American gourmets eager for beauty, tradition and authentic living cultural landscape, *Tinawon rice* is no longer for local consumption or rituals. Taking advantage of the classification of the rice terraces as a UNESCO World Heritage in 1995, the American Eighth Wonder company selects the rice variety and farmers' associations according to organic farming criteria or 'good' cultural practices. It also checks the compliance with global market attributes (Chapter 9).

The emphasis given to label differentiation puts forward a set of multidimensional qualities attesting to the superiority of the rice: in addition to the specificity of the rice (which can be measured with technical equipment), traditional know-how, cultural rituals, living landscape, organic farming, health and heritage transfer emphasize specific qualities which are codified through a set of marketing mechanisms. In practice, local farmers no longer control their own agriculture production processes: international exports criteria dominate local ways of growing the rice.

The dependency path, which is common in global standard markets, is also true for 'niche' markets: small farmers do not benefit from the high prices overseas, as they are not empowered to negotiate the distribution of the benefits from the export. In effect, the value created by the elements of cultures that belong to the farmers is captured by the company that is able to market them. As in the Chinese examples studied earlier, the question of private property is raised: who 'owns' the cultural values? As indicated earlier, corporate interests dominate, because they are able to control the way markets are organized. Nevertheless, the answer is not once and for all, and Filipino farmers are challenging this interpretation.

Food safety?

The old industrial model has established basic conditions for food safety: standard food control and daily compulsory check-ups are regular practices. With the new global quality and origin trade regime, audits and assessments grow each day and in each small area. Food designations contribute to building a complex and sophisticated governance system. The importance given to labels, management schemes and monitoring of signs, such as GIs, is central to the creation of new segments of markets. The very large companies, with brand equity and famous goods, exert a pressure on governments to set the rules to give them the rights of pursuit or the rights of anticipation. Governments involved in the protection of their heritage value and/or of origin and quality intervene to legitimize the practices of the formalization of 'know-how'. The consensus for the strengthening of intellectual property rights according to global quality and origin is shared by a growing number of private and public entities. Japan, China and the Philippines are developing specific strategies to extend the scope of the protection.

Thus, whether the ASEAN and other Asian countries will lean towards the US or European proposals for monitoring food might change the balance of power. Qualification methods, such as labels or GIs, create new barriers but also new opportunities. While luxury markets may expand globally, the issues of food security, food safety, food quality and food crises remain fundamental. The social dimension, the citizens' expectation, and the issues of utility and equity have to be taken in to consideration.

Notes

1. http://ec.europa.eu/commission_2010-2014/ciolos/headlines/news/2011/03/20110322_en.htm

'The dossiers have been treated and examined on each side according to the exacting standards for approval set out in law and administrative procedures, including the right of any interested party to oppose registration.

The EU list comprises: Grana Padano; Prosciutto di Parma; Roquefort; Pruneaux d'Agen/Pruneaux d'Agen mi-cuits; Priego de Cordóba; Sierra Mágina; Comté; White Stilton Cheese/Blue Stilton Cheese; Scottish Farmed Salmon and West Country Farmhouse Cheddar.

The Chinese list comprises: Dongshan Bai Lu Sun (asparagus), Guanxi Mi You (honey pomelo), Jinxiang Da Suan (garlic), Lixian Ma Shan Yao (yam), Longjing cha (tea), Pinggu Da Tao (peach), Shaanxi ping guo (apple), Yancheng Long Xia (crayfish), Zhenjiang Xiang Cu (vinegar) and Longkou Fen Si (vermicelli).'

Index

Note: Page spans given in bold indicate that an entire section of the book is devoted to the subject.